T0332002

Standardizing the World

Standardizing the World

EU Trade Policy and the Road to Convergence

Edited by

FRANCESCO DUINA

and

CRINA VIJU-MILJUSEVIC

OXFORD
UNIVERSITY PRESS

OXFORD
UNIVERSITY PRESS

Oxford University Press is a department of the University of Oxford. It furthers
the University's objective of excellence in research, scholarship, and education
by publishing worldwide. Oxford is a registered trade mark of Oxford University
Press in the UK and certain other countries.

Published in the United States of America by Oxford University Press
198 Madison Avenue, New York, NY 10016, United States of America.

CIP data is on file at the Library of Congress

ISBN 978–0–19–768188–6

DOI: 10.1093/oso/9780197681886.001.0001

Printed by Integrated Books International, United States of America

Contents

Acknowledgments

This volume is proof that we are, indeed, all connected. It could not have been envisioned, written, or published without the support and collaboration of people from many countries and organizations.

To start, both of us began exploring the idea for this volume as participants in the Jean Monnet Network on Transatlantic Trade Politics, funded by the Erasmus + Programme of the European Union. Led by Achim Hurrelmann at Carleton University (Canada), the network brought together scholars from Carleton, the University of Antwerp (Belgium), Bates College (United States), the Paris Lodron University of Salzburg (Austria), and the University of Warwick (United Kingdom). The network provided us with an intellectual home for our effort, financial support, and the opportunity to gather invaluable feedback on all our volume's chapters. In particular, Gabriel Siles-Brügge (Warwick) and Gabriele Spilker (Salzburg) devoted many hours assessing the chapters. They did so at a workshop we held in May 2022 and later—with further comments to the authors and editors. We are deeply grateful to them.

We looked around the world to invite the best possible scholars to contribute to our volume. The responses were positive from the start, and we believe we succeeded in bringing together a stellar group of authors. An initial workshop in February 2022 allowed us to lay the groundwork for the volume, hear everyone's thoughts, and plan for the work ahead. At the May 2022 workshop, authors presented their chapters and gathered feedback. Throughout, we benefited greatly from having James Cook, senior editor at Oxford University Press (OUP), express his interest in the volume. He understood immediately our aims for this project and guided us along wisely. In the process, he relied on the input of four reviewers. We thank those reviewers for their encouraging and constructive comments. The conceptual and empirical scope of the volume improved significantly because of their insights.

Any volume on EU trade policy will necessarily involve technical terms and data, legal material, consideration of evidence from disparate geographies, countless acronyms, and many other matters that would challenge even the most talented of copyeditors. Knowing her level of expertise and precision from a previous project, we turned to Anna Zuschlag, hoping she would be able to help us prepare the manuscript for submission to OUP. Thankfully, she agreed to take this project on. As expected, her work was exceptional and far beyond anything either of us could have achieved. We are very grateful to Anna for her help.

The production work at OUP was flawlessly managed by Senior Project Editor Emily Benitez. We thank Emily for her outstanding support.

Francesco Duina (Cumberland, Maine, US) and Crina Viju-Miljusevic
(Ottawa, Ontario, Canada)
September 27, 2022

Contributors

Gerry Alons, Associate Professor of Sustainable Agri-Food Governance, Institute for Management Research, Department of Political Science, Radboud University

Andrea C. Bianculli, Assistant Professor, Institut Barcelona d'Estudis Internacionals

Ferdi De Ville, Associate Professor, Department of Political Science, Ghent University

Francesco Duina, Charles A. Dana Professor of Sociology, Department of Sociology, Bates College

Julia Grübler, Economic Affairs Officer, United Nations Conference on Trade and Development; Visiting Lecturer, Central European University

Sangeeta Khorana, Professor, International Trade Policy, Bournemouth University

Rodrigo Polanco, Senior Lecturer and Researcher, World Trade Institute, University of Bern; Legal Adviser, Swiss Institute of Comparative Law

Evgeny Postnikov, Senior Lecturer, School of Social and Political Sciences, University of Melbourne

Maryna Rabinovych, Post-doctoral Researcher, Department of Political Science and Management, University of Agder

Daniela Sicurelli, Professor, Department of Sociology and Social Research, University of Trento

Charlotte Sieber-Gasser, Senior Researcher, Geneva Graduate Institute; Lecturer, Faculty of Law, University of Zurich and University of Lucerne

Crina Viju-Miljusevic, Director and Associate Professor, Institute of European, Russian and Eurasian Studies, Carleton University

Introduction

In the EU's Image?

Francesco Duina and Crina Viju-Miljusevic

The European Union (EU) has pursued a large number of trade agreements across the world.[1] This has been part and parcel of its foreign policy. As the third largest economy (after the United States and China) in the world and lacking "hard" power, the EU has relied on those agreements to project its interests and objectives across every continent (Keukeleire and Delreux 2014; Szymanski and Smith 2005). These are often complex and far-reaching initiatives that have the potential to shape not only economic but also political and social life in the EU and its trading partners.

One of their most important dimensions has involved regulatory standardization. Whereas the EU's "older" (i.e., prior to the twenty-first century) types of trade agreements focused primarily on tariff reductions, the "new generation" has sought to advance convergence in regulatory approaches to goods, services, capital, and labor (Siles-Brügge 2013; Young 2016). This is because regulatory divergences—for instance, around product safety or quality requirements—have historically prevented trade from happening (Young 2017). They have been "trade diverting" for two main reasons. On the one hand, divergences can mean that an item is categorized as non-compliant according to domestic laws, and thus as impossible to import. On the other hand, divergences can drive differences in production costs and thus prices. This can make those items that are more expensive due to higher regulatory standards less competitive (Efrat 2016). Regulatory standardization has sought to do away with those differences.

It seems reasonable to think of this process in mostly economic, legalistic, or technical terms. But regulatory standardization has entailed something more than that: the production of agreed-upon *definitional* and *normative* *principles* around a huge array of matters—many of which may be highly sensitive, may extend beyond strictly market concerns, and may have

Francesco Duina and Crina Viju-Miljusevic, *Introduction* In: *Standardizing the World*. Edited by: Francesco Duina and Crina Viju-Miljusevic, Oxford University Press. © Oxford University Press 2023. DOI: 10.1093/oso/9780197681886.003.0001 far-reaching implications for many aspects of social life. Issues from labor rights to the environment, consumer health, product safety, food quality, human rights, gender equality, e-commerce, and data privacy have all been affected. The very essence of regulatory standardization involves the elimination of definitional and normative differences in those and many other areas. What, for instance, constitutes "safe" or "sustainable" food? What is "gender discrimination at the workplace"? What uses should technology companies make of consumer data? How should manufacturers dispose of toxic waste?

Thus, in the broadest sense and consistent with economic sociology's insights into the making of markets, we may say that the process of standardization has entailed the articulation and acceptance, by the trading partners, of specific *worldviews*. At stake is ultimately how citizens, organizations, and governments make sense of and behave in the world around them. Put differently, we may say that EU trade agreements contain cultural material that contributes to the social construction of reality, as countless aspects of daily life become defined and are subjected to normative perspectives of how things should be.

Not surprisingly, the EU has sought to promote its own regulatory approaches in those trade agreements—that is to say, it has aimed to project its own worldviews onto its trading partners across the globe. In this regard, the Lisbon Treaty's provisions, in Article 21 of the Treaty on European Union (TEU) and Chapter 1 of Title V of the Treaty on the Functioning of the European Union, linking more or less directly a series of high-level general principles (such as the promotion of human rights and sustainable development) to EU trade policy (and other dimensions of external policy), have provided an important driver (Leblond and Viju-Miljusevic 2019; Pelkmans 2021). The same can be said of the ambitious 2006 Global Europe Strategy communication formulated by the European Commission Directorate-General for Trade (DG Trade) on a more assertive EU in world markets (Siles-Brügge 2014), and the Commission's 2015 Trade for All Strategy. The European Commission's publication, in February 2021, of its Trade Policy Review, titled *An Open, Sustainable and Assertive Trade Policy*, in turn will no doubt offer further impetus for this (Jacobs et al. 2023).

Also unsurprisingly, those trading partners have often sought to do the same—wishing to have their own approaches serve as the blueprints or otherwise looking for compromises. The result has been an amazingly rich and complex tapestry of EU trade agreements across the globe, preceded in some cases by intense negotiations, lobbying, and varying degrees of public mobilization. It follows that the EU has not always secured what it wants, and efforts have not always led to the adoption of an agreement. As with the Transatlantic Trade and Investment Partnership (TTIP) with the US, failure and the abandonment of negotiations have also occurred.

This volume seeks to grasp and understand this process of standardization. In particular, it has two objectives. *First, it aims to generate an overall picture of the main contours of the standardizing content of the EU trade agreements across major policy areas and with major trade parties across the world.* Such a picture is currently missing from the existing scholarship which, as we shall discuss, is fragmented both when it comes to analytical approaches to standardization and regulatory convergence, and the empirical cases considered. We are interested, in other words, in identifying the worldview(s) that are emerging from those agreements. More specifically, this means answering a number of related questions: What issue areas appear to have been especially targeted by standardization in EU trade agreements? What are the main features (tendencies, positions, etc.) of that standardizing content? And what are the variations—in issue areas and features—of that standardization across trading partners?

Second, this volume seeks to explain the observable outcomes. What can account for the emerging patterns? More specifically, what explains which issue areas are subject to standardization, the content of that standardization, and the variations we see across geographies (where we find considerable differences in the amount and content of that standardization)? As we address these questions, we also wish to understand why the EU has succeeded in some instances at securing a projection of its worldviews but not in others. Importantly, while we view the process of standardization in sociological and constructivist terms, we start from the premise that a number of rather different driving forces have shaped that process. Political, institutionalist, economic, civil society, and other factors all have an impact. We foresee *multiple causal pathways*. Moreover, we expect the relevant factors to be at work at various levels: the subnational, national, and international/global. Our aim is to shed light on this complex causal reality.

To be clear, our intent is not to catalog and then account for every instance of standardization in every EU trade agreement. Rather, we wish to identify and explain major patterns of standardization (i.e., definitional and normative passages) in those agreements. Our focus is on the overall tendencies in EU trade agreements that could not possibly be understood by simply producing an exhaustive list of all things subject to standardization, or, for that matter, by examining any single trade agreement or a set of agreements in a given policy area.

Given this, we are interested in not only "positive" cases where we see standardization, but also "negative" ones, where the EU has not been able to project its worldviews or there has been a broader failure to reach trade agreements in the first place. The negative cases can reveal important information about what the EU can and cannot achieve.

In addition, we are not assuming a static picture. Indeed, we recognize the likelihood that the EU's standardizing efforts in a particular subject area or vis-à-vis a given trading partner can change over time due to a variety of factors. If so, we wish to understand and explain that variance. Thus, we also expect multiple methodologies—quantitative and qualitative, historically oriented and time-specific, single versus multiple case studies, etc.—to be useful for analysis as we move across the relevant empirical cases.

Throughout, we direct our spotlight squarely on EU trade agreements and not broader policy statements, speeches, press releases, and other such materials. Trade agreements are binding under international law. They are consequential and represent the outcome of concerted negotiations and efforts. The same cannot be said of the other materials. With that said, those other materials can, of course, be relevant for our analysis because they can inform the explanation or may serve as background context that can help grasp the content of the agreements.

Consistent with that, we are, above all, interested in the mandatory regulatory passages in trade agreements. At the same time, we recognize that those agreements often include aspirational passages that may offer some context for the binding ones or point to what may come in the future. To the extent that it seems useful to note these sorts of passages, we do so.

Our aims in this volume are obviously considerable. To achieve them, we (the editors) invited contributions from leading experts in Europe and Australia in political science, economics, and law, and at trade institutes. With their help, we refined the analytical framework that guided their empirical analyses.

We proceed in this Introduction as follows. First, we specify how this volume speaks to existing literatures on the EU, standardization, and globalization. Second, we detail the analytical framework guiding the contributors in their work. Third, we offer a brief overview of the organization of the volume. We then report on the findings both in terms of observable outcomes and driving factors.

Why This Volume? Understanding the Existing Research

This volume is in "conversation" with several research strands, overlapping with some of their key concerns but also contributing a new perspective that is currently missing from them.

Most obviously, there exists a substantial body of research, largely informed by international political economy (IPE), on the EU's new generation of trade agreements. Given the significant departure that these agreements represent from their tariff-reduction-oriented predecessors, scholars have sought to account for that shift, to identify what their primary aims are (partly due, as already noted, to the priorities set out in the Lisbon Treaty but also later documents such as the 2006 Global Europe Strategy statement, and, most recently, the 2021 Trade Policy Review), and to explain the contestation that some have generated (see, e.g., De Bièvre et al. 2020; Young 2017). A subset of these works has certainly considered standardizing principles as understood in this volume. Yet, those analyses share important limitations: they either focus on trade agreements with single trading partners (e.g., the Common Market of the South (MERCOSUR) or Japan) or partners in a particular region (e.g., North America or East Asia), or they consider single-issue areas (e.g., standards on labor rights or services). Such selective focus is reasonable if the objective is to illustrate how EU trade agreements have shifted toward substantive regulatory harmonization as a result of new ways of approaching market integration with external partners. It makes it difficult, however, to arrive at an overarching assessment of those agreements *based on what they actually contain* when it comes to standards across issues and trading partners.

This is especially so given that these works adopt different analytical perspectives and theoretical orientations. Many do not differentiate between soft and hard requirements, for example, while others largely ignore definitional standardization in favor of normative passages. Most do not appreciate the cultural dimensions of standardization. As such, though certainly useful as references, these works amount to a valuable but disparate and disconnected set of insights and data with only limited relevance for this volume. Simply put, when it comes to standardization within trade agreements, they cannot be woven together into a coherent whole in general, or in keeping with our objectives.

This volume speaks to a second strand in EU research: the EU's "normative" power in the world (see, e.g., Lenz 2021; Neuman 2018; Poletti and Sicurelli 2018; Velluti and Martines 2020; Whitman 2011). In this literature, scholars have sought to identify, account for, and assess the impact of a number of high-level principles (such as democracy, good governance, and sustainable development) that the EU has over time advanced through a variety of means, such as foreign policy initiatives, the provision of international aid, influence over the institutional design of other trade blocs (e.g., MERCOSUR or the Southern African Development Community), enlargement to future member states, and trade itself. This is a rich and well-developed literature. Yet, we note that when trade agreements do appear in the analyses they do so as part of a broader consideration of the tools available to the EU (see, e.g., Whitman 2011), or with a focus on specific issue areas, such as labor and human rights (see, e.g., Manners 2009). This volume contributes to this research program by turning specifically and systematically to EU trade agreements and by subscribing to a more expansive concept of "normative" that includes much more than abstract and high-level principles of interest in this literature.

Third, this volume connects to the rather specialized literature on standardization and the EU. These works tend to subscribe to a rather narrow understanding of "standards" as involving mostly technical requirements for products or activities (see, e.g., Bradford 2020; Drexl et al. 2014; Egan 2001; Eliantonio and Cauffman 2020; Van Leeuwen 2017). The focus, moreover, is on the EU's internal market or, in some cases, how the EU's Internal standards indirectly influence corporations and other actors outside the EU because they must trade with the EU, or selected regions with which the EU trades. Our view is that there is no inherent reason to limit the notion of "standard" to technical considerations. Statements identifying acceptable or unacceptable behavior (e.g., around discrimination based on gender or ethnic origins) or definitional statements on what, for instance, is meant by "the right to strike" can certainly be viewed as setting standards. We also see considerable merit in broadening the analysis beyond the EU internal market and to trade agreements.

Returning to research on EU trade agreements, we note that a large number of works has paid attention to what those texts might state on a wide range of policy areas—from the environment to finance, agriculture, and competition (see, e.g., Ferraris 2020; Griller et al. 2017; Jordan and Gravey 2021; Papadopoulos 2010). While potentially relevant for this volume, each work tends to be siloed in a subject area. Moreover, the works are not easily comparable in terms of findings because they adopt different investigative approaches. Some, for example, certainly focus on regulation; others, however, may focus on other dimensions of those agreements, such as their broader links to the EU's foreign policy goals or its officials' discursive practices. It is difficult to draw overarching conclusions across these works when it comes to regulatory standardization.

In the broadest sense, this volume speaks to the various research strands on globalization and cultural, political, and economic convergence (see, e.g., Meyer et al. 2021; Turner 2010; Holzer et al. 2015). These constitute the high-level "intellectual home" of this volume. Scholars have examined the general tendency toward homogeneity at the world level from many angles. A recent example is Yates and Murphy's (2019) work on the spread of voluntary private standards in many industries across the globe since the late 1800s. Much attention is also devoted to power dynamics and which actors seem especially influential. Here, a good deal of research tries to assess the competition between the US and the EU when it comes to setting standards in a wide variety of areas (e.g., the automotive industry in relation to the environment (Crippa et al. 2016), banking, or internet service providers). Such influence, scholars observe, may be direct or indirect. Instances of direct influence include the EU seeking to shape global regulatory bodies (Newman and Posner 2015). Indirect include cases of the "Brussels Effect" (Bradford 2020), whereby actors around the world embrace EU standards not because they are necessarily required to by law, but rather, because of the size of the EU market and the advantages of adopting EU standards in all their operations.

It is clear that some of these works on globalization and convergence focus on the EU itself as a driver of those processes (Fahey 2020). What is still missing, however, is an appreciation for the EU's contribution via its trade agreements to such global convergence, accompanied by a systematic in-depth analysis of those agreements (for an initial brief analysis, see Hoffmeister 2020). Again, this volume is thus unique in its sustained and pointed analysis of standardization in EU trade agreements. What has been the EU's contribution? How extensive has it been, substantively and geographically? What can explain its patterns? *Standardizing the World* seeks to answers these questions with a clear analytical framework and methodical empirical assessment.

The Guiding Analytical Framework

We draw from economic sociology as our starting point. Economic sociologists have argued for some time that market exchanges, in order to occur, require an alignment among participants in the perceived characteristics of what is being traded. Goods, services, labor, and capital are not simply "there." Markets are not "spontaneously generated by the exchange activity of buyers and sellers" (Abolafia 1996, 9). Instead, what is exchanged must be endowed with ascribed properties—from very specific ones around functionalities, for example, to more abstract ones such as "healthy," "safe," or "environmentally sustainable" (see, e.g., Beardsworth and Bryman 1999; Brown 2011; Fourcade and Healy 2007; Spillman 1999). Sociologists thus refer to markets as being "embedded" in cultural, and then often institutional (regulatory, etc.) contexts (Duina 2011; Granovetter 1985).

Historically, when it came to the expansion of trading routes or exchanges between distant societies, the process of alignment occurred gradually (Curtin 1984). Initial contacts became more permanent; trust was established, and a small volume of products was first exchanged. As mutual understandings grew, so did the exchanges, along with contracts that specified expectations more formally. In national economies, markets have been embedded in shared cultural and existing regulatory contexts that have evolved in fairly organic fashion over time. By contrast, the planned process of establishing integrated markets via trade agreements at the international level poses special challenges. Those agreements commit the partners, who typically subscribe to different perspectives on what is being traded, to deeper integration in short periods of time. Once agreement is reached on the economic goals, attention must necessarily go to those disparate perspectives (Duina 2006). How should those be addressed?

The explosion of regional trade agreements (RTAs) after the end of the Cold War shows the emergence of two distinct approaches (Duina 2016). In some cases, such as the North American Free Trade Agreement, the member states have tried to rely on the principle of mutual recognition or, as with the Association of Southeast Asian Nations, a combination of mutual recognition and extensive standardization through regulation. That route to market integration has proven successful but of course has been limited: much that could be traded is not, since non-alignment, especially when significant, can act as a barrier. Put differently, many non-trading barriers have thus been left intact—a limitation experienced, we can note here, by the World Trade

Organization (WTO) at a more global level over time, given its focus on tariff-barriers and its struggles to go beyond those.

By contrast, in other cases the preferred approach has been one of significant standardization. Among the most prominent examples are the EU itself (with its push for the completion of the internal market starting in the 1980s) and then MERCOSUR and the Andean Common Market. Here, the participants have committed to deep levels of standardization through regulation, as scholars have documented in great detail, especially when it comes to the EU but also other cases.

The EU's pursuit of trade agreements across the globe represents the latest step in the expansion of markets. The EU has turned outward, seeking integration with potential partners across the world. This, as we have already observed, has come in the form of the "new generation" of trade agreements (i.e., by way of deeper integration by way of standardization through regulation). The move is, of course, logical: having essentially completed its own market integration through a good deal of standardization, the EU is seeking something similar, albeit not as comprehensive, with many of its trading partners. Given this, and in line with our sociological understanding of markets, a major challenge in this pursuit has been precisely that of standardization. What has been standardized across the EU's various trading agreements? And what seems to be driving the observable patterns?

The question, which by now should be clear, is more than a technical or legal one. At stake is the construction of worldviews—of ways of understanding and making sense of the world, and of aspirations about what should and should not happen in the world. The spotlight is on the articulation of what, in line with economic sociology, we would call elements of culture that concern the EU and its trading partners.

We note that this perspective on EU trade agreements is not only consistent with economic sociology's basic insights about markets, but also echoes constructivist accounts in IPE of the constitution of actors and markets in the international arena. While realists assume pre-constituted and unitary actors and markets, constructivists see these as emergent and composite outcomes. Rather than taking them as "givens," constructivists recognize that they must be "built" (Katzenstein 1996, 4–6). Accordingly, their accounts pay considerable attention to the way in which norms, values, and cognitive processes interact and overlap with market and political processers (Jacobs et al. 2023).

With all this in mind, we specify below the two dimensions of standardization used in this volume for empirical investigation: definitional and normative standardization as present in trade agreements between the EU and its partners. We then identify a priori (based on existing paradigms in IPE, comparative politics, and sociology) a set of possible explanatory frameworks for the observable patterns. The contributors were asked to keep those in mind in their work, so as to subscribe at least at the start to similar disciplinary and analytical concepts in their analysis in order to enable fruitful comparisons across the findings.

Standardization

"Standardization" is the core object of our interest. Specifically, drawing from our earlier work (Duina 2006), by standardization we mean the presence in the relevant EU trade agreements of two sorts of passages. The first are those passages that state something *definitional* about objects/things (e.g., "green energy," "monopoly," "human rights," "fresh fish"), processes/actions (e.g., "investing," "discriminating," "data streaming"), or actors (e.g., "driver," "doctor," "farmer"). This means that those passages specify something about the essential qualities of those objects/things, processes/actions, or actors. This can include listing key ingredients or components, purposes, origins, and other such defining factors.

The second are those passages that state something *normative* about the world: desired practices and outcomes (e.g., pollution thresholds, maximum hours worked, admissible pesticides, required safety features) or unacceptable practices and outcomes (e.g., unfair use of consumer data, racism, abusive market practices). Rather than describing aspects of the world, therefore, these passages describe how the world should be.

By "standards," we therefore mean anything from a very specific set of technical requirements to statements about very high-level matters. Standards can apply to many aspects of "reality," and we are looking to see, ultimately given all that we can observe, what "worldviews" are emerging in EU trade agreements. We are interested, then, in understanding what is being standardized (definitionally and normatively) and, given that, the content of that standardization.

Three additional specifications are in order. First, while our attention is squarely on mandatory or binding passages, we recognize that trade agreements often include aspirational passages (both definitional and, more often, normative). To the extent that these seem worthy of note because of what one day may follow, for instance, or because they help contextualize (and thus better grasp) the mandatory passages, it seems useful to consider them in our analyses.

Second, we understand that texts can vary from very explicit to implicit. Certain perspectives—especially normative ones—can be advanced indirectly, perhaps less powerfully so, as a way to introduce them into the framework of what is important. Again, we wish to be sensitive to this and capture, when it seems consequential, implicit statements.

Third, the spotlight is on the standardizing content of EU trade agreements and not on the question of how those passages are implemented in practice. Implementation can, of course, vary a great deal and, as a subject matter, connects to the rich literature on compliance with EU law as well as international law. As we discuss in our concluding chapter, the issue should certainly inform future research efforts.

Explaining the Patterns

We wish to explain why standardization looks as it does across EU trade agreements, including if the EU has failed to advance its views. We stress that, while we have described the outcomes of interest in sociological and constructivist terms, we recognize that *multiple causal pathways* are certainly at work in influencing the observable patterns of standardization. Thus, we identified, a priori, for our contributors a varied set of possible frameworks in which to "house" or ground their explanations. The frameworks drew from basic insights in IPE, comparative politics, and sociology about causal dynamics in economic and political life, and international trade more specifically (see, e.g., Allee and Elsig 2019; Buonanno 2017; Dür 2019; Gamso and Postnikov 2021; Lechner and Spilker 2022; Milner and Mansfield 2012).

This was in no way intended to constrain what the contributors would discover and argue, but was instead meant to provide them with shared analytical terms and tools that hopefully were useful and enable them to categorize their explanations in ways that we, the editors (and ultimately, the readers), could then connect. Put differently, we wanted to ensure that the contributors used, to the extent possible, a similar social scientific language in their investigations. With that said, we also engaged in early conversations with the contributors themselves to gather what they thought might be especially important causal factors given their expertise and knowledge. This helped us refine the articulation of the guiding explanatory frameworks.

We identified five types of frameworks:

1. Rational choice/political economy frameworks, with attention to the interests of especially powerful economic or political actors in the EU and its trading partners: here, the preferences of powerful business groups are often seen as shaping outcomes. Explanatory power is also assigned to national political leaders and officials in the EU and its trading partners who are able to take positions that are consistently reflective of their constituents' economic or geopolitical interests.

2. Frameworks that focus on the political dynamics and power asymmetries *between* the EU and its trading partners: Here, attention goes to market-size differences, collective action problems, the available resources for bargaining, and various dependencies on the EU (from aid to the possibility of accession).

3. Frameworks that see institutional contexts as especially important: Drawing from historical and sociological institutionalism, neo-functionalism, and related traditions, these explanations put a premium on legacies, path dependencies, bargaining rules and structures, modes of representation, regulatory contexts, and the linkages between issue areas. The focus is less on interests or intentions, and more on structural and temporal dimensions.

4. Frameworks that emphasize the impact of interest groups and other civil society actors, who may operate internationally or at more local levels.

5. Cultural and identity-driven accounts: Values, norms, discursive frames, myths, and other such factors are presented as independent causal variables that influence what actors want and how they pursue their goals.

Importantly, these explanatory frameworks not only focus on distinct causal factors, but also point to the different levels at which they are at work: the transnational, national, and subnational. In one case, for instance, attention might go to the balance of power between the EU and the trading partner, while in another case it might turn to the relevance of certain food traditions in particular countries or regions. This is to be expected: the process of "construction" is complex, multifaceted, and even messy. It proceeds according to multiple logics and at different levels from the local to the international.

The Organization of This Volume

What follows are ten chapters from as many leading scholars from across the world. Each chapter offers answers to the two driving questions of this volume: What has been standardized? What explains the observable outcomes? Throughout, special attention goes to what the answers reveal about the EU's ability to project its interests onto the world. Has the EU been able to standardize the world according to its preferences?

Given this, the first five chapters (Part I) are substantively focused. They examine the EU's standardizing efforts in some of the most important issue areas across a large number of trade agreements: agriculture and food quality, services, rule of law and anti-corruption, investments, labor rights, and the environment. The analyses reveal broad outcomes in those issue areas, as well as the possible drivers of those outcomes.

The subsequent five chapters (Part II) are geographically focused. The spotlight is aimed at EU agreements with major trading partners: the US, Canada, MERCOSUR, Japan, South Korea, and India. Smaller trading partners are also considered, including Indonesia, Malaysia, and Vietnam. These chapters allow for more in-depth analyses of outcomes given any one trading partner, as well as for the possibility of comparisons across trading partners—in terms of factors such as developing and developed economies, market sizes, and different political economies. Some cases also allow for consideration of policy areas (e.g., intellectual property rights [IPR], public procurement, the auto industry, rules of origin) not highlighted in the first chapters.

We discuss the main findings from these analyses in the following section. A concluding chapter reflects on the implications of these findings for future trade agreements, the EU's place in the world, and lines of future research.

The Main Findings

Let us consider the observable outcomes first, and then causality.

Outcomes

We identify here four primary outcomes.

The *first* is that the EU has, indeed, used trade agreements to advance standardizing material in a variety of policy areas. Sometimes this has been done in reference to standards found in the materials of the WTO, International Labour Organization (ILO), World Health Organization (WHO), and other international organizations. But, in many cases, we also see an expansion beyond international standards or a more original process of articulation that does not "take off" from those international standards. The result has been the articulation of new definitional and normative content. We observe this not only across policy areas, but also with different types of trading partners in terms of economic development, market size, and political economies.

Our contributors present highly detailed data in their chapters. We highlight here some of the most important findings:

- **Services:** Sieber-Gasser (Chapter 2) reports that the EU has ratified twenty preferential trade agreements (PTAs) across the world, covering services between 2000 and 2021, a period where it gained near-exclusive competence in this area thanks in part to the 2017 Court of Justice of the European Union (CJEU)'s Singapore Opinion. The pattern has been to include the definitional and normative materials found in the Trade in Services Agreement (an initiative launched in 2013 by a subgroup of WTO members now with over twenty members, including the EU, with the hope of turning it into a WTO agreement for all members), but also, as Sieber-Gasser puts it, to go cautiously beyond it.
  o This has happened in various aspects of services. The PTAs offer definitions, for example, of new services that did not exist at the time of previous WTO agreements in areas such as e-commerce and computer services, services and services-related economic activities, "cross-border services trade," establishment and investment, and the temporary presence of natural persons for business purposes. The PTAs offer new normative notions around electronic communication services and internet-related services more generally. By contrast, areas such as sustainability in services and culture-related services are not covered in the PTAs.

- **Investments**: As Polanco (Chapter 4) reports, post-TTIP negotiations the EU—with its increasing, though not exclusive, competence in this area—has entered into a growing number of PTAs with EU-driven content on investment liberalization and on investment protection. Previous agreements in the 2010s did not have such scope. Among other things, important principles now recognize the category of investments as different from services and extend equal treatment rights to foreign investors.

- **Geographic indications (GIs) and sanitary and phytosanitary measures around food safety, animal health, and plant health**: Alons (Chapter 1) writes that EU trade agreements contain definitional and above all normative principles that go beyond WTO baselines and reflect EU internal standards, which, among other things, treat GIs as a class of intellectual property. This can be seen in not only the agreement with Japan but also those with MERCOSUR and Canada (the Comprehensive Economic and Trade Agreement, [CETA]), and especially around GIs. When it comes to food safety (such as around genetically modified organisms [GMOs] and hormones), CETA with Canada and the EU-MERCOSUR agreement point to considerably more limited alignment with EU normative standardization preferences. Those preferences entail an understanding of consumer rights and food quality as deeply related to the rejection of GMOs, hormones, and other practices that are seen as potentially harmful.

- **Rule of law (RoL) and anti-corruption with developing countries**: Rabinovych (Chapter 3) reports that the EU has projected internal principles (as articulated in a 2004 Commission Framework statement as later reinforced by the CJEU) onto trade agreements with a large number of developing countries across the globe. These principles translate into definitional and normative standards around transparency, non-discrimination, accountability, legal certainty, and judicial independence.

- **Labor and environment**: Both Postnikov (Chapter 5) and Sicurelli (Chapter 8) present evidence of considerable standardization in labor and the environment. Grübler (Chapter 9) also notes the overall commitment to sustainable development in EU FTAs with East Asian economies (Korea, Japan, Singapore, and Vietnam). While the EU has pushed for mostly (but not only) ILO standards when it comes to labor, it has secured more stringent and pronounced standards in the case of the environment since the Global Europe Strategy of 2006. Biofuels, fisheries, biodiversity, and forestry are examples.

- **Trade facilitation and IPR**: The EU-MERCOSUR agreement, finalized after negotiations stretching over two decades, contains extensive provisions on trade facilitation and IPR. Bianculli (Chapter 7) observes that on trade facilitation the agreement relies on established international standards (e.g., the WTO Trade Facilitation Agreement and the International Convention on the Harmonized Commodity Description and Coding System). This is something that Grübler (Chapter 9) notes as well in relation to EU agreements with East Asian economies, whereby the parties agree to follow the standards set by the World Customs Organization. Importantly, though, the MERCOSUR agreement also articulates notions around transparency, good practices, and the need for consultation with business communities that—though consistent with preexisting international principles—represent novel specific articulations.

- **Rules of origin**: Grübler (Chapter 9) finds that the EU-Japan chapter on rules of origins makes no referral to WTO agreements on the matter. Instead, it is rich with definitions for terms as basic as "exporter," "importer," "material," "product," and "production" in order to then elaborate articles on requirements for originating products and their sophisticated technical specifications (e.g., for wholly obtained products, insufficient processing of goods, or the treatment of packaging materials).

- **Intellectual property**: In relation to IPR and especially patents, Bianculli (Chapter 7) writes that the EU-MERCOSUR agreement leverages existing WTO and WHO principles. In the case of patents, it encourages (thus in non-binding fashion) further regulatory compliance and commitments that are consistent with, but also extend beyond, international principles as set forth in the Patent Cooperation Treaty. Importantly, the agreement also articulates principles around GIs that cannot be reduced to existing international standards. In addition, the text expresses a commitment to social and economic welfare, and the advancement of the public interest. Thus, when it comes to IPR, the EU-MERCOSUR agreement includes new standardizing material worthy of note.

- **Digital commerce and the automotive industry**: Turning to East and Southeast Asia, Grübler (Chapter 9) observes that agreements with Japan and Korea not only build significantly from existing international standards and the work of standard-setting bodies when it comes to the auto industry, but also lay the groundwork for additional standardization (e.g., around safety and with the aspiration of influencing global standards). In the case of digital commerce, aspirations for future and novel standardization are asserted in agreements with Japan, Korea, Vietnam, and Singapore (e.g., in relation to the liability of intermediary service providers, intellectual property, and electronic government). Moreover, with Japan in particular, the principle of technological neutrality in e-commerce is recognized as important. The text also contains normative notions on topics that feature in plurilateral negotiations at the WTO, such as access to source code, electronic contracts, e-signatures, and unsolicited commercial electronic messages. Thus, regarding digital commerce specifically, though specific standards have yet to be really agreed upon, the groundwork appears set for future work and output.
- **Procurement**: In relation to the EU-Japan agreement, Grübler (Chapter 9) mentions government procurement as an example where the level playing field of WTO agreements is extended to a greater number of goods, services, and institutions to include central and subcentral government authorities, bodies governed by public law (such as universities and hospitals), additional services, and the transport sector.

Taken together, the evidence suggests considerable and original standardizing content in EU trade agreement. Importantly, some of the contributors point to an additional trend—one that suggests an "amplification" of the relevance of those agreements well beyond trade with the partners onto other agreements not involving the EU or in multilateral settings. This is the case for labor and environmental standards as well as investments, and it is the stated ambition in the auto industry and digital commerce (Postnikov, Chapter 5; Polanco, Chapter 4; and Grübler, Chapter 9). This is reminiscent of the "Brussels Effect," but, in this case, with the baseline being EU trade agreements with other partners (rather than the EU's internal rules) and the adopting actors being non-EU partners entering into agreements among themselves.

In addition, at least in the case of services (Sieber-Gasser, Chapter 2), the resulting standardization in EU trade agreements has actually enabled the EU to introduce measures within its internal market that for various reasons (including a lack of competence internally) the EU has not been able to advance. A similar point can probably be made around investments (Polanco, Chapter 4): an active EU on the international stage has offered opportunities for further EU internal regulatory consolidation in an area where competency has been contested with the member states.

The *second* central finding is that the standardizing material in EU's trade agreements has particular characteristics. Most obviously, it is often highly granular and specific. In line with the expectations of economic sociology, definitionally the objective is clearly to identify, categorize, and ascribe the key properties of objects/things, processes/actions, and actors—often in those areas left vague or untouched by existing international arrangements for various reasons, not least of which is the fact that certain industries or sectors are rapidly evolving due to technological innovations. In the same vein, normatively, while high-order principles are frequently present, we also see the articulation of specific parameters for desired or inadmissible practices and outcomes. The EU, along with its partners, has explicitly recognized the need to produce for market participants detailed blueprints for the world that ultimately facilitate—and indeed, in many cases make possible—economic exchanges. The world must be defined, and behavior guided, for international markets to deepen.

In addition, especially when the content is a projection of the EU's existing internal regulatory or otherwise stated approaches to market liberalization, we observe a tendency toward a measured and socially minded approach to trade and capitalist markets. This is in contrast to what might be viewed as a more direct neoliberal approach. Examples include RoL and anti-corruption measures (present in broad terms already in the TEU and later echoed in the Commission's 2015 Trade for All Strategy) and RoL principles with developing countries (Rabinovych, Chapter 3); standards for digital trade and emerging technologies, with a view to ensuring high levels of consumer protection (Grübler, Chapter 9); sustainability standards in general and as set out in 2009 with the Renewable Energy Directive and the case of biofuels (and its links to palm oil and deforestation) (Postnikov, Chapter 5; Sicurelli, Chapter 8); and a whole host of labor standards (Postnikov, Chapter 5).

Such characterization of the standardizing material in EU trade agreements deserves qualification. Some might view it as consistent with neoliberal objectives, insofar as the material might be seen as a tool to ensure market access to the benefit of EU businesses, and to protect domestic interests from otherwise more competitive foreign businesses or ones that might challenge existing domestic standards. The EU wants its trading partners to be ultimately attractive in economic terms, and this cannot happen when corruption, for instance, or poor environmental practices are widespread, or when opening its markets to products that might undermine current food or health standards. If so, we could describe this standardizing material as serving market-making liberalization ends—not unlike the apparently more technical standardizing material in other areas, and, according to some, the entire EU internal market project itself (Jacobs et al. 2023).

Third, the chapters ahead show that while the EU is quite successful at advancing its views, in several cases—both across policy areas and when it comes to specific partners—the results speak to compromises or even failures to reach agreement. Important examples include the following:

- The US and Canada: The EU has achieved very little in terms of standardization when it comes to transatlantic trade. As De Ville (Chapter 6) observes, early ambitions at standardization with the US with TTIP were quickly abandoned. Mutual recognition was instead pursued—with that, too, ultimately failing. The less ambitious CETA with Canada, which does include provision for potential future standardization, proved more palatable. The EU and US have now set up the Trade and Technology Council, with the hope of developing standards together for future services and products.
- GIs and food safety: As Alons (Chapter 1) writes, with CETA over 1,000 existing EU GIs have been permanently excluded from future consideration. Only 173 EU GIs were included. With Japan and MERCOSUR, additions are allowed but only after consultations and mutual agreement. Most consequentially perhaps, GIs and food safety were primary causes (along with investor protector clauses) for the failure to reach a deal (TTIP) with the most important trading partner in the world: the US.
- Procurement and human rights with India: As Khorana (Chapter 10) reports, negotiations with India collapsed around public procurement and human rights. While the EU pushed for principles in those areas, India resisted. Ultimately, the entire agreement project was shelved.
- Sustainable biofuels: While the EU secured standards with Vietnam, it failed with Malaysia and Indonesia (Sicurelli, Chapter 8).

Importantly, as the above data points suggest, such mixed or negative outcomes have happened not only with partners of considerable economic size or geopolitical relevance; developing countries with limited resources can clearly also shape outcomes. The EU has standardizing powers yet experiences obstacles as well.

Fourth, we observe that even in cases where the EU shows considerable success, the resulting outcomes do not always amount to a consistent pattern. This contrasts with the consistency we can see in some areas, such as services, where, regardless of trading partner, most EU free trade agreements follow a similar blueprint (Sieber-Gasser, Chapter 2).

In the case of RoL, the EU has, for instance, pursued different standardizing objectives (Rabinovych, Chapter 3). Investments offer a second clear example: After 2010, we see a general move toward protection of investments and a definitional split between the right to establishment and capital movement. However, differences abound across agreements. Consider investor protection. CETA provides protection, but the agreement with Japan and others (including the EU-Organisation of African, Caribbean, and Pacific States Partnership Agreement initiated on April 15, 2021, as a replacement for the Cotonou Agreement) do not (Polanco, Chapter 4). Similar variations appear in terms of investor dispute-settlement mechanisms, where we see them missing in the case of China (Agreement in Principle with China—the Comprehensive Agreement on Investment—made public in January 2021). The automotive industry offers a further example: very detailed streamlined standardization is pursued but is applicable to a substantially varying product space across trading partners (Grübler, Chapter 9).

To this, we can add that the EU has systematically excluded, a priori and not because of failed negotiations, from trade agreements certain industry sectors. Services (Sieber-Gasser, Chapter 2) offer an illustration: audiovisual services (themselves often related to cultural material), health services, and education services are not covered in the PTAs. This is less a matter of consistency in terms of content across PTAs and is more one of whether the EU has in fact sought to standardize in a particular subject area.

Overall, the picture that emerges is one of a sustained effort toward standardization that is, however, still in process, given the partial successes and multiplicities of substantive outcomes. We should hence resist the temptation to attribute to the EU a single, coordinated intentionality. We will turn to the question of whether it may be attainable in the future in the Conclusion.

Explanations

What might explain the observable patterns? Are there certain kinds of explanatory frameworks that appear to be especially important? We are interested in accounting for the presence and specific characteristics of the standardizing principles, the varying extent to which the EU manages to assert itself, and the unevenness in consistency in the EU's preferred outcomes as we move across cases and time. To varying degrees, all five causal frameworks identified earlier in this chapter have explanatory power.

Several chapters point to various *institutional* factors as particularly relevant. We consider each institutional factor in turn.

Path dependency and neo-functionalist dynamics appear especially important. These sorts of explanations shed valuable light on the growth of standardizing material while also allowing for more open-ended substantive outcomes: they are more revealing about the impetus and opportunities for more standardization than the specific content it takes.

Rabinovych (Chapter 3) argues as much when considering standardizing principles around RoL and anti-corruption in EU agreements with developing countries. The new generation of trade liberalization expands beyond goods to areas such as public procurement and financial markets. This, logically, spills over into the RoL and anti-corruption domains—with subnational actors mobilizing to lobby for good governance principles in trade agreements (we return to this point later when discussing interest groups). The result is a considerable amount of definitional standardization. Evidence comes from RTAs with developing countries, from Vietnam to the EU-Central America Trade Agreement, to Ukraine.

Polanco (Chapter 4), in turn, discusses an unintended spillover effect caused by the Maastricht Treaty, which established a common external capital regime governing capital flows between the member states and third countries. This gave the EU a shared competence to regulate investment market access, even when member states had expressed opposition to the idea beforehand. In a similar vein, Bianculli (Chapter 7) observes that standardization around trade liberalization rules in the EU-MERCOSUR agreement cannot be understood without appreciating the fact that it emerged from twenty years of negotiations. She describes processes of socialization, communication, persuasion, and learning-by-doing whereby earlier steps informed later ones. Inertia built and eventually the negotiators were able to agree on a number of standardizing principles.

Institutional factors also include internal EU constitutional and regulatory tendencies and shifts that open the way for standardization in trade deals with external partners and also explain some of its specific content and consistency. Polanco (Chapter 4) offers examples in the area of investments, where increased EU competency has allowed the EU to move forward with standardizing material that it deems necessary for trade liberalization. Postnikov (Chapter 5), in parallel, points to the Commission's ability to limit, via its organizational design (and in a path-dependent fashion), the influence of civil society actors when it comes to labor and environmental standards. DG Trade has had considerable latitude to advance particular visions in tune with business interests.

In the case of services, Sieber-Gasser (Chapter 2), rather counterintuitively at first, suggests that the EU's limited competence to regulate services internally has prompted it to move forward externally with noteworthy substantive consistency (at least in part to eventually turn inward and have a conceptual road map). Thus, she notes, EU trade agreements look remarkably similar in their definitional and normative standards regardless of trading partners, market size, or other factors. At the same time, she writes that the EU has held back from standardization in certain areas, such as audiovisual and education, because of entrenched national protectionism within the EU. Polanco notes something similar when it comes to investments.

Still on the institutional front, Alons (Chapter 1) views regulatory "gaps" on GIs between the EU and its trading partners as limiting what the EU has managed to project onto its trading agreements. The bigger the gaps, the less the EU has attained. More GIs could thus be protected with MERCOSUR and Japan than with CETA.

Similarly, in the case of India and public procurement, Khorana (Chapter 10) describes that country's multilayered and fragmented regulatory and administrative environment as making any agreement with the EU very difficult. To that, she adds that procurement was in any event essentially closed to foreign competition until recently. Regulatory "gaps" also figure in Sicurelli's account (Chapter 8) on sustainable biofuels. The EU's limited influence on that front is partly due to the perception, among some trading partners, of questionable scientific legitimacy and suspicions of protectionism as driving forces of standardizing priorities that have no equivalents in those partners.

A final institutional factor is the presence or absence of international standards in any given area. We see that international standards already in place can serve as the core or the basis for eventual agreements. The cases of the WTO Trade Facilitation Agreement serving as the basis for EU-MERCOSUR (Bianculli, Chapter 7) is one example, as are United Nations regulations on motor vehicles in CETA and FTAs with East Asian economies (De Ville, Chapter 6; Grübler, Chapter 9). While the EU may have been influential in shaping those international standards in the first place, their existence appears to serve as a ready-to-take model that the EU (and its trading partners) can find convenient to use. At the same time, the case of services (Sieber-Gasser, Chapter 2) suggests that when relatively little exists internationally (because of factors such as the relevance of that sector for global trade, or the difficulty associated with regulating matters) the EU may be limited in its aspirations with its partners. With this said, it is also the case that the EU may also take advantage of that absence by taking the initiative, as has happened in the emerging area of digital trade.

Our contributors highlight, in turn, the importance of *political economy*. Most prominently, business interests, including in developing countries, play a role in shaping the amount and content of standardization. We see this with GIs and Southern European producers (Alons, Chapter 1; Bianculli, Chapter 7), biofuels in Malaysia and Indonesia (Sicurelli, Chapter 8), MERCOSUR with trade facilitation (Bianculli, Chapter 7), and the protection of domestic providers when it comes to procurement in India (Khorana, Chapter 10). Regarding India, for example, the fact that government procurement comprises 30 percent of its gross domestic product is of enormous importance, as is the fact that this market was essentially closed to foreign providers through the first decade of the twenty-first century, even as the EU began negotiations with India. Such interests can significantly shape the extent and content of standardization.

Asymmetries of power must in turn always be taken into consideration. The chapters show that the EU gets a good deal of what it wants, especially when it comes to aid-dependent countries (Rabinovych, Chapter 3), countries hoping to join the EU (Rabinovych, Chapter 3), and to some extent economically weaker partners such as MERCOSUR, though often by having to offer something in return (as we explain in the next paragraph) (Bianculli, Chapter 7). By contrast, it can fail when dealing with stronger countries who might have divergent perspectives. These include the US around most issues (with whom the initial attempt to pursue regulatory convergence set the negotiations up for failure, as De Ville writes in Chapter 6), autocratic partners like China and the Gulf Cooperation Council countries (Rabinovych, Chapter 3), Canada with CETA and GI limits (Alons, Chapter 1; though some were secured, as De Ville notes in Chapter 6, while pointing out as well that Canada was the weaker negotiator at the table given its smaller economic size), and India to a good extent in relation to procurements (Khorana, Chapter 10).

But our contributors report surprises too. The EU does not always get its way with developing or weaker countries. On sustainable biofuels, Sicurelli (Chapter 8) writes that while the EU secured its preferred standards with Vietnam, it did not with Indonesia and Malaysia. With MERCOSUR, a compromise was struck around IPR—and was indeed explicitly mentioned in the texts themselves. Specifically, the EU agreed to yield when it came to patents, with MERCOSUR negotiators pushing (based on a consensus between its member states, the business sector, and civil society) for what they thought was an important public health matter (Bianculli, Chapter 7). Those outcomes are thus explained by different causal factors—above all, those related to political economy, such as the strength of the relevant business interests, what else might be on the table, and low dependence on the EU for exports.

The EU is continuously evolving, growing in reach, and taking more pronounced and public steps to articulate what its stands for. Values, norms, discursive frames, and myths inform and advance that process. The EU has strong elements of *culture* and *identity*. Our contributors stress that these have shaped the standardization found in its trade agreements. Hence, Rabinovych (Chapter 3) highlights the relevance of the "power through trade" idea, as set out in the Commission's 2015 Trade for All Strategy, as especially important for normative standardization. The EU's overall successful push so far for good governance and human rights in its trade agreements can be directly linked to those visions. Sicurelli (Chapter 8) notes something similar when it comes to sustainable energy: many scholars have linked the EU's "green" objectives to an internal understanding of environmentalism and managed economic growth. When assessing the regulatory depth of the EU-MERCOSUR agreement, Bianculli (Chapter 7) assigns causal relevance to the ideas expressed in the EU's 2006 Global Europe Strategy and its earlier foundations. In the context of FTAs with East Asian countries, the EU stresses the designation of "like-minded" partners, repeatedly underlining shared normative values such as consumer protection and safe and ethical use of emerging technologies (Grübler, Chapter 9).

Relatedly, the EU's approach to GIs is deeply rooted in the long-standing farming and food traditions of its southern member states, as Alons (Chapter 1) argues. It is impossible to understand the existentialist position of the EU vis-à-vis Canada and the US around GIs—but also GMOs and other food matters—without an appreciation for their cultural significance, and long history of importance to the EU itself over time. They have become in part a symbol of what the EU represents in a global world. This is why they jeopardized an agreement with the US despite their relatively minor economic significance and why the EU sought to secure some concessions around GIs with Canada (Alons, Chapter 1; De Ville, Chapter 6).

Our contributors point to some degree of influence by *interest groups* and *civil society*. Specifically, consistent with neo-functionalist expectations, spillover dynamics have invited democracy-oriented actors to pressure the EU for RoL and anti-corruption measures (Rabinovych, Chapter 3). TTIP's failure and various CETA's features around investor rights and food were, in turn, considerably affected by the mobilization of interest groups and civil society (Alons, Chapter 1; De Ville, Chapter 6). Bianculli (Chapter 7) notes in turn the relevance of non-governmental organizations when it comes to MERCOSUR and pressuring the EU on patents.

Multiple factors, then, shape outcomes. These factors are obviously distinguishable from each other in terms of the sorts of actors and dynamics that they point to. But close analysis also suggests that they differ in terms of whether they see causality at work at the *subnational, national, regional,* or *international levels*. Explanations that emphasize power asymmetries between the EU and its trading partners are global/international in nature, for instance, as are those explanations highlighting the centrality of WTO or other international organizations' standards. Those that point to the EU's efforts to craft an identity and sets of values are more regionally focused. But nations are also depicted at times as being particularly impactful. Southern European countries, for instance, have been the driving force behind the EU's GIs regime.

Yet, the subnational can also be highly relevant: business groups, interest groups, and civil society actors mobilize sometimes within, and influence the position of, an EU member state or that of its trading partners. Subnational administrations may have distinct regulatory powers and contexts, along with control over markets in certain sectors—as we saw in India and the public procurement sector. If correct, all this suggests that we must also view the standardizing outcomes of EU trade agreements, while themselves existing at the *international level*, as reflective of forces that extend from the global to the rather *local levels*.

Taken together, the findings paint a picture of a dynamic EU that is nonetheless not always consistent or successful. Multiple causal factors are at work, complicating the picture and precluding easy predictions. We are, of course, still in the early phases of the new generation of trade agreements, and it may seem reasonable to expect the EU to continue pushing for standardization in future agreements. But perhaps other approaches may prove attractive too, including unilateral standardization by the EU with the expectations that business and other actors will comply. Overall, the findings thus raise questions about the future of multilateral trade, competition with other standard setters such as the US and China, the EU's own future interest and abilities to pursue standardization, the design of trade agreements among non-EU countries, and more. We turn to these points in the concluding chapter.

Note

1. For an updated list of the EU's current trade agreements (including those being negotiated or awaiting adoption/ratification), see https://ec.europa.eu/trade/policy/countries-and-regions/negotiations-and-agreements/#_in-place.

References

Abolafia, M. Y. 1996. *Making Markets: Opportunism and Restraint on Wall Street.* Cambridge, MA: Harvard University Press.

Allee, T., and M. Elsig. 2019. "Are the Contents of International Treaties Copied and Pasted? Evidence from Preferential Trade Agreements." *International Studies Quarterly* 63 (3): pp. 603–661.

Beardsworth, A., and A. Bryman. 1999. "Late Modernity and the Dynamics of Quasification: The Case of the Themed Restaurant." *The Sociological Review* 47 (2): pp. 228–257.

Bradford, A. 2020. *The Brussels Effect: How the European Union Rules the World.* Oxford: Oxford University Press.

Brown, K. R. 2011. "Interaction Ritual Chains and the Mobilization of Conscientious Consumers." *Qualitative Sociology* 34 (1): pp. 121–141.

Buonanno, L. 2017. "The New Trade Deals and the Mobilisation of Civil Society Organizations: Comparing EU and US Responses." *Journal of European Integration* 39 (7): pp. 795–809.

Crippa, M., G. Janssens-Maenhout, D. Guizzardi, and S. Galmarini. 2016. "EU Effect: Exporting Emission Standards for Vehicles Through the Global Market Economy." *Journal of Environmental Management* 183 (Pt 3): pp. 959–971.

Curtin, P. D. 1984. *Cross-Cultural Trade in World History*. New York: Cambridge University Press.

De Bièvre, D., P. Garcia-Duran, L. J. Eliasson, and O. Costa. 2020. "Editorial: Politicization of EU Trade Policy across Time and Space." *Politics and Governance* 8 (1): pp. 239–242.

Drexl, J., H. Grosse Ruse-Khan, and S. Nadde-Phlix. 2014. *EU Bilateral Trade Agreements and Intellectual Property: For Better or Worse?* Cham: Springer.

Duina, F. 2006. *The Social Construction of Free Trade: The European Union, NAFTA, and MERCOSUR*. Princeton, NJ: Princeton University Press.

Duina, F. 2011. *Institutions and the Economy*. Boston: Polity Press.

Duina, F. 2016. "Making Sense of the Legal and Judicial Architectures of Regional Trade Agreements Worldwide." *Regulation & Governance* 10 (4): pp. 368–383.

Dür, A. 2019. "How Interest Groups Influence Public Opinion: Arguments Matter More than the Sources." *European Journal of Political Research* 58 (2): pp. 514–535.

Efrat, A. 2016. "Promoting Trade Through Private Law: Explaining International Legal Harmonization." *The Review of International Organizations* 11 (3): pp. 311–336.

Egan, M. P. (2001). *Constructing a European Market: Standards, Regulation, and Governance*. Oxford: Oxford University Press.

Eliantonio, M., and C. Cauffman. 2020. *The Legitimacy of Standardisation as a Regulatory Technique*. Cheltenham, UK: Edward Elgar.

Fahey, Elaine, ed. 2020. *Framing Convergence with the Global Legal Order*. London: Bloomsbury.

Ferraris, L. 2020. *The Pursuit of Sustainable Agriculture in EU Free Trade Agreements*. Wageningen: Wageningen Publishers.

Fourcade, M., and K. Healy. 2007. "Moral Views of Market Society." *Annual Review of Sociology* 33: pp. 285–311.

Granovetter, M. 1985. "Economic Action and Social Structure: The Problem of Embeddedness." *American Journal of Sociology* 91 (3): pp. 481–510.

Griller, S., W. Obwexer, and E. Vranes. 2017. *Mega-Regional Trade Agreements: CETA, TTIP, and TiSA—New Orientations for EU External Economic Relations*. Oxford: Oxford University Press.

Hoffmeister, F. 2020. "The EU's Free Trade and Investment Agreements: European Convergence with World Trade Law?" In *Framing Convergence with the Global Legal Order*, edited by E. Fahey, pp. 25–48. London: Bloomsbury.

Holzer, B., F. Kastner, and T. Werron. 2015. *From Globalization to World Society: Neo-Institutional and Systems-Theoretical Perspectives*. London: Routledge.

Gamso, J., and E. Postnikov. 2021. "Leveling-up: Explaining the Depth of South-South Trade Agreements." *Review of International Political Economy* 29 (5): pp. 1601–1624.

Jacobs, T., N. Gheyle, F. De Ville, and J. Orbie. 2023. "The Hegemonic Politics of 'Strategic Autonomy' and 'Resilience': COVID-19 and the Dislocation of EU Trade Policy." *Journal of Common Market Studies* 61 (1): pp. 3–19.

Jordan, A., and V. Gravey. 2021. *Environmental Policy in the EU: Actors, Institutions and Processes*. London: Routledge.

Katzenstein, P., ed. 1996. *The Culture of National Security: Norms and Identity in World Politics*. New York: Columbia University Press.

Keukeleire, S., and T. Delreux. 2014. *The Foreign Policy of the European Union*. London: Palgrave Macmillan.

Leblond, P., and C. Viju-Miljusevic. 2019. "EU Trade Policy in the Twenty-First Century: Change, Continuity and Challenges." *Journal of European Public Policy* 26 (12): pp. 1836–1846.

Lechner, L., and G. Spilker. 2022. "Taking It Seriously: Commitments to the Environment in South-South Preferential Trade Agreements." *Environmental Politics* 31 (6): pp. 1058–1080.

Lenz, T. 2021. *Interorganizational Diffusion in International Relations: Regional Institutions and the Role of the European Union.* Oxford: Oxford University Press.

Manners, I. 2009. "The Social Dimension of EU Trade Policies: Reflections from a Normative Power Perspective." *European Foreign Affairs Review* 14 (5): pp. 785–803.

Meyer, T., J. L. de Sales Marques, and M. Telò, eds. 2021. *Towards a New Multilateralism: Cultural Divergence and Political Convergence?* London: Routledge.

Milner, H. V., and E. D. Mansfield. 2012. *Votes, Vetoes, and the Political Economy of International Trade Agreements.* Princeton, NJ: Princeton University Press.

Neuman, M. 2018. *Democracy Promotion and the Normative Power Europe Framework: The European Union in South Eastern Europe, Eastern Europe, and Central Asia.* Cham: Springer.

Newman, A. L., and E. Posner. 2015. "Putting the EU in Its Place: Policy Strategies and the Global Regulatory Context." *Journal of European Public Policy* 22 (9): pp. 1316–1335.

Papadopoulos, A. S. 2010. *The International Dimension of EU Competition Law and Policy.* Cambridge: Cambridge University Press.

Pelkmans, J. 2021. "Linking 'Values' to EU Trade Policy—A Good Idea?" *European Law Journal* 26 (5–6): pp. 391–400.

Poletti, A., and D. Sicurelli. 2018. *The Political Economy of Normative Trade Power Europe.* Cham: Springer.

Siles-Brügge, G. 2013. "The Power of Economic Ideas: A Constructivist Political Economy of EU Trade Policy." *Journal of Contemporary European Research* 9 (4): pp. 597–617.

Siles-Brügge, G. 2014. *Constructing European Union Trade Policy: A Global Idea of Europe.* London: Palgrave Macmillan.

Spillman, L. 1999. "Enriching Exchange: Cultural Dimensions of Markets." *American Journal of Economics and Sociology* 58 (4): pp. 1047–1071.

Szymanski, M., and M. E. Smith. 2005. "Coherence and Conditionality in European Foreign Policy: Negotiating the EU-Mexico Global Agreement." *Journal of Common Market Studies* 43 (1): pp. 171–192.

Turner, B. S. 2010. *The Routledge International Handbook of Globalization Studies.* London: Routledge.

Van Leeuwen, B. 2017. *European Standardisation of Services and Its Impact on Private Law: Paradoxes of Convergence.* Portland, OR: Hart.

Velluti, S., and F. Martines. 2020. *The Role of the EU in the Promotion of Human Rights and International Labour Standards in Its External Trade Relations.* Cham: Springer.

Whitman, R. G. 2011. *Normative Power Europe: Empirical and Theoretical Perspectives.* London: Palgrave Macmillan.

Yates, J., and C. Murphy. 2019. *Engineering Rules: Global Standard Setting since 1880.* Baltimore, MD: Johns Hopkins University Press.

Young, A. R. 2016. "Not Your Parents' Trade Politics: The Transatlantic Trade and Investment Partnership Negotiations." *Review of International Political Economy* 23 (3): pp. 345–378.

Young, A. R. 2017. "The Politics of Deep Integration." *Cambridge Review of International Affairs* 30 (5–6): pp. 453–463.

PART I
MAJOR POLICY AREAS

1

Agricultural Regulations in Free Trade Agreements

The EU's Ambitions as Rule-Maker on Food Safety and Geographical Indications

Gerry Alons

Introduction

Agriculture and food policy issues have since long been contentious and sensitive in both the multilateral (e.g., General Agreement on Tariffs and Trade [GATT], World Trade Organization [WTO]) and bilateral trade negotiations and agreements that the European Union (EU) engages in. When the focus was still on negative integration—focusing on eliminating at-the-border barriers to trade, such as tariffs and quotas—sectoral economic interests and broader national interests, such as food security, were already important reasons for states' reticence toward agricultural trade liberalization. Once trade negotiations on agriculture shifted toward positive integration in the first decade of the twenty-first century (involving efforts to align beyond-the-border regulatory regimes), they engendered the interest of an increasingly broad array of (societal) actors and became significantly more contested. While compromises with respect to tariffs mainly involve economic costs, regulations and standards tend to be grounded in (national) traditions, principles, and values, which cannot simply be exchanged for benefits in other domains in a package deal. Instead, states seek to export their own worldviews, projecting their norms and standards by means of trade agreements.

This is specifically the case in the field of agriculture—the domain par excellence that is considered to be able to make or break free trade negotiations. Regulations and standards with respect to food safety (think of the contestation over hormone-treated cows and pigs and the use of genetically modified

Gerry Alons, *Agricultural Regulations in Free Trade Agreements* In: *Standardizing the World*. Edited by: Francesco Duina and Crina Viju-Miljusevic, Oxford University Press. © Oxford University Press 2023.
DOI: 10.1093/oso/9780197681886.003.0002

organisms [GMOs]) and intellectual property (geographical indications [GIs]) are particularly important topics for the EU in their trade negotiations and agreements. Interestingly, these topics are also stakes in a global regulatory competition between the EU and the United States (US), in which both major powers seek to project their preferred principles and approach globally: the American emphasis on a science-based risk-assessment approach competing with the EU's precautionary approach toward food safety and the EU's sui generis approach toward GI protection clashing with the US focus on trademarks. Regulation of these domains in trade agreements is thus a domain of regulatory competition in agri-food governance.

This chapter will investigate to what extent and how four different EU trade negotiations and agreements—the Comprehensive Economic and Trade Agreement (CETA) with Canada, the Transatlantic Trade and Investment Partnership (TTIP) with the US (no agreement), the Economic Partnership Agreement with Japan, and the Free Trade Agreement (FTA) with the Common Market of the South (MERCOSUR)—have contributed to the standardization of food safety and GI regulations. These four cases were selected because they provide for interesting variation expected to be relevant for arriving at explanations of different standardization outcomes. Canada and the US are close political partners of the EU, but their policy ideas with respect to risk management in food safety policy and on the conceptualization and protection of GIs differ significantly from the EU's policy ideas. Furthermore, from an economic perspective, these countries are major trading partners for the EU. The contribution of trade with Japan and the MERCOSUR countries to overall EU trade is more limited, while Japan's policies particularly with respect to food safety were relatively more aligned with EU policy ideas. With respect to MERCOSUR, potential competition from agricultural producers (beef in particular) and the level of food safety standards were specific concerns from the perspective of the EU.

As set out in the Introduction of this volume, two dimensions of standardization—definitional and normative—are distinguished in this chapter and are applied to the trade agreement or negotiating texts. Definitional statements refer to passages in the agreements that specify essential qualities of objects, actors, or processes, such as the definition of what a GI is, or lists of GIs that the agreement applies to. These are essentially descriptive in nature, whereas normative standardization involves statements that are prescriptive in nature, stating something normative about practices, procedures, or outcomes (see this volume's Introduction as well).

The next two sections of the chapter provide analyses of the type and degree of standardization with respect to, first, GI regulations and, second, sanitary and phytosanitary (SPS) measures in the four cases. In each of these sections, I will first set the stage by elaborating on EU policies and ambitions in the domain and the worldview in which these are embedded, before moving to the comparative analysis of standardization in the agreements. Each of these sections ends with an analysis of the extent to which the EU may be considered to have been successful in exporting its standards and values. Applying economic and ideational variables and their interactions with the political process, the chapter's fourth section moves toward explaining the variation in standardization found and the degree of EU success in the different agreements. The chapter concludes with a concise conclusion of the main findings.

Geographical Indications

GI Regulation and Contestation

GIs are signs used on products that have a specific geographical origin and possess qualities or a reputation that are (considered) due to that origin.[1] Well-known examples are Champagne, Roquefort cheese, and Parma ham. Agricultural producers of these products are interested in having an exclusive and protected right to use such product names (usually with higher price premiums), while consumers have an interest in being correctly informed on the geographical origin of a product, particularly when a higher quality is ascribed to the product on the basis of this origin.

EU member states—particularly the Southern states—have a large collection of GIs they wish to see protected, in both their intra-EU and external trade. The EU has developed a sui generis regulatory system for the protection of GIs, setting them apart as a separate class of intellectual property (next to, for example, trademarks, patents, designs, and copyrights). In this system, public institutions are tasked with the enforcement of the regulation (Marette et al. 2008). If usurpation is found, it is dealt with summarily, without the GI producers having to instigate and pay for court proceedings and without having to prove that consumers were misled, and financial damage accrued. In its negotiations with trading partners, the EU seeks to internationalize the protection of GIs, projecting the EU norms and the method and degree of protection globally in order to secure the protection of GIs in third-country markets, supporting the interests of EU producers and ascertaining reliable information for consumers (Josling 2006).

Not all EU-trading partners share the EU's approach to GIs. The US, in particular, has almost diametrically opposed preferences on GI regulation (Matthews 2016b). It argues that many product names that are considered GIs in the EU are actually generic names, indicating *types* of cheese or wine, for example, which do not warrant protection (Monten 2006). They consider GIs to be potential trade barriers and argue that GIs do not require a sui generis system of protection (Goldberg 2001; Josling 2006). Instead, the US treats GIs as private property rights to be protected through the existing trademark system (Matthews 2016b). Contrary to the role of public administration in the sui generis system of protection of GIs in the EU, in the US, it is private actors' own responsibility to protect their product names through the existing legal infrastructure of the trademark system and to ascertain enforcement of the ensuing property rights (Josling, 2006; Marette et al. 2008).

Apart from protecting economic (producer) and social (consumer) interests, GI policies are also grounded in policy ideas that represent a particular worldview that negotiating partners may not share. Trade negotiations, therefore, are also an instrument for the EU to export its worldview. With respect to GIs, this worldview is based on a perception of GIs as an issue of food quality and cultural heritage, rooted in traditional production methods. State regulation is deemed appropriate to promote and protect GIs. In this vein, GI is also considered a tool that opposes neoliberal globalization and its homogenizing tendencies (Fracarolli 2021), or even a form of identity politics when consumers identify with particular foods. Huysmans (2022, 990) uses the concept "gastronationalism" in this respect, presenting GI protection through trade agreements as "a symbolic affirmation of its value, an expression of national identity, and a source of pride."

Outside of bilateral agreements, the use and protection of GIs is also governed through a number of multilateral agreements, dating back as early as the 1883 Paris Convention for the Protection of Industrial Property. However, membership in these agreements was limited, and the WTO Trade-Related Investment Property Rights (TRIPS) agreement of 1994 was the first agreement with a genuinely global reach, establishing a minimum level of protection for GIs. Since TRIPS, the WTO's binding dispute-settlement mechanism also extends to GI policies (Viju et al. 2013). In its trade agreements, the EU seeks to go beyond TRIPS commitments by

Table 1.1 GI Dimensions in the Trade Agreements

Element/Dimension	Options	EU Preference
Legal status of GIs	Separate class of IP or not	Separate IP class
GI list	Fewer or more GIs included in the list of protected GIs	Include as large a number as possible
Level of protection	Correctives (like, style, etc.) allowed or not	No correctives allowed
	Automatic protection based on register/list or not	Automatic protection
	Weight of the "burden of proof" for protection (conditions: e.g., misleading public, proof of damage)	No or "light" burden of proof
Relation between trademarks and GIs	First-in-time-first-in-right, question of primacy, coexistence	GIs replacing origin trademarks, phaseout of trademarks that coincide with EU GIs
System of protection	Free choice, versus primacy of particular system	Primacy for a public enforcement system

agreeing on a list of EU GI foodstuffs to be protected in the partner country at an extended level of protection—protection whether misuse of the name misleads the public or not, and preventing correctives such as "like" and "style" as well as origin symbols—by finding agreement on coexistence with prior trademarks and by including mandatory administrative protection (Matthews 2016b).

In order to gauge the degree to which the EU has succeeded in projecting its standards through standardization with regard to GIs in its trade negotiations, five elements or dimensions (Table 1.1) will be included in the comparative case analysis.

Comparative Analysis of Standardization in the Trade Agreements

The CETA, EU-MERCOSUR, and EU-Japan agreements contain subsections on GIs in their chapters on intellectual property, addressing the five issues of relevance. Negotiations on GIs in TTIP had not yet advanced to a stage of a consolidated text (Trade-leaks.org 2016) at the time that the negotiations collapsed. However, the EU put forward its own proposal, and secondary sources reflect on the differences in preferences between the EU and the US.

CETA, the EU-Japan, and the EU-MERCOSUR agreements all recognize GIs as a *separate class of intellectual property* (with a separate section in the intellectual property chapter in each of the agreements) and include annexes listing the GIs that will receive a certain level of automatic protection based on the agreement. The definition of GI applied (art. 14.22.2 EU-Japan treaty and art. 20.16 CETA) or referred to (art. X.3.1) in each of these agreements largely follows the art. 22.1 definition as laid down in the WTO TRIPS treaty. A variation in the definitions in the treaties is that CETA only includes agricultural products and foodstuffs—the EU and Canada already have an existing agreement on wine and spirits (Viju et al. 2013)—while in the treaties with Japan and MERCOSUR the more general term "good" is applied. This translates into differences in the classes of products that are part of the lists of GIs annexed to the different treaties: 173 EU GIs in CETA Annex 20-A, 238 EU GIs in Annex 14-B EU-Japan agreement, and over 300 EU GIs in Annex II to the intellectual property chapter in the EU-MERCOSUR agreement. Interestingly, both CETA and the EU-MERCOSUR treaty also include a separate annex which lists a number of terms connected to EU GIs for which no protection is sought, while the EU-Japan treaty does not include such a list. Apart from achieving protection for foodstuff GIs in the TTIP, the EU (European Commission 2016) also aimed to integrate existing bilateral agreements with the US on spirits (1994 agreement) and wine (2006 agreement) in order to gain protection for twenty-two additional names of spirits and to "claw back" seventeen names of wines that were not yet granted exclusive protection on US territory under the 2006 agreement. The US opposed this proposal.

Regarding the *GI lists*, all three treaties also include normative standardization, specifying the appropriate processes and procedures (e.g., opposition/objection procedures, consultations) by which the lists can be adapted and the proper role of specific actors in the process (CETA art. 20.22; EU-Japan art. 14.30; EU-MERCOSUR art. 33.4), albeit that the options are more circumscribed in CETA than in the other treaties. In the case of CETA, the list of GIs that could, in theory, be added at a later date is severely limited by art. 20.22.2, which indicates that "no GIs that were already registered in the EU on the day of signing of this agreement" qualify to be added at a later point in time through this procedure. This effectively means that over 1,000 current EU GIs cannot be added in the future. Furthermore, CETA art.

20.22.3 provides that, after the agreement's signing date, new GIs cannot be added if a trademark with the same name already exists.

With respect to the *scope and level of protection*, the agreements specify not only what constitutes wrongful or prohibited use of GI names but also establish exceptions that circumscribe the situations qualifying for protective action. While this is definitional standardization to the extent that it defines specific behavior as proper use or prohibited use, the adjectives "proper" and "prohibited" indicate that norms are at play here. Normative standardization can further be found in provisions on what GI protection should (at a minimum) entail. CETA (art. 20.19) and the EU-MERCOSUR Agreement (art. 35) indicate that protection should entail "provid[ing] the legal means for interested parties" to prevent usurpation of their GIs, while the EU-Japan treaty even sets out an explicit list of minimum requirements for the system of protection (art. 14.23). The general indication of what constitutes wrongful or prohibited use of GIs that warrant protection includes the same three elements in each of the treaties (CETA art. 20.19; EU-Japan art. 14.25; EU-MERCOSUR art. 35.1-2): use of the GI for products that do not qualify for the term; means of designation or presentation (e.g., by origin-invoking images) that wrongfully suggest the good originates in a geographical area; and unfair competition. These acts are considered prohibited, even if the true origin of the product is indicated (e.g., Australian feta), the GI is used in translation, or is accompanied by correctives such as "kind," "style," "type," or "imitation." This essentially brings the foodstuff GIs to the level of protection awarded by TRIPS art. 23 (see also Matthews 2016b). While the EU aimed to achieve a similar level of protection in TTIP, there was no agreement with the US on this issue. For homonymous GIs—GIs that are spelled or sound alike but originate from different countries (e.g., when two countries have regions with similar names)—procedures for coexistence are put in place (CETA art. 20.29; EU-Japan art. 14.25; EU-MERCOSUR art. X.35.8). However, the agreements, particularly CETA, also include exceptions that circumscribe the level of protection for specific GIs listed in the treaty annexes, such as temporary (EU-Japan treaty art. 14.29) or indefinite (CETA art. 20.21) continued use of GIs by prior (pre-CETA agreement) users of a specific GI. Similar exceptions in MERCOSUR contain very particular descriptions of the MERCOSUR country or countries where continued use is allowed, and very precise labeling requirements.[2] The homonym procedures and provisions for exceptions constitute normative standardization, indicating what are proper behaviors and procedures under different circumstances.

The three FTAs provide only limited normative standardization with respect to the *system of protection* required to protect GIs. Enforcement by administrative action is required (CETA art. 20.19), but the parties are largely left free "to determine the appropriate method of implementing the provisions of th[e] Agreement within its own legal system and practice" (CETA art. 20.2; EU-Japan art. 14.28; EU-MERCOSUR art. 1.2, 33.2, and 35.1) and to provide enforcement "to the extent provided by its law" (CETA art. 20.19). A difference between CETA and the other two treaties is that CETA states that enforcement is required if reference to a GI is used "in a manner that is false, misleading or deceptive or is likely to create an erroneous impression regarding origin," while the other two treaties do not include such a precondition. The EU-Japan treaty even provides further normative standardization by setting out minimum systemic and procedural requirements for the system of protection (art. 14.23), including a registration system, publication of GI lists, administrative processes to verify GIs, opposition procedures, and procedures for the cancellation of GI protections.

On the required action with regard to the relation between GIs listed and new trademarks (or existing trademarks and new or newly protected GIs as a result of the agreement), all three treaties provide normative standardization by including the rules on how GIs and trademarks are to coexist. New trademarks should be registered if a GI with the same name already exists (e.g., EU-Japan art 14.27). With respect to existing (prior) trademarks in a party's territory and the GIs for which protection is established through the trade agreement, the rules foresee coexistence. The reasoning in CETA (art. 20.21) and EU-Japan (art. 14.27.5) is that preexisting trademarks cannot be denied eligibility or validity for registration or use "on the basis that the trademark is identical with, or similar to, a geographical indication." In addition, however, the EU-Japan treaty (art. 14.27.4) also states that the existence of a prior conflicting trademark "would not completely preclude the protection under this Agreement of a subsequent geographical indication for like goods"; this also appears to be the case for future GI registrations. CETA does not allow GIs that existed at the date of the agreement's signing and were not included in the Annex to be added to the Annex at a later date, according to art. 20.21.9. The EU-MERCOSUR treaty provides the strongest description of the coexistence and protection of GIs listed despite existing trademarks requiring protection "also where a prior trademark exists" (art. 35.3d). Relatedly, art. 6.1 in this treaty (in the subsection on trademarks) already indicates that geographical indications can provide for exceptions to the rights conferred by a trademark. In TTIP, the EU aimed for coexistence between GIs and prior trademarks, but it is unclear to what extent progress had been made on this issue by the time the negotiations collapsed in 2016.

The comparative analysis of the three agreements with respect to GI-related standardization is summarized in Table 1.2. Because the potential outcome of TTIP on GIs was so uncertain—for example, Matthews (2016b) elaborated on three different scenarios around the time the negotiations collapsed—and the positions of both parties were still wide apart, TTIP is not included in Table 1.2.

Reflecting on the degree to which the EU succeeded in exporting its standards by means of trade agreements, the results are mixed. On the positive side, in all agreements, the degree of protection goes beyond the default option of art. 22 of the WTO TRIPS, shifting a number of the EU's foodstuff GIs to the stronger level of protection of art. 23. Furthermore, in each of the agreements, a system and procedure for enforcement is foreseen—even though in many cases this would require legal action on the part of the GI-holders as the domestic rules and procedures apply—which goes beyond WTO dispute settlement provided through TRIPS. CETA is more limited than the other two agreements with respect to the number of EU GIs protected, the relatively extensive exceptions to this protection, and the curtailment of future additions to the protected GI list. Nevertheless, as Huysmans (2022) argues, getting 143 GIs accepted in a country with important trade relations with the US is a significant success. Exceptions to protection are most limited in the EU-Japan agreement, and this agreement provides clear minimum requirements for the system of protection. Exporting EU standards was, therefore, most successful in the agreement with Japan, followed by MERCOSUR and then CETA.

Food Safety

Food Safety and Contestation

Trade agreement chapters on so-called SPS measures involve the arrangements made with respect to food safety, animal health, and plant health. SPS regulations—or divergence in such regulations between trading partners—can constitute barriers to trade. For example, if a product for the Canadian market is required to meet other product (or production)

Table 1.2 Regulation and Standardization with Respect to GIs

Element/ Dimension	CETA	EU-Japan	EU-MERCOSUR
Conceptualization of GIs	Art. 22 TRIPS, foodstuffs only	Art. 22 TRIPS	Art. 22 TRIPS
Legal status of GIs	Separate class of IP	Separate class of IP	Separate class of IP
GI list	173 EU GIs	238 EU GIs	> 300 GIs
	Separate list of non-protected terms	Procedure for adding new GIs, no a priori limitations	Separate list of non-protected terms
	Procedure for adding new GIs but: (a) EU GIs registered at time of signing agreement do not qualify, (b) no GIs if trademark with the same name exists		Procedure for adding new GIs, no a priori limitations
Level of protection	Essentially art. 23 TRIPS	Essentially art. 23 TRIPS	Essentially art. 23 TRIPS
	No correctives allowed	No correctives allowed	No correctives allowed
	Coexistence of homonymous GIs	Coexistence of homonymous GIs	Coexistence of homonymous GIs
	Extensive exceptions to the protection	Very limited exceptions to the protection	Exceptions to the protection
Relation between trademarks and GIs	Existing trademarks coexist with the agreement-protected GIs	Existing trademarks coexist with the agreement-protected GIs	Existing trademarks coexist with the agreement-protected GIs
	No new trademarks allowed similar to protected GIs	No new trademarks allowed similar to protected GIs	No new trademarks allowed similar to protected GIs
	No protection for new GIs similar to existing trademarks	Potential protection for new GIs similar to existing trademarks	Potential protection for new GIs similar to existing trademarks
System of protection	Administrative action within own legal system and practice	Administrative action within own legal system and practice	Administrative action within own legal system and practice
	Enforcement only in case of misleading or deceptive use and to the extent provided by its law	Minimum requirements for system of protection	

requirements than the same product for the EU market, producers in both countries may need double production lines, or the products will be required to undergo multiple checks on both sides of the Atlantic before they can be imported in the other country. This involves costs for producers and eventually consumers. Therefore, the objective of regulatory cooperation in general, and of SPS agreements in the case of agri-food trade specifically, is to diminish trade barriers, while safeguarding human health, animal health, and other values.

Diverse ideas on food safety, indicative of different worldviews—or cultures (Echols 1998)—exist between the EU and the US, resulting in disparities in policies and levels of protection (Schroeder 2016). A focal point is the precautionary principle that, in the perception and application of the EU, results in products not being allowed on the market unless they are indisputably proven safe. The principle allows policymakers to "elaborate provisional, non-discriminatory and proportionate health protection strategies in response to situations where there is a potential health risk but little scientific data is available at the time" (McEvoy 2016, 513). As a result, EU policies involve a substantial degree of state regulation and intervention. US policy ideas come with higher risk tolerance and are more business-oriented, allowing for a large degree of industry self-regulation and accepting products unless they are scientifically proven harmful (Duina 2019). Echols (1998) argues that such transatlantic variations are grounded in cultural differences, where citizens in the EU prefer traditional foods (think also of GIs), minimal processing, and value naturalness over new food technologies (e.g., GMOs), whereas the US represents greater willingness to accept new technologies and the scientific progress associated with them.

The development of food safety legislation in the EU over time has significantly been shaped by different food crises. Concerns about the effect of residues of hormonal growth promoters applied in animal husbandry were an important driver of EU food safety regulation in the 1980s and 1990s (McEvoy 2016). In the late 1990s, the BSE (bovine spongiform encephalopathy) crisis gave rise to the creation of a Directorate-General for Health and Consumer Protection; together with the Belgian dioxin crisis in 1999, this caused a fundamental change in EU food legislation. In 2000, the Commission presented a White Paper on Food Safety (European Commission 1999) which included an action plan for numerous (legislative) initiatives and introduced the concept of the *precautionary principle* (which it later elaborated in additional legislation [Regulation EC No 853/2004]). Contrary to contestation of this principle by trading partners (Matthews 2016a), the resulting strict food safety regulations are in high demand with European consumers and civil society organizations (CSOs), partly instigated by fear of adverse health effects of beef from hormone-treated cattle, poultry washed in anti-microbial rinses ("chlorinated chicken"), and GMOs.

International norms on food safety, animal, and plant health have been established in the Codex Alimentarius (Codex), the International Plant Protection Convention (IPPC), and by the World Organisation for Animal Health (Office International des Epizooties [OIE]). These international standards are voluntary and non-binding. However, the WTO agreements on SPS measures and technical barriers to trade (TBT) identify Codex, IPPC, and OIE standards as international benchmarks (e.g., SPS art. 3). National regulations that are consistent with these standards are considered lawful under the SPS and TBT agreements. While the SPS agreement grants WTO member states the right to decide on their national safety standards (SPS, art. 2), implementing national standards that are more stringent than the Codex, IPPC, or OIE standards must be based on risk assessment and underpinned by scientific justification (SPS, art. 3.3 and 5). The SPS agreement (art. 4 on equivalence) also requires WTO member states to accept the SPS measures of other member states as equivalent, if the exporting state demonstrates that its measures produce the same level of protection as those of the importing state. The burden of proof thus rests with the exporting state, and checks, inspection, and approval procedures to ensure the fulfillment of SPS measures are allowed. The existing WTO dispute-settlement system applies to the SPS agreement. EU trade disputes with the US and Canada on hormone-treated beef have been decided in favor of the US and Canada, as the EU import ban was judged to be based "neither on a scientifically sound risk analysis for life and health nor on internationally relevant rules" (Schroeder 2016, 498). Food safety can thus be considered a defensive trade issue for the EU. In its trade negotiations with third parties, the EU seeks to emphasize the "freedom to regulate"—to ascertain that the trade agreement does not circumscribe and constrain their power to install emergency regulation when health risks warrant such actions—to gain recognition for the EU perception of the precautionary principle, and to secure a high level of protection.

The CETA, EU-Japan, and EU-MERCOSUR trade agreements and the negotiating texts in TTIP include provisions on five issues that are relevant for analyzing whether and how the agreements accomplish standardization and result in obligations beyond the SPS agreement: (1) equivalence, (2) trade facilitation and audits, (3) risk assessment and emergency measures, (4) information exchange and consultation, and (5) SPS committee and dispute settlement. These themes are the basis for the comparative analysis below.

Comparative Analysis of Standardization in the Trade Agreements

The four agreement or negotiating texts include provisions on obligations and procedures with respect to establishing *equivalence* between the parties' SPS measures (CETA, art. 5.6; TTIP, art. X.4; EU-Japan, art. 6.14; EU-MERCOSUR, art. 9). All texts reiterate that the burden of proof of equivalence lies with the exporting party and that the parties shall agree to consultations on the equivalence of specific SPS measures if one of the parties makes such a request. This is in line with the existing SPS agreement and thus creates no additional obligations. Furthermore, the CETA agreement and TTIP negotiating texts include (plans for) lists of SPS measures that the parties recognize as equivalent based on existing veterinary agreements the EU already established with the US in 1998 and Canada in 1999. CETA essentially does not include further mutual recognition beyond the existing veterinary agreement (Rudloff 2014; Schroeder 2016). It is with respect to principles and guidelines for determining the recognition and maintaining of equivalence that the agreements, with the exception of the EU-Japan agreement, aim to move beyond existing arrangements. Annex 5-D to CETA aims to specify these principles and guidelines but only included maintenance of equivalence at the time the treaty was signed; for TTIP, this Annex was not yet developed. The EU-MERCOSUR agreement leaves the procedure for recognition of equivalence to the Subcommittee on SPS that the treaty establishes.

How should these provisions be considered in terms of standardization? First, mutual recognition or equivalence does not introduce new common standards, nor does it set existing national or international standards as guidelines for future relations between the two trading partners. In the context of this volume, it therefore constitutes an outcome of non-standardization of SPS norms. That said, in terms of procedures for *determining equivalence—* which would qualify as normative standardization—CETA, TTIP, and EU-MERCOSUR aim to introduce normative standards, but these are largely not yet included in the actual agreements. The agreements, therefore, barely standardize procedures of conformity assessment, while the mutual recognition of standards does not go beyond existing agreements (see also, De Ville, Chapter 6 in this volume).

With respect to *risk assessment*, the agreements with Canada, Japan, and MERCOSUR do not contain standardization applied to SPS. The topic is included in the TBT chapters in CETA and the EU-Japan agreement, but these chapters explicitly do not apply to SPS. References made to risk assessment and scientific evidence in the SPS chapters are restricted to topics for future bilateral dialogue (CETA art. 5.14), general notes that SPS measures should be based on risk assessment, with reference to SPS art. 5 (EU-Japan art. 6), and reiteration of SPS art. 5.7 that in cases of insufficient scientific evidence, provisional measures have to be based on risk assessment and reviewed within a reasonable term (EU-MERCOSUR art. 11). Only the TTIP negotiating text contains an elaborate provision on "science and risk" (art. X.5), proposed by the US, which would have implied normative standardization of procedures in line with US preferences. Emergency SPS measures are allowed under all four agreements to protect human, animal, or plant life or health (CETA art. 5.13; EU-Japan art. 6.13; EU-MERCOSUR art. 14; TTIP art. X.18) and the agreements set normative standards with respect to the required notification and appropriate response times in case of a request for consultations by the other party.

Provisions concerning *trade facilitation* are included in CETA (art. 5.7 and Annex 5-F), EU-MERCOSUR (art. 7), EU-Japan (art. 6.7), and TTIP (art. X.3 and X.11). These aim to simplify the procedures and potentially reduce the inspections required for trading food products. All agreements and the TTIP negotiating text foresee or spell out procedures for recognizing each other's "authorized establishments" for a commodity and their control systems. Exports authorized by these establishments do not require pre-clearance or inspections. The authorized establishments ascertain that the products comply with the importing state's SPS conditions. The provisions on these procedures are most specific and elaborate in the CETA and EU-MERCOSUR agreements: for example, with respect to deadlines for import approval (EU-MERCOSUR art. 7.5) and conditions for recognition of establishments (CETA Annex 5-F). Such procedures and the concomitant simplification of and reduction in inspections constitute normative standardization and go beyond existing obligations based on the SPS agreement. The agreements also allow *audits* or verification of the control programs of the competent authorities in the other party, including provisions for reports and right of the other party to comment (CETA art. 5.8; EU-Japan art. 6.8; EU-MERCOSUR art. 15; TTIP art. X.9). To this end, the EU-MERCOSUR agreement stipulates a procedure in art. 15. CETA intended Annex 5-H to set principles and guidelines for audit or verification, but the parties did not agree on a text here, while the EU-Japan treaty does not include further specification either. Finally, in the consolidated negotiating text of TTIP, the EU included an elaborate text emphasizing the right of audit and verification of the other party's control system, with a frequency determined by the importing party, and procedures and guidelines to be laid down in a separate Annex. Normative standardization of the guidelines for verification procedures is clearly the aim of EU-MERCOSUR, CETA, and TTIP, but only the first includes more specific procedures in the actual agreement text.

With respect to *information exchange*, the EU-Japan agreement (art. 6.11) explicitly follows the SPS agreement art. 7 and Annexes B and C, including information on SPS regulations in force in the territory and control and inspection procedures. The EU-MERCOSUR agreement (art. 11) and CETA (art. 5.11) additionally include information on pest status, lists of regulated pests, and risk analysis and/or scientific information with respect to SPS standards that are not based on existing international standards. The CETA text does not create a strict obligation for the latter, however, and only speaks of "endeavour to exchange information," while the EU-MERCOSUR agreement specifies that, upon request, the parties "shall" exchange this information. The latter agreement also sets a fifteen-working-day deadline for responses to information requests. The EU's proposal for a TTIP agreement largely resembles the CETA text. The US proposal is more elaborate, however, and includes information exchange on regulations that the other party is developing, where "the Party shall ensure that any person, regardless of domicile, has an opportunity, on no less favorable terms than any person of the Party, to submit comments on the regulation" (art. X.7.3). Although this provision would obviously work both ways and would also provide actors from the EU the opportunity to submit comments on US plans for SPS measures (Matthews 2016a), the European Commission opposed this provision. In case one of the parties is concerned about food safety, plant health, or animal health, or an SPS measure that the other party has proposed or implemented, all four agreements and negotiating texts include provisions for *technical consultation*, albeit with different degrees of specificity and commitment. The EU-Japan treaty (art. 6.12) and CETA (art. 5.12) appear to provide the least commitment: they do not provide deadlines for a party within which to respond, and the EU-Japan treaty explicitly allows for termination of consultations by notification of the other party in writing. The provision in the EU-MERCOSUR agreement (art. 13) is more elaborate and includes deadlines for responses and the option of referring an issue to the SPS sub-committee. The EU's proposal in the consolidated text of TTIP (art. X.17) mirrors the article in CETA, with the exception of a fifteen-day deadline to respond to a request for consultation. The US proposal additionally includes a sixty-day deadline for the first consultations to take place and elaborate provisions on appointing a facilitator. Despite deadlines and specification of procedures, the provisions in the agreements eventually only oblige to make an *effort* to reach a mutually acceptable solution, not an obligation to find a solution and implement it. Nonetheless, the provisions on relevant information and the proper procedures agreed on constitute normative standardization.

CETA (art. 5.14), the EU-Japan (art. 6.15), and the EU-MERCOSUR agreements establish *special committees* on SPS to monitor implementation of the SPS chapter and provide a forum for discussion, with the possibility of establishing ad hoc working groups to address specific SPS issues. For TTIP, the US proposal also included standing, instead of ad hoc, technical working groups. While these committees are allowed to discuss many themes, the treaty provisions do not give them actual decision-making powers on standards. Decisions on developing and implementing SPS measures and binding decisions about harmonization or mutual recognition of measures maintain the prerogative of the states (Schroeder 2016, 500), albeit that they have to follow the proper procedures—normative standardization—as set out above with respect to risk assessment, notification, and consultation. With respect to *dispute settlement*, CETA (ch. 29), the EU-Japan agreement (ch. 21), and the EU-MERCOSUR agreement include a separate chapter on dispute settlement. In the case of the EU-Japan agreement (art. 6.16), this chapter does not apply to important provisions on risk assessment, the justification of checks, and the guidelines for equivalence. However, in CETA and the EU-MERCOSUR agreement, these chapters provide for consultation, mediation, arbitration, compliance, and remedies in case of non-compliance and appear to be applicable to the SPS chapter as well.

The comparative analysis of the three agreements and TTIP consolidated negotiating text with respect to food safety–related regulation and standardization is summarized in Table 1.3. Overall, the different agreements do not set actual SPS standards (either new or based on existing standards)

Table 1.3 Regulation and Standardization with Respect to Food Security

Issue	CETA	TTIP	EU-Japan	EU-MERCOSUR
Equivalence	Annex with list of equivalent standards. No further mutual recognition than existing veterinary agreement. Partial procedural principles and guidelines	EU proposes to integrate existing veterinary agreement in TTIP. Procedural principles and guidelines foreseen	Standards of SPS agreement apply	Standards of SPS agreement apply. SPS subcommittee tasked with developing procedural principles and guidelines
Risk assessment and emergency measures	Topic for future dialogue. Emergency measures allowed with appropriate procedures for notification and consultation	US proposes procedures for science and risk. Emergency measures allowed with appropriate procedures for notification and consultation	Risk assessment reference to SPS agreement. Emergency measures allowed with appropriate procedures for notification and consultation	Risk assessment reference to SPS agreement. Emergency measures allowed with appropriate procedures for notification and consultation
Trade facilitation and audits	Procedures with specific conditions for recognizing "authorized establishments". No pre-clearance and inspections on regulated products. Audits and verification allowed (no procedural guidelines)	EU emphasizes right of audit and verification, frequency decided by importing part. No procedural guidelines	Aim to recognize "authorized establishments," but no specific procedure described. Audits and verification allowed (no procedural guidelines)	Procedures for recognizing "authorized establishments". Elaborate specification of procedure for audits and verification
Information exchange and consultations	Information requirements beyond SPS agreement. Consultations on request by one of the parties, relatively unspecified process requirements and no outcome obligations	US proposal foresees requirements beyond SPS agreement, including inclusive consultation on planned SPS measures	Follows SPS agreement. Consultations on request by one of the parties, relatively unspecified process and no outcome obligations. Parties can individually terminate consultations	Information requirements beyond SPS agreement. Consultations on request by one of the parties, specified process, but no outcome obligations
SPS committee and dispute settlement	Joint Management Committee on SPS. Separate chapter on dispute settlement, also applicable to SPS	Committee on SPS. US proposal also includes standing working groups	Committee on SPS. Separate chapter on dispute settlement, only partially applicable to SPS	Subcommittee on SPS. Separate chapter on dispute settlement, also applicable to SPS

but particularly provide a degree of normative standardization with respect to the principles and guidelines for procedures to follow. The EU-Japan agreement remains closest to the SPS agreement, while CETA and the EU-MERCOSUR move further beyond existing obligations, by including more guidelines and procedural specifications and introducing separate dispute-settlement mechanisms next to WTO dispute settlement. Since the TTIP negotiations broke down, the consolidated text from 2016 shows many outstanding issues, with the US clearly aiming for standardization beyond the SPS agreement. Did the EU export its own standards by means of these trade agreements? The results are mixed. While the principle of "freedom to regulate" is laid down in the agreements and allows for emergency measures, this freedom is (and already was through the SPS agreement) procedurally circumscribed by provisions in the trade agreements. Furthermore, the EU perspective on the precautionary principle is not explicitly included in the SPS chapters. While it is included in the sustainable development chapters of the agreements, the provisions in these chapters are usually not enforceable (Treat 2020). That said, considering that the SPS issues were a defensive trade domain for the EU, its SPS standards being under pressure from trading partners, the fact that the agreements entail only limited standardization and concomitant obligations and commitments, most of which the EU already meets (Matthews 2016a), can be considered in line with EU interests. In this vein, Young (2015, 1263) argues that the European Commission's objective was not so much "to export its food safety rules through PTAs: Rather it has kept cooperation intentionally limited in order to preserve domestic regulatory autonomy" and thus not give up its own standards (Duina 2019).

Explaining the Pattern of Observed Variation

In order to explain the variation in standardization and the degree to which the EU has been successful in projecting its values and standards through the bilateral trade agreements, I use a combination of (rational choice) economic interest variables, and (constructivist) ideational variables in interaction with political mechanisms that shape the negotiation process and outcome. Regarding economic interests, I focus on producer and trade interests, as well as differences in market size that are likely to feed into differences in negotiating power. Economic interests give rise to mobilization of producer organizations (and also member states in the EU case), producing political pressure on decision-makers. The ideational variables focus on the policy ideas embedded in the worldviews discussed in the second section, assuming that larger distances between these variables among the trading partners, and between the policies to which they give rise, reduce the likeliness of far-reaching agreements and standardization. This is the result not only of the associated difference in policy preferences that impede agreement, but also of the politicization and political pressure to which more extensive differences in worldviews are likely to give rise. Once political pressure based on the protection of worldviews and identities increases, making concessions becomes politically costly, and hence, the overall likelihood of reaching an agreement diminishes. That said, combined with large market size (and thus the economic interest of the third party in gaining improved access to this market), such ideationally instigated political constraints could also contribute to one's negotiating power and result in a favorable agreement.

Geographical Indications

In the second section of this chapter, it was concluded that standardization in line with EU preferences was most extensive in the EU-Japan agreement, with a long list of protected GIs with limited exceptions and a well-specified system of protection; intermediate in the case of MERCOSUR due to more exceptions to protection; and more limited in CETA, with extensive exceptions to the list and curtailment of options for adding additional GIs to the protected list. This variation can be explained on the basis of the variables introduced above.

In terms of economic interests, GIs were a mostly defensive issue for Canada in the negotiations. While Canada had few GIs of its own for which it could seek protection in CETA, the interests of Canadian producers (particularly cheese producers) would be harmed by extending protection to important EU GIs. Protection for these GIs would prevent them from selling their products under the same name on the Canadian market. In the case of CETA, it would also affect US producers with a significant stake in the Canadian market. US producer organizations and the United States Trade Representative exerted political pressure on Canada regarding GIs, and Canada feared that inconsistencies between obligations based on CETA and the North American Free Trade Agreement (NAFTA) could result in complaints by US producers, potentially making Canada liable for damages (Viju et al. 2013). For producers in MERCOSUR and Japan, economic interests were mixed. The share of valuable EU GIs was smaller in their markets compared to Canada, and they had GIs of their own for which they could seek protection in exchange. Nevertheless, Blasetti (2020) still considers GIs a more defensive issue for MERCOSUR, as the interests of different member states varied, with Argentina and Brazil having the most GIs but for different product types. This internal variation and the lack of regionally harmonized intellectual property standards inhibited speaking with a single voice and eventually also resulted in bilateral deals with respect to exceptions for specific GIs for individual MERCOSUR countries. EU producers had high economic stakes, particularly with respect to CETA and in the TTIP negotiations. Producer and product organizations lobbied with the European institutions, and Southern member states warned that they would not vote in favor of a trade agreement if it did not contain sufficient coverage of their GIs (Huysmans 2022).

The distance between preexisting policy ideas and legal approaches toward GIs was most extensive between the EU and Canada, which applied a US-style trademark system to protect GIs. While Japan initially also protected GIs by means of a trademark system, it had a more developed history and culture of designations of origin and was in the process of introducing sui generis legislation for GI protection in 2015 (Port 2015; Van Uytsel 2015). MERCOSUR was characterized by heterogeneity with respect to legal systems of protection, with Argentina and Uruguay operating genuine sui generis systems, while Brazil maintained a mixed system and Paraguay's regulations focused on trademarks (Fracarolli 2021).

The variation in economic producer interests helps explain why the agreements with Japan and MERCOSUR had longer lists of protected GIs and a relatively higher level of protection than that offered by CETA for GIs. It also explains the exceptions that were included in the EU-MERCOSUR and CETA agreements—mostly concerning GIs that are important on the market of the partner countries. Its market size contributed to EU negotiating power with respect to Japan and MERCOSUR, where it is also assumed that MERCOSUR compromised on GIs in order to gain market access in other domains (Blasetti 2020). The fact that the EU consistently presented an agreement on GIs as a *conditio sine qua non* for a trade deal (see De Ville, Chapter 6 in this volume) added credibility to its negotiating position. While these arguments in principle also hold with respect to CETA, the ideational distance between preexisting policy ideas and legal approaches, and the significant political pressure on CETA emanating from its own producers and from the US, resulted in a compromise in which the EU was relatively less able to export its values and standards.

Food Safety Regulations

In the third section of this chapter, it was found that neither of the agreements provides for standardization through complete harmonization of standards, but rather they contain (limited) normative standardization of procedures and guidelines relevant for establishing equivalence, audit, and verification. Of the agreements, the EU-MERCOSUR FTA contains the most elaborate specifications of such procedures in the agreement.

Standardization with respect to food safety regulation, even if not harmonizing the standards itself but procedures for conformity assessment, for example, is in the economic interest of producers, as it facilitates trade and can reduce costs by eliminating duplicate testing. While producers certainly stated their interests and preferences, in the EU case, their mobilization was overshadowed by the ideationally grounded critique and concerns propounded by civil society groups (Gheyle 2019). The issue of food safety was particularly politicized in CETA and TTIP, where CSOs claimed that the Commission was lowering EU standards through these trade agreements and compromised the precautionary principle (Duina 2019; Stoll et al. 2016). Later, the same claims were also made with respect to the EU-MERCOSUR agreement (Treat 2020), but mobilization on this agreement was less pronounced.

Matthews (2016b) argues that civil society critique with respect to the leaked TTIP consolidated text was overstated, as it would leave EU food standards and the right to regulate its own standards untouched, while the obligations with respect to procedures and processes would be limited. Justified critique or not, the key explanation of both the mobilization and eventually the variation in outcomes between the agreements lies in ideational differences in worldviews and how these interacted with political forces. The distance between worldviews was, again, greatest between the US and Canada on the one side and the EU on the other. The North American relatively risk-tolerant and business-oriented approach clashed with the EU's perspective focusing on the precautionary principle (see previous discussion). After CSOs started scrutinizing the negotiations on the basis of ideational arguments—the agreement affecting not only food safety per se but also European culture and even democracy—the European Commission responded by likewise adopting an ideational discourse, promising to defend the "European way of life" (Duina 2019, 1875). This confirmed and entrenched the ideational perspective on SPS and explains why standardization in CETA was limited and agreement could not be reached in TTIP.

Preexisting MERCOSUR regulations on SPS were heterogeneous, defined at the national level and aligned with export market requirements. Original plans for full harmonization of SPS policy within MERCOSUR had not materialized, with the important exception of the dairy sector (Delich and Lengyel 2014). There was less pronounced contestation on SPS regulations between the EU and MERCOSUR, and the negotiations were less politicized (Duina 2019). This helps explain why more elaborate specifications for guidelines and procedures could be agreed upon in MERCOSUR than in CETA. The outcome in the EU-Japan agreement is puzzling, however. Considering that the Japanese regulatory regime around food safety policies had a similar development trajectory and largely aligned with EU policy ideas and instruments, and consumer demands are important instigators of strict food safety regulations in both the EU and Japan (Berends 2015; Duina 2019), one would have expected agreement on more elaborate provisions on, for example, the (procedures for) mutual recognition of standards. However, such normative standardization was actually least specified in exactly this agreement. One potential explanation would be that neither of the parties felt the need to make very specific arrangements in the agreement, as they judged one another's existing regulations as adequate, while the similarity in existing food regulations did not require bilateral regulation to prevent adverse trade effects. However, considering that Japanese food exports to the EU are negligible while EU food product exports to Japan are somewhat more significant and EU producers have complaints about some Japanese SPS measures (Berends 2015), another possibility is that Japan simply did not consider specific SPS regulations in its interest, and the EU did not push the matter.

Conclusion

The comparative analysis of standardization of GI and SPS regulations in the CETA, EU-Japan, and EU-MERCOSUR agreements and the TTIP negotiations showed a number of striking variations. First, most standardization involved normative standardization. Second, the degree of standardization was more enhanced with respect to GIs than SPS. Third, the EU was more successful in exporting its GI standards than its SPS standards. And, finally, MERCOSUR and Japan made more concessions than Canada, particularly regarding GIs. This variation could be largely explained by differences in economic interests, differences in worldviews in which the countries embedded their policies, and how these interacted, shaping political incentives and constraints on government actors in the negotiating process. While the expectation that a larger gap between worldviews reduces the odds of a successful negotiating outcome and extensive standardization was generally confirmed, the EU-Japan agreement's SPS chapter showed that close alignment of existing policies can also diminish the incentive for regulating SPS in a bilateral trade agreement. The ideational variable of worldviews proved highly significant in these agri-food cases and was arguably a decisive factor with respect to SPS.

What do these findings imply for agri-food regulations in future bilateral and multilateral agreements and for the transatlantic regulatory competition? The significance of contrasting worldviews in and the (political) sensitivity of these domains are likely to inhibit far-reaching standardization, both on a multilateral level and in bilateral agreements. The EU and US will undoubtedly continue their aspirations for exporting their standards and values through bilateral trade agreements. Mixed successes for both parties on GIs in their bilateral agreements, combined with the fact that many trading partners have established or are negotiating trade agreements with both the EU and the US, could, in time, however, contribute to the emergence of coexistence between GIs and trademarks across large parts of the globe. Similar developments are unlikely with respect to food safety measures.

Notes

1. They are, therefore, more than merely indications of source (a connection between products and a given region or place) because of the quality, reputation, or other product characteristics that are considered related to this geographical origin.
2. For example, that they are *not commercialized using references* (graphics, names, pictures, flags) to the genuine origin of the GI and/or provided the *term is displayed* in a font character substantially smaller than the brand name. Such exceptions, for example, apply to well-known cheeses, such as Fontina and Gruyère.

References

"Agreement between the European Union and Japan for an Economic Partnership." 2018. *Official Journal of the European Union* L 330, vol. 61. December 27, pp. 3–899.

Berends, G. 2015. "Food Fights or a Recipe for Cooperation? EU-Japan Relations and the Development of Norms in Food Safety Policy." In *The European Union and Japan: A New Chapter in Civilian Power Cooperation?*, edited by P. Bacon, H. Mayer, and H. Nakamaru, pp. 115–130. Farnham, UK: Ashgate.

Blasetti, R. 2020. "Geographical Indications: A Major Challenge for MERCOSUR." *GRUR International* 69 (11): pp. 1113–1122.

"Comprehensive Economic and Trade Agreement (CETA) between Canada, of the one part, and the European Union and its Member States, of the other part." 2017. *Official Journal of the European Union* L 11, vol. 60. January 14, pp. 23–1079. https://eur-lex.eur opa.eu/legal-content/EN/TXT/PDF/?uri=CELEX:22017A0114(01)&from=EN.

Delich, V., and M. Lengyel. 2014. "Can Developing Countries Use SPS Standards to Gain Access to Markets? The Case of Mercosur." In *Connecting to Global Markets*, edited by M. Jansen, M. S. Jallab, and M. Smeets, pp. 87–99. Lausanne: WTO Publications. https://www.wto.org/english/res_e/booksp_e/cmark_full_e.pdf.

Duina, F. 2019. "Why the Excitement? Values, Identities, and the Politicization of EU Trade Policy with North America." *Journal of European Public Policy* 26 (12): pp. 1866–1882. doi: https://doi.org/10.1080/13501763.2019.1678056.

Echols, M. A. 1998. "Food Safety Regulation in the European Union and the United States: Different Cultures, Different Laws." *Columbia Journal of International Law* 4: pp. 525–543.

European Commission. 1999. *White Paper on Food Safety.* COM (1999) 719. https://eur-lex.europa.eu/legal-content/EN/TXT/?uri=celex%3A51999DC0719.

European Commission. 2002. "Regulation (EC) No 178/2002 of the European Parliament and of the Council of 28 January 2002 laying down the general principles and requirements of food law, establishing the European Food Safety Authority and laying down procedures in matters of food safety." *Official Journal of the European Union* L 31, vol. 45. February 1, pp. 1–25.

European Commission. 2004. "Regulation (EC) No 853/2004 of the European Parliament and of the Council of 29 April 2004 laying down specific hygiene rules for food of animal origin." *Official Journal of the European Union* L 139, vol. 47. April 30, pp. 55–205 [p. 55 corrected and republished in *Official Journal of the European Union* L 226, June 25, p. 22].

European Commission. 2016. "Outline of Text on Geographical Indications." https://trade.ec.europa.eu/doclib/docs/2016/march/tradoc_154385.%20Paper%20-%20GIs%20skeleton%20FINAL.pdf.

European Commission. 2019. EU-Mercosur Agreement: The Agreement in Principle. https://policy.trade.ec.europa.eu/eu-trade-relationships-country-and-region/countr ies-and-regions/mercosur/eu-mercosur-agreement/agreement-principle_en.

Fracarolli, G.S. 2021. "The Effects of Institutional Measures: Geographical Indication in Mercosur and the EU." *Sustainability* 13 (6): pp. 3476–3492.

Gheyle, N. 2019. *Trade Policy with the Lights On: The Origins, Dynamics, and Consequences of the Politicization of TTIP.* Ph.D. dissertation, Gent University. https://lib.ugent.be/en/catalog/rug01:002773477.

Goldberg, S. J. 2001. "Who Will Raise the White Flag: The Battle Between the United States and the European Union over the Protection of Geographical Indications." *University of Pennsylvania Journal of International Law* 22 (1): pp. 107–151.

Huysmans, M. 2022. "Exporting Protection: EU Trade Agreements, Geographical Indications, and Gastronationalism." *Review of International Political Economy* 29 (3): pp. 979–1005.

Josling, T. 2006. "The War on *Terroir*: Geographical Indications as a Transatlantic Trade Conflict." *Journal of Agricultural Economics* 57 (3): pp. 337–363.

Marette, S., R. Clemens, and B. Babcock. 2008. "Recent International and Regulatory Decisions about Geographical Indications." *Agribusiness* 24: pp. 453–472.

Matthews, A. 2016a. "Much Ado about Nothing in TTIP Leaks on Food Safety Standards." *Cap Reform*. May 17. capreform.eu/much-ado-about-nothing-in-ttip-leaks-on-food-safety-standards/.

Matthews, A. 2016b. "What Outcome to Expect on Geographical Indications in the TTIP Free Trade Negotiations with the United States?" In *Intellectual Property Rights for Geographical Indications: What Is at Stake in the TTIP?*, edited by F. Arfini, M. Mancini, M. Veneziani, and M. Donati, pp. 2–18. Newcastle upon Tyne: Cambridge Scholars.

McEvoy, J. D. G. 2016. "Emerging Food Safety Issues: An EU Perspective." *Drug Testing and Analysis* 8 (5–6): 511–520. doi: https://doi.org/10.1002/dta.2015.

Monten, L. 2006. "Geographical Indications of Origin: Should They Be Protected and Why? An Analysis of the Issue from the US and EU Perspectives." *Santa Clara High Tech Law Journal* 22 (2): pp. 315–349.

Port, K. L. 2015. "Regionally Based Collective Trademark System in Japan: Geographical Indicators by a Different Name or a Political Misdirection?" *Cybaris* 6 (2): Article 2, pp. 2–56. https://open.mitchellhamline.edu/cybaris/vol6/iss2/2.

Rudloff, B. 2014. "Food Standards in Trade Agreements." *SWP Comment* 49: pp. 1–8.

Schroeder, W. 2016. "Transatlantic Free Trade Agreements and European Food Standards." *European Food and Feed Law Review* 11 (6): pp. 494–501.

Stoll, P. T., W. T. Douma, N. Sadeleer, and P. Abel. 2016. *CETA, TTIP and the EU Precautionary Principle*. Foodwatch. https://www.foodwatch.org/fileadmin/Themen/TTIP_Freihandel/Dokumente/2016-06-21_foodwatch-study_precautionary-principle.pdf.

Trade-leaks.org. 2016. "Sanitary and Phytosanitary Measures: Consolidated Proposals." https://trade-leaks.org/ttip/.

Treat, S. 2020. *Food Safety and the EU-Mercosur Agreement: Risking Weaker Standards on Both Sides of the Atlantic*. Institute for Agriculture and Trade Policy. https://www.iatp.org/sites/default/files/2020-12/Factsheet_EU%20Mercosur%20FTA_FOOD%20SAFETY.pdf.

Van Uytsel, S. 2015. *The New Japanese Act on Geographical Indications—An Intangible Cultural Heritage Perspective*. November 18. doi: http://dx.doi.org/10.2139/ssrn.2692449.

Viju, C., M. Yeung, and W. A. Kerr. 2013. "Geographical Indications, Conflicted Preferential Agreements and Market Access." *Journal of International Economic Law* 16 (2): pp. 409–437.

Young, A. R. 2015. "Liberalizing Trade, Not Exporting Rules: The Limits to Regulatory Co-ordination in the EU's New Generation Preferential Trade Agreements." *Journal of European Public Policy* 22 (9): pp. 1253–1275.

2

(New) EU Standards in Preferential Services Trade Liberalization

Charlotte Sieber-Gasser

Introduction

In the past decade, the European Union (EU) has constantly been exporting more services to non-EU countries than it imported, with a (temporary) maximum of services exports of €1.072 trillion in 2019 (Eurostat n.d.). Therewith, the EU remains the largest exporter of services worldwide.[1] Perhaps due to the underreporting of services trade statistics compared with goods trade statistics, it is comparatively little known that the EU is the undisputed world leader in services exports.[2] It is, thus, no surprise that services trade with non-EU countries still accounted for 25.1 percent of gross domestic product in the EU in 2020, even after a decrease due to the pandemic (World Bank n.d.). Given its status in the global services market, EU services trade policy, therefore, inevitably has an impact on the global regulatory framework in services trade.

It should not be forgotten that services not only are traded for the sake of trading services, but also are a key ingredient of successful global value-added chains: they enable high-quality production and are necessary for markets to converge. In an increasingly specialized and globalized economy, essential know-how is often transferred through services, and services therewith are at the heart of overall economic performance (Sieber-Gasser 2016, 30). Particularly in a strong service economy like that of the EU, services trade also accounts for a considerable number of jobs in the market.[3] Liberalization in trade in services therefore serves the purpose of increasing global market access and extending growth opportunities for the EU service industry, but at the same time needs to take into account that an increase in competition within the EU market might lead to negative spillovers, such as job losses among service suppliers.

Charlotte Sieber-Gasser, *(New) EU Standards in Preferential Services Trade Liberalization* In: *Standardizing the World.*
Edited by: Francesco Duina and Crina Viju-Miljusevic, Oxford University Press. © Oxford University Press 2023.
DOI: 10.1093/oso/9780197681886.003.0003

General Agreement on Trade in Services

Contrary to other fields in international trade regulation, services trade rules originate in the multilateral and not in the preferential forum: the first comprehensive set of rules for the liberalization of services trade was established in the General Agreement on Trade in Services (GATS) as part of the Uruguay Round of negotiations of the World Trade Organization (WTO) in the late 1980s and early 1990s (GATS 1994). Regulation of and obligations in the liberalization of trade in services were new and largely untested at the time. Hence, the GATS was seen as a stepping stone to further, more elaborate services trade regulation and to an expanding scope of liberalization through subsequent rounds of negotiations. WTO members therefore remained cautious with regard to the level of liberalization to which they committed under the multilateral GATS. Instead, they quickly turned to negotiations of preferential trade agreements (PTAs) in services in parallel to the GATS negotiations and shortly after the conclusion of the GATS, in which they committed to more extensive trade liberalization in services with hand-picked partners. Meanwhile negotiations at the multilateral level (i.e., the Doha Round) regarding the initially envisaged gradual modernization of the GATS rules have remained blocked (Sieber-Gasser 2016, 110–115; Sieber-Gasser 2022, 60–61).

EU Internal Services Market Liberalization

Services trade within the EU is not as standardized or liberalized as intra-EU goods trade: national legislation continues to create barriers to intra-EU services trade, at times creating complex administrative procedures which may be considered outdated or even unnecessary (see van Leeuwen 2018). The European Commission (EC)—in an effort to fully implement the 2006 Services Directive (EU 2006)—presented, in January 2017, proposals for a services e-card which renders intra-EU trade in services easier, particularly in the sectors of business services and construction services (EC 2017). However, the proposal failed to secure the required support and agreement in the legislative process, and the EC withdrew the proposal in 2021 (European Parliament n.d.). This leaves the identified unnecessarily burdensome regulatory obstacles to intra-EU services trade still unresolved. In this regard, PTAs are actually one way in which the EU can achieve progress also in the harmonization and standardization of *internal* services trade (Fiorini and Hoekman 2020, 265).

In addition, the scope of EU-only competence in services trade in foreign trade policy remained unclear until recently. Typically, the EU would conclude a PTA covering services as a "mixed" agreement, meaning that the PTA had to also be ratified by each EU member individually, in addition to the EU itself (see, e.g., Chaisse 2012, 61; Leal-Arcas 2001, 512; Reinisch 2014, 122). This practice obviously had implications for the ambition in the negotiations of services trade liberalization in PTAs: services chapters in EU PTAs tended to be rather cautious.

It was in the so-called Singapore Opinion in 2017 that the scope of EU-only competence in services trade in foreign trade policy was legally appraised for the first time (CJEU 2017). The Court held that only portfolio investments and the investor-state dispute settlement procedures in the EU-Singapore PTA did not fall within the scope of EU-only competence. All other policy areas—including substantial obligations in trade in services—were found to be within the scope of exclusive EU competence (see Conconi et al. 2021, 4–6). This clarification with regard to EU competence in the negotiation of preferential trade liberalization in services is expected to contribute to more ambitious outcomes in services trade liberalization in EU PTAs, along with preferential services trade obligations which also may incentivize the full implementation of the free movement of services within the EU internal market.

Trade in Services Agreement

In 2016, the negotiations of the Trade in Services Agreement (TiSA)[4] came close to modernizing trade in services rules on the plurilateral level (limited to the signatories of the agreement) (see also Kerneis 2017, 143–144). Modernizing the GATS rules not only corresponds with the initial plan to use the GATS as a stepping stone to further and deeper services trade liberalization, but it also became more urgent due to technological advancements, cheaper and more accessible transportation, and internet access, which all rendered services substantially more "tradeable" and relevant than was the case when the initial GATS rules were negotiated. In consequence, critical regulatory aspects of services trade liberalization remain unaddressed by the GATS, along with rules for new types of services which did not exist at the time of the negotiation of the GATS. For instance, the supply of services through the internet—arguably the most common cross-border supply of services today—and all other, new internet-related services are not specifically addressed by the GATS. Regulatory issues regarding services which form an integral, inseparable part of manufacturing also remain unaddressed at the multilateral level: they may, at times, play a critical role in international goods trade even if supplied domestically (Antimiani and Cernat 2018; Peng 2020).

In particular, TiSA negotiations focused on rules regarding e-commerce, the cross-border supply of telecommunication services, and aspects of the temporary movement of service suppliers, along with transparency and recognition of licenses and diplomas. They were indefinitely suspended in 2016. Therewith, PTAs remain the preferred forum for the advancement and modernization of applicable rules in services trade liberalization, along with selected services-related plurilateral initiatives. PTAs are also a means to essentially move ahead with like-minded members of the plurilateral TiSA negotiations: the more TiSA members agree with a certain regulatory structure in their PTAs, the more likely it is that this particular structure will ultimately also prevail at the plurilateral or even multilateral level. EU PTAs negotiated simultaneously or after the last round of TiSA negotiations are, therefore, closely in line with the EU TiSA offer, typically include new standards in selected topics of services trade liberalization, and feature more ambitious services trade chapters than earlier EU PTAs (see Sieber-Gasser 2022, 60–61).

Plurilateral Initiatives in Services Trade

Of the services-related plurilateral initiatives aside from TiSA, negotiations of the Joint Initiative on Services Domestic Regulation were successfully concluded in December 2021 (WTO 2021). The initiative addresses overly burdensome bureaucracy in attaining the permission to trade in services. Therewith, it is inherently linked with the EC's 2017 services e-card proposal, though not identical. The EU participated in negotiations, and all EU member states are among the sixty-seven original signatories. Members will inscribe the agreed disciplines in their existing GATS schedules of commitments. Therewith, the agreed new rules regarding procedures of attaining the permission to trade in services will apply vis-à-vis all GATS members and are not limited to the participants in the joint initiative. The agreed minimum standards in the applicable national rules for authorization to supply a service address, among other issues, the maximum number of competent authorities required to approach for authorization (one), a reasonable period of time for the submission of applications (all year, reasonably long time windows if applicable), applications in electronic format (acceptance of electronic documents), transparency during processing of applications (time frame, information sharing, resubmission), authorization fees (not restrictive), as well as the frequency of examinations of qualifications (at reasonable intervals).[5]

With regard to the mutual recognition of certificates and diplomas, participants in the joint initiative agreed on a rule which is similar to that of the Comprehensive Economic and Trade Agreement (CETA) between the EU and Canada:[6] if professional bodies of members are mutually interested in establishing a dialogue on the recognition of professional qualifications, members should support them appropriately.[7] This approach is interesting because it moves the responsibility for the advancement of mutual recognition away from the public to the private sector. In consequence, the state intends to play a passive role in this regard, limiting itself to providing support to private-sector initiatives. The fact that this rule has been agreed to by all participants in the joint initiative indicates to services industries that it is up to their professional bodies to become active if they wish to further facilitate cross-border trade in services.

In January 2022, negotiations of a plurilateral agreement on e-commerce resumed. The eighty-six WTO members participating in negotiations already agreed on a fair deal of common new rules for e-commerce: agreed text exists on spam, electronic signatures and authentication, e-contracts, online consumer protection, and open government data. Three main topics remain disputed: restricting the free flow of data, network neutrality, and customs duties on electronic transmissions (Geneva Trade Platform n.d.). As mentioned earlier, by addressing trade realities in a twenty-first-century global market in which internet constitutes a key factor in cross-border trade, these negotiations are closely linked with updating the applicable rules for trade in services beyond the GATS.

Preferential Trade Agreements in Services

Based on notifications to the WTO, there are currently twenty EU-PTAs in force which cover services trade liberalization (notified under GATS art. V).[8] The first extra-European trade agreement covering services trade liberalization was EU-Mexico (2000). Between 2000 and 2010, the EU ratified six PTAs in services,[9] and between 2011 and 2021, an additional fourteen.[10] Hence, the focus of EU foreign trade policy has not always been on PTAs in services; this is rather a comparatively recent phenomenon.

In order to qualify for the most-favoured nation (MFN) exception in GATS art. V, PTAs in services need to fulfil substantial sectorial coverage (in terms of number of sectors covered, volume of services trade covered, and without a priori exclusion of any of the modes of supply). Furthermore, PTAs in services in principle have to establish the absence or elimination of substantially all discrimination within covered sectors. In order to comply with the quantitative requirements of GATS art. V, WTO members may exclude one to two services sectors from their PTAs in services as long as these sectors are not substantial in the sense of covered volume of services trade (GATS 1994, art. V; Sieber-Gasser 2016, 135–137). The EU typically excludes audiovisual services from the scope of its PTAs, as well as parts of cabotage services and of air transport services. The qualitative requirement of GATS art. V of "absence or elimination of substantially all discrimination" is generally considered to be fulfilled if market access obligations and national treatment obligations in the PTA go beyond the scope of the respective GATS commitments (Sieber-Gasser 2016, 137–153).

Not all EU PTAs in services clearly fulfil the requirements of GATS art. V;[11] however, they have not been challenged to date with regard to their GATS compliance.[12] Hence, the GATS members are typically both legally and practically quite free to define the kind of rules and the levels of liberalization they wish to apply to their bilateral and preferential services trade. PTAs therewith constitute the ideal instrument to advance and perhaps even experiment with trade liberalization in services. Given the identified urgency of updated rules on services trade liberalization and the reach of EU services exports in the global market, ambitious services chapters in EU PTAs are likely to contribute to global standard setting in services.

Sample and Methodology

Of interest to the study of standardization in EU preferential services trade are particularly the EU PTAs since EU-Korea (2010), which entered into force in 2011. The six earlier EU PTAs in services will either be replaced with a more modern agreement (EU-Mexico, EU-Chile)[13] (see European Commission n.d.), entail an asymmetric services chapter (EU-CARIFORUM) (see European Commission 2008), or essentially consist of standstill obligations with a goal of progressive further liberalization of trade in services (EU-North Macedonia, EU-Albania, and EU-Montenegro). It is EU-Korea (2010) which entails substantial trade liberalization of services, including the subsequently pursued particular EU-structure of services trade liberalization, which separates modes 1–2 from mode 3 and mode 4, each with a separate chapter.

Findings in this chapter are, thus, based on data from the services chapters and the chapters tightly linked with specific aspects of services in EU PTAs since 2010, along with the corresponding EU schedules of commitments. Data from EU PTAs are complemented with data from the EU GATS schedule of commitments, the EU TiSA offer of 2016, and the TiSA draft core text of 2016. The total sample of agreements consists of the following treaties, including Annexes:

1. GATS (1994)
2. EU-Korea (2010)
3. Colombia-EU-Peru (2012)
4. Central America–EU (2012)
5. EU-Moldova (2014)
6. EU-Georgia (2014)
7. EU-Ukraine (2014)
8. EU-Kosovo SAA (2015)
9. EU-Bosnia Herzegovina (2015)
10. EU-Kazakhstan (2015)
11. Canada-EU or CETA (2016)
12. TiSA (2016)
13. Armenia-EU (2017)
14. EU-Japan (2018)
15. EU-Singapore (2018)
16. EU-Vietnam (2019)
17. EU-UK or TCA (2020).

The main treaty texts, along with the EU schedules of commitments, were coded for scope of liberalization (scope of commitments in individual sectors compared with GATS, MFN, and NT obligations; procedural obligations for mutual recognition; excluded sectors/services) and for regulatory innovation (regulatory structure of services trade liberalization, GATS-extra services, and services-related rules and obligations).

Of the fifteen coded EU PTAs, twelve cover substantial services trade liberalization,[14] while two agreements contain a ratchet-clause in services trade in combination with a declaration of intent to further liberalize trade in future negotiations (EU-Kosovo SAA and EU-Bosnia Herzegovina), and one agreement contains a ratchet-clause in services trade in combination with commitments regarding the temporary movement of natural persons, rules regarding domestic regulation and licensing and qualifications, and rules on international maritime transport (EU-Kazakhstan). Of particular interest with regard to the analysis of standardization are the twelve substantive EU PTAs, along with the GATS and the TiSA.

Of these twelve substantive EU PTAs since 2010, five were concluded between the EU and industrialized, services-strong economies,[15] and seven between the EU and developing to emerging markets, with less competitive service industries.[16] Interestingly, the scope of market access, along with the regulatory structure of the services chapters, does not substantially differ from one EU PTA to another, and appears to be rather independent from the level of competitiveness of the services industries in the respective PTA partner.[17] Instead, Figure 2.1 shows that EU PTAs in services list on average a clearly broader scope of commitments after CETA than before.[18]

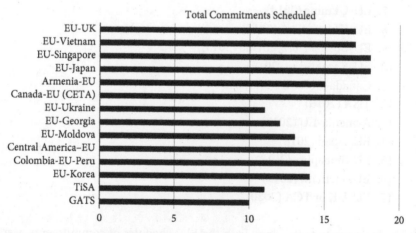

Figure 2.1 Depth of liberalization.

Note: Individual schedules (business, communication, construction, distribution, education, energy, environment, financial, health, tourism, transport, e-commerce, mode 4) coded as follows: few or almost no reservations = 2; considerable reservations = 1; few or almost no commitments = 0. Maximum score (almost no restrictions in all sectors and mode 4) would be 26.

Furthermore, clearly on average all the EU PTAs in the sample are GATS-plus, even if in some instances commitments in individual sectors are actually less in scope than GATS commitments.[19]

Hence, it would appear that the level and scope of commitments regarding market access and national treatment in the EU depend less on the respective negotiations/partner, and more on the EU services trade policy in general. The fact that more recent agreements entail more substantial commitments may indicate that the EU is binding the existing levels of openness in the respective negotiations, rather than using the PTA to expand services market access and national treatment beyond current practice.[20] This renders the subsequent analysis of standardization in EU preferential services trade potentially intertwined with regulatory and practical developments in intra-EU services trade facilitation.

From a market access and national treatment perspective, intra-EU and extra-EU services trade is not always as clearly distinguishable as intra-EU and extra-EU goods trade. This is due to the fact that barriers to trade in services typically are of a regulatory nature and are not tariffs. As long as intra-EU services trade is not fully harmonized, facilitation of market access and national treatment for extra-EU services in the EU, therefore, continue to encounter regulatory limitations.

It goes beyond the scope of this study to analyze the extent to which preferential rules in extra-EU services trade deviate from the applicable rules of individual EU members in intra-EU services trade. What we can tell from the analysis of standardization in EU PTAs in services, however, is the type and extent of global rules for the liberalization pursued—and pushed through—by the EU.

Definitional Standardization

Definitional standardization in the context of services trade regulation deals, for instance, with the definition of (new) types of services, with the definition of the kind of economic activities which are considered "cross-border trade in services," or what constitutes a barrier to trade in services. While PTAs in general and at a global level closely follow the structure of the GATS and typically incorporate definitions as established in the GATS, there is room for regulatory development of definitional standardization, particularly in (1) the definition of new services which did not exist at the time of the ratification of the

GATS, (2) with regard to the distinction between services and services-related economic activities, and (3) with regard to "green services" (see Sieber-Gasser 2021). While the analysis finds EU definitional standardisation in the first two aspects, none could be found in the third aspect.

Prominently, EU PTAs address aspects of definition with regard to internet-related services trade. In separate chapters on computer services[21] and on postal and courier services,[22] elements of definitional standardization are entailed. The same can be said about the inclusion of e-commerce in the context of services trade liberalization. The separate chapter on computer services is particularly relevant with regard to definitional standardization: it is typically limited to the joint declaration that the parties to the agreement define "computer and related services" as services within the meaning of United Nations Code CPC 84.[23] A similar footnote can be found in the EU TiSA offer; hence, it appears that the inclusion of "computer and related services" in CPC 84 is in the process of becoming an international standard.

All of the coded substantive EU PTAs define cross-border trade in services as limited to GATS modes 1 (cross-border supply) and 2 (consumption abroad). The initial GATS mode 3 (commercial presence) is merged with liberalization in establishment, therewith covering the commercial presence not only of service suppliers but also of suppliers of all other economic activities. The initial GATS mode 4 (presence of natural persons), on the other hand, is typically covered in a separate chapter on the temporary presence of natural persons for business purposes, therewith also extending the right of temporary stay of natural persons to non-service sectors.

This division of services trade regulation into "services-only" and "services-plus" chapters based on the respective mode of supply is not mirrored in the TiSA draft core text of 2016. It is unlikely that the EU would oppose incorporating its preferred regulatory structure and its own definition of "cross-border trade in services" at the plurilateral level. However, given the accompanying extension of liberalization to the goods sector, incorporating the EU definition and regulatory structure does not currently fit within TiSA's mandate (which is limited in principle to services trade).

The limitation of the definition of "cross-border trade in services" to modes 1 and 2 benefits overall levels of liberalization in trade in general—since establishment and temporary movement are not limited to services industries—but ignores the fact that today most of global trade in services is supplied on the basis of mode 3 (establishment) (Rueda-Cantuche et al. 2016). Hence, the re-definition of "cross-border trade in services" as can be found in EU PTAs is not actually in line with de facto realities of trade in services, unless we no longer consider the supply of services through commercial presence to indeed constitute "trade in services."

Services trade statistics remain shaped by data limitations. Nevertheless, a more recent EU study on the share of trade in services along the four modes of supply suggests that by disregarding mode 3, mode 1 accounts for more than two-thirds of international services trade in the EU (Rueda-Cantuche et al. 2016, 18). Temporary presence of natural persons (mode 4) typically accounts for the least amount of international services trade. Thus, by limiting the definition of "cross-border trade in services" to modes 1 and 2, the EU manages to focus rules of services trade liberalization on the core of international services trade, which is unrelated to goods trade.

This new definition of "cross-border trade in services" creates, however, regulatory inconsistencies with GATS: GATS rules continue to apply in principle to all modes of supply, even if in an EU PTA supply of services through commercial presence is excluded from the general scope of the rules governing trade in services. Furthermore, excluding one or two modes of supply from the scope of a PTA would constitute in principle a violation of GATS art. V. The only reason why the redefinition of "cross-border services trade" by the EU does not constitute a serious problem is to be found in the fact that de facto, modes 3 and 4 are covered in the respective chapters on establishment/investment and on temporary presence of natural persons. Interestingly, EU PTAs are not explicitly addressing this potential conflict with GATS, while they address the relation to WTO agreements in other chapters.[24] However, there have not been any disputes in this regard to date, and therefore the matter might qualify under legal cosmetics with limited practical implications.

It can, thus, be concluded, that the EU is establishing its own definitional standard of "cross-border services trade," and in combination with this, its own definitional standard of establishment/investment and of temporary presence of natural persons for business purposes. Because all the assessed EU PTAs entail these definitions, the EU is clearly successful in pushing these definitions through. This is remarkable also since EU partners are otherwise not incorporating these definitions in their PTAs with other countries.[25]

Normative Standardization

Normative standardization in the context of international services trade deals, for instance, with the modernization and specification of the rules and obligations applicable to services trade liberalization. Normative standardization therewith creates additional obligations compared with GATS. TiSA negotiations essentially dealt with normative standardization in international services trade. Given that TiSA negotiations were well advanced until they were suspended, a considerable share of normative standardization in EU PTAs essentially constitutes the implementation of the EU's TiSA offer. Particularly interesting are therefore new normative standards in EU PTAs which go beyond the scope of TiSA negotiations.

All agreements cover separate chapters in the main treaty text on financial services, e-commerce, telecommunication services, international maritime transport, temporary presence of natural persons, and on domestic regulation and licensing and qualification. In principle, this is where normative standardization is potentially found. The scope of these additional service-chapters, however, differs, particularly with respect to the scope of rules in procedures for mutual recognition and in e-commerce: newer agreements tend to cover binding obligations in mutual recognition procedures and in e-commerce, while older agreements focus on outlining transparency rules and cooperation.

In the eight services trade–related fields covered in separate chapters in EU-PTAs, emerging new normative standards in services trade regulation can be found. While in telecommunication services, these new regulatory standards are already included in the TiSA, other emerging regulatory standards in services trade with the EU are comparatively new.

Normative Standardization in Computer Services

As already mentioned above, the separate chapters on computer services primarily serve the purpose of clarifying the definition of computer services. Therewith, services provided by electronic means remain covered by the respective EU PTA. But through the definition of computer services, EU PTAs also create normative standards in the sense that they therewith extend rules and obligations governing services trade along with the scope of GATS schedules of commitments. The understanding essentially ensures that services traded via network, including the internet (i.e., services which did not exist at the time of the negotiation of the GATS), do not fall outside of the scope of services trade liberalization.

In the most recent agreement in the dataset, the TCA, the understanding on trade in computer and related services is part of the separate chapter on digital trade (see art. 212). However, the outcome effectively stays the same since the understanding lists the types of services which are considered "computer and related services" regardless of whether they are delivered via network. These listed services therewith essentially fall within the scope of the chapter on cross-border trade in services. Hence, why the understanding on computer and related services was moved to the chapter on digital trade is not immediately clear.

Normative Standardization in Postal and Courier Services

Chapters on postal and courier services—titles differ between agreements, sometimes the respective rules fall under only postal (Central America–EU) or only courier (Armenia-EU) services, and more recently under delivery services (TCA)—have the main purpose of establishing basic rules regarding competition. They typically cover rules and obligations regarding licensing, anti-competitive practices, universal service, and independence of the regulatory body. These rules and obligations have become relevant due to the important role these services play today in the global market, along with the fact that postal and courier service suppliers are increasingly operating across borders and have therefore begun to compete with national suppliers of postal and courier services.

These normative standards in EU PTAs are typically in line with TiSA.[26] Thus, while they might not be considered just EU standards, the EU appears to be using its PTAs to implement the rules and obligations in postal and courier services which had already been agreed to in the TiSA negotiations. By implementing a plurilateral minimum standard, EU PTAs therefore contribute substantially to the global standard setting in new rules on competition in postal and courier services.

Normative Standardization in Telecommunication Services

These chapters basically establish the regulatory framework for electronic communication services. They address definitions, authorization, access and interconnection, scarce resources, universal service, confidentiality, and dispute settlement, along with, more recently, submarine cable landing stations (e.g., EU-Singapore), roaming (TCA and EU-Japan), and open internet (TCA). Obviously, these rules and obligations in electronic communication services are to some extent new, given that they did not exist at the time of the negotiation of the GATS or were not as critical for the economy as a whole as they are today.

These chapters tend to be quite substantive and similar, therewith covering substantial normative standardization. Given that the TiSA covers a similar—and to some extent even identical—structure and scope compared with EU PTAs, it appears that also in this regard the EU is already implementing the plurilateral TiSA standard, therewith substantially contributing to global standard setting in new rules and obligations in electronic communication services.

The question remains open, to what extent the division between electronic telecommunication services and e-commerce remains durable. Possibly, both regulatory fields will eventually fall within the scope of "digital trade."

Normative Standardization in E-Commerce

Newer EU PTAs not only recognize the fact that electronic commerce exists, and that cooperation is required, but they also establish binding obligations so as not to impose customs duties on electronic transmissions (e.g., art. 8.58 in EU-Singapore). Three EU-PTAs establish liability obligations in the respective e-commerce chapters (Armenia-EU, EU-Moldova, and EU-Georgia); however, this does not seem to have become a new normative standard for the EU just yet.

These are all new rules and obligations which are not covered by the GATS and have become increasingly critical for the maintenance of fair and safe trade relations at the international level. It is therefore somewhat surprising that plurilateral negotiations on e-commerce appear more advanced than the rules and obligations entailed in individual EU PTAs.[27] In addition, given that at the plurilateral level, the prohibition to impose customs duties on electronic transmissions constitutes one of the three main obstacles to the conclusion of the negotiations (developing countries do not agree with this prohibition), particularly the inclusion of this prohibition in a number of EU

PTAs can be interpreted as an attempt by the EU to push through their pre-ferred standard also at the plurilateral level.

Normative Standardization in Presence of Natural Persons

As mentioned earlier, GATS mode 4 has been substantially extended in EU PTAs to also cover, most notably, the presence of natural persons for business purposes unrelated with the provision of services. Furthermore, the scope of commitments regarding the presence of natural persons is broader in EU PTAs than in the TiSA and in the GATS with respect to categories of cov-ered natural persons.[28] Therewith, the EU creates substantive new rules and obligations in the temporary movement of natural persons—for themselves but also for their partners, since these rules and obligations are entailed in a separate chapter in the main treaty text and therewith apply to both sides equally.

Due to the size of the EU internal market, commitments by the EU in temporary movement of natural persons are particularly attractive for all potential trading partners of the EU. Because not all markets are equally at-tractive for the temporary movement of natural persons, it is rather unlikely that the particular normative standards in EU PTAs will become the new global standard. On the contrary, typically PTAs remain comparatively si-lent on rules and obligations in the temporary movement of natural persons (Gootiiz et al. 2020, 135). It appears, hence, that the normative standardi-zation in EU PTAs in the presence of natural persons corresponds with a template which the EU itself developed for the regulation of presence for business purposes of extra-EU citizens.

The EU approach of extending rules and obligations to the presence of nat-ural persons for business purposes unrelated to trade in services contributes to simplification of the corresponding rules and therewith supports effective implementation: distinguishing the temporary movement of natural persons for the supply of services from the supply of goods may contribute to un-necessarily burdensome bureaucracy in attaining the permission to enter a market. Hence, if practical experience with the EU approach to normative standardization in the movement of natural persons turns out to be positive, it could be of interest also to other markets and therewith has the potential to become a new international standard.

Normative Standardization in Mutual Recognition

Normative standardization in mutual recognition is tricky here. On the one hand, mutual recognition qualifies as quite the contrary of standardization given that it explicitly accepts different standards as equal and given that it applies only to a "club of a few privileged service suppliers." On the other hand, the rules applying to the procedures for mutual recognition can indeed fall within the scope of normative standardization in the sense that they establish new, binding obligations in EU PTAs which regulate when and how mutual recognition is to be granted.

As mentioned above, more recent EU PTAs cover not only rules regarding transparency and fairness in the recognition of licences and qualifications but also binding obligations regarding the procedures for mutual recognition. These binding obligations go beyond the scope of TiSA and substantially beyond the scope of GATS and therewith introduce new rules and obligations for the EU and their partners. The currently applied procedure was introduced for the first time in CETA and basically builds on recommendations for mutual recognition of relevant professional bodies in both territories of the PTA. The parties to the EU PTAs are obliged to take necessary steps to negotiate a mutual recognition agreement if the recommendation is found to be consistent with the EU PTA (e.g., art. 8.16 EU-Singapore).[29]

In the meantime, these obligations have been incorporated to some extent in the Joint Initiative on Services Domestic Regulation and will therefore apply at a plurilateral level shortly. This creates opportunities for the private sector to engage in standardization across borders in order to facilitate services trade liberalization by reducing burdensome bureaucracy in attaining the permission to trade in and with a foreign market.

Absent Standardization

Given that the EU has been active for years in the creation of more sustainable trade relations, it is genuinely striking that none of the EU PTAs in services is considering the role of services trade in sustainable development. Services play a critical role in trade in environmental goods and in the promotion of sustainability and environmental protection in general; specialized expert services are required for the construction, maintenance, and repair, for instance, for any kind of green energy plant (solar, wind, geothermal, hydro, etc.). Access to high-quality services is therefore decisive for the longevity and effectiveness of environmental goods (Sieber-Gasser 2021).

Furthermore, schedules of commitments are not distinguishing between maintenance services of a gas-fired power plant and maintenance services of a wind power plant. In consequence both services have to be treated the same, while one—maintenance services for wind power plants—clearly has a positive impact on climate change mitigation, while the other has quite the contrary impact. The narrow scope of the WTO's sectoral classification list has been criticized for years for failing to reflect the current market characteristics of the environmental services sector (Sauvage and Timiliotis 2017). The Organisation for Economic Co-operation and Development (OECD)/ Eurostat even specifically proposed in 1999 to include services provided "to measure, prevent, minimise or correct environmental damage to water, air, soil, as well as problems related to waste, noise and ecosystems" in the sectoral classification of "environmental services." Notably, the initiative for an Agreement on Climate Change, Trade and Sustainability (ACCTS) is incorporating the OECD/Eurostat proposal and expanding it to include also environmental goods (New Zealand n.d.). The EU is not currently participating in this initiative and appears also to not consider the initiative's objectives in its PTAs.[30]

Considering the scope of EU standardization in preferential services trade otherwise, expanding or redefining "environmental services" would constitute a perfect case for EU leadership in standardization. It is, hence, quite possible that the EU will eventually join the ACCTS effort, or at least will begin to incorporate its objectives in EU PTAs in services.

Conclusion

The liberalization of trade in services is a delicate matter: in addition to the obvious cultural and language barriers, it inevitably touches upon domestic law and national administrative processes; it is hampered by a serious lack of data and reliable, comprehensive statistics; and it renders globalization more visible through human interaction across borders than trade liberalization in goods (Rueda-Cantuche et al. 2016, 6). Not even within the EU internal market is services trade fully liberalized. It is arguably for these reasons that the EU treads comparatively cautiously in extra-EU preferential services trade liberalization: legislative differences between EU members in services trade have to be accounted for and the EU cannot overstep the scope of their exclusive competence in foreign trade policy, which still remains somewhat blurry when dealing with services trade liberalization.

In consequence, the EU appears to use plurilateral negotiations[31] and high-stakes PTAs in services (CETA) to internally agree on new standards in international trade in services, which are then implemented in and through PTAs. Clearly, the EU is prepared to go beyond minimum standards established in the GATS and also in plurilateral negotiations in its PTAs. Therewith, the EU contributes—despite its relatively cautious approach—in particular to the normative advancement of standardization in international services trade in internet-related services, and in the comprehensive liberalization of the presence of natural persons for business purposes and in establishment/investment.

It is striking that despite the comparatively low level of liberalization, the EU continues to remain the world's leading market for services exports. This raises the question: to what extent is it in the genuine interest of the EU to engage in trade liberalization in services? After all, the existing regulatory framework seems to work reasonably well for EU services industries so far. Unfortunately, due to a lack of data, we do not know the answer to this.

EU services industries will have to prepare for increasing competition from abroad with or without PTA. Given that emerging markets continue to catch up in expertise and technology and are already absorbing a number of initially European services jobs, it is quite possible that European services industries will have to innovate more in the future in order to defend their position as the number one export market for services worldwide. Standardization will support this endeavour and hence contribute to the protection of many services-related jobs and businesses in the EU.

Notes

1. As a single country, the US exports more services than EU members individually, but less than the EU as a whole (see UNCTAD 2021).
2. For example, in 2021, the EU exported an estimated US$1.212 trillion in services, whereas the US is estimated to have exported US$0.771 trillion in services (see WTO Stats n.d.).
3. Of the 36 million jobs supported by EU exports, 61 percent are in services (see Kerneis 2019, 72).

4. TiSA had twenty-one negotiation rounds until November 17, 2016; negotiations between the twenty-three WTO members (including the EU and Australia) have been on hold since. For more information, see https://ec.europa.eu/trade/policy/in-focus/tisa/.

5. Section II—Disciplines on Services Domestic Regulation, Annex 1, Declaration on the Conclusion of Negotiations on Services Domestic Regulation, 2 December 2021, WT/L/1129. Section III then entails specific rules regarding financial services domestic regulation.

6. Chapter Eleven—Mutual Recognition of Professional Qualifications, CETA.

7. See 11. Recognition, Section II—Disciplines on Services Domestic Regulation, Annex 1, Declaration on the Conclusion of Negotiations on Services Domestic Regulation, 2 December 2021, WT/L/1129.

8. Treaty on European Union and European Economic Area Treaty not included (WTO n.d.).

9. EU-Mexico (2000), EU–North Macedonia (2004), EU-Chile (2005), EU-CARIFORUM (2008), EU-Albania (2009), and EU-Montenegro (2010).

10. In the same period of time (2011–2021), the EU also ratified five PTAs covering only goods trade: EU–Eastern and Southern Africa States (2012), EU-Cameroon (2014), EU–Côte d'Ivoire (2016), EU–Southern African Development Community (2016), and EU-Ghana (2016).

11. Some might even be considered GATS-minus (failing the qualitative and quantitative requirements). See, for example, Adlung and Miroudot (2012).

12. To date, the only WTO dispute dealing explicitly with GATS art. V is Canada—Autos (see WTO 2000, para. 10.270). See also Sieber-Gasser (2016, 150–153).

13. An Agreement in Principle was reached in 2018 and is awaiting ratification (see European Commission 2018).

14. EU-Korea (2010), Colombia-EU-Peru (2012), Central America–EU (2012), EU-Moldova (2014), EU-Georgia (2014), EU-Ukraine (2014), CETA (2016), TiSA (2016), Armenia-EU (2017), EU-Japan (2018), EU-Singapore (2018), EU-Vietnam (2019), and EU-UK (2020).

15. EU-Korea (2010), CETA (2016), EU-Japan (2018), EU-Singapore (2018), and EU-UK (2020).

16. Colombia-EU-Peru (2012), Central America–EU (2012), EU-Moldova (2014), EU-Georgia (2014), EU-Ukraine (2014), Armenia-EU (2017), and EU-Vietnam (2019).

17. For instance, EU-Vietnam (2019) and EU-UK (2020) score equally well, while Armenia-EU (2017) entails overall more substantial commitments than EU-Korea (2010).

18. This is not only because in all EU PTAs, commitments in mode 4 (temporary movement of natural persons) are broader than in GATS (GATS-plus), but is also due to the fact that eight of the twelve EU PTAs entail commitments in e-commerce (GATS-extra).

19. For instance, commitments in tourism are less broad in scope than in GATS (GATS-minus) in EU-Moldova (2014), EU-Georgia (2014), and EU-Ukraine (2014).

20. Given that CETA (2016) is clearly more substantial than all the previous EU PTAs in services, subsequent EU PTAs may have benefited from the levels of openness established through CETA (2016) negotiations (binding of existing levels post-CETA [2016]).

21. No separate chapter on computer services in CETA (2016) or EU-Japan (2018).
22. No separate chapter on postal and courier services in CETA (2016).
23. See, for example, art. 108 of EU-Ukraine (2014).
24. For instance, Chapter 12, "Subsidies," in EU-Japan (2018) explicitly clarifies in art. 12.4 that "nothing in this Chapter shall affect the rights and obligations of either Party under [. . .] Article XV of GATS." No comparable provision is to be found in the chapters covering (among others) cross-border services trade and establishment or investment liberalization.
25. For example, Japan-Australia (2014) covers all four modes of supply in its services chapter (art. 9.2(n)); the Comprehensive and Progressive Agreement for Trans-Pacific Partnership (2016) covers modes 1, 2, and 4 in its services chapter (art. 10.1), which corresponds with the US template in this regard (see, for example, art. 12.13 US-Korea [2012]). Globally, the majority of PTAs in services follow the US template (see Gootiiz et al. 2020, 125).
26. See Wikileaks (2015) for draft TiSA Annex on Competitive Delivery Services.
27. See previously under 1.d.
28. EU PTAs cover the categories of independent professionals, managers or executives, specialists, and trainee employees. See, for example, art. 8.13 EU-Vietnam (2019), and art. 99 and art. 102 EU-Ukraine (2014).
29. See also here under 1.d.
30. Current members are New Zealand, Costa Rica, Fiji, Iceland, Norway, and Switzerland.
31. See TiSA, Joint Initiative on Services Domestic Regulation, plurilateral agreement on e-commerce. See https://www.europarl.europa.eu/legislative-train/theme-a-balanced-and-progressive-trade-policy-to-harness-globalisation/file-trade-in-services-agreement-(tisa); https://www.wto.org/english/tratop_e/serv_e/jsdomreg_e.htm; https://www.wto.org/english/tratop_e/ecom_e/joint_statement_e.htm.

References

Adlung, R., and S. Miroudot. 2012. "Poison in the Wine? Tracing GATS-Minus Commitments in Regional Trade Agreements." WTO Staff Working Papers ERSD-2012-04.

Antimiani, A., and L. Cernat. 2018. "Liberalizing Global Trade in Mode 5 Services: How Much Is It Worth?" *Journal of World Trade* 52 (1): pp. 65–83.

Chaisse, J. 2012. "Promises and Pitfalls of the European Union Policy on Foreign Investment—How Will the New EU Competence on DFI Affect the Emerging Global Regime?" *Journal of International Economic Law* 15 (1): pp. 51–84.

Conconi, P., C. Herghelegiu, and L. Puccio. 2021. "EU Trade Agreements: To Mix or Not to Mix, That Is the Question." *Journal of World Trade* 55 (2): pp. 231–260.

Court of Justice of the European Union (CJEU). 2017. Opinion 2/15 of the Court (Full Court), 16 May 2017. ECLI:EU:C:2017:376.

European Commission (EC). n.d. "Trade: Chile." https://policy.trade.ec.europa.eu/eu-trade-relationships-country-and-region/countries-and-regions/chile_en.

European Commission. 2008. "The EU-CARIFORUM Economic Partnership." https://trade.ec.europa.eu/access-to-markets/en/content/eu-cariforum-economic-partnership-agreement.

European Commission. 2017. A Services Economy That Works for Europeans. Press Release. January 10. Brussels. https://ec.europa.eu/commission/presscorner/detail/en/IP_17_23.

European Commission. 2018. EU-Mexico Trade Agreement. https://policy.trade.ec.europa.eu/eu-trade-relationships-country-and-region/countries-and-regions/mexico/eu-mexico-agreement_en.

European Parliament. n.d. "Services e-card." Legislative Train Schedule. https://www.europarl.europa.eu/legislative-train/theme-a-europe-fit-for-the-digital-age/file-services-e-card.

European Union. 2006. Directive 2006/123/EC of the European Parliament and of the Council of 12 December 2006 on Services in the Internal Market. *Official Journal of the European Union*. L376/36. https://eur-lex.europa.eu/legal-content/EN/TXT/?uri=celex%3A32006L0123.

Eurostat. n.d. "International Trade in Services." https://ec.europa.eu/eurostat/statistics-explained/index.php?title=International_trade_in_services.

Fiorini, M., and B. Hoekman. 2020. "EU Services Trade Liberalization and Economic Regulation: Complements or Substitutes?" *The Review of International Organizations* 15: pp. 247–270.

General Agreement on Trade in Services (GATS). 1994. Annex 1B. April 15. https://www.wto.org/english/docs_e/legal_e/26-gats.pdf.

Geneva Trade Platform. n.d. Joint Statement Initiative on Electronic Commerce. https://wtoplurilaterals.info/plural_initiative/e-commerce/.

Gootiiz, B., G. Jonetzko, J. Magdeleine, J. Marchetti, and A. Mattoo. 2020. "Services." In *Handbook of Deep Trade Agreements*, edited by A. Mattoo, N. Rocha, and M. Ruta, pp. 111–142. World Bank Group. Washington, DC.

Kerneis, P. 2017. "Gains for Trade in Services in an EU-Australia Free Trade Agreement: A European Perspective." In *Australia, the European Union and the New Trade Agenda*, edited by A. Elijah, D. Kenyon, K. Hussey, and P. van der Eng, pp. 139–162. Canberra: Australian National University Press.

Kerneis, P. 2019. "EU Trade Policy and Services: The Perspective from the Private Sector." In *Perspectives on the Soft Power of EU Trade Policy*, edited by S. Bilal and B. Hoekman, pp. 71–78. London: CEPR Press.

Leal-Arcas, R. 2001. "The European Community and Mixed Agreements." *European Foreign Affairs Review* 6 (4): pp. 483–513.

New Zealand Foreign Affairs and Trade. n.d. Agreement on Climate Change, Trade and Sustainability (ACCTS) Negotiations. https://www.mfat.govt.nz/en/trade/free-trade-agreements/trade-and-climate/agreement-on-climate-change-trade-and-sustainability-accts-negotiations/.

Peng, S-Y. 2020. "A New Trade Regime for the Servitization of Manufacturing: Rethinking the Goods-Services Dichotomy." *Journal of World Trade* 54 (5): pp. 669–726.

Reinisch, A. 2014. "The EU on the Investment Path—Quo Vadis Europe? The Future of EU BITs and Other Investment Agreements." *Santa Clara Journal of International Law* 12 (1): pp. 111–157.

Rueda-Cantuche, J. M., R. Kerner, L. Cernat, and V. Ritola. 2016. "Trade in Services by GATS Modes of Supply: Statistical Concepts and First EU Estimates." *Chief Economist*

Note no. 3 (November): pp. 1–27. https://trade.ec.europa.eu/doclib/docs/2016/decem ber/tradoc_155119.pdf.

Sauvage, J., and C. Timiliotis. 2017. "Trade in Services Related to the Environment." OECD Trade and Environment Working Papers 2017/02.

Sieber-Gasser, C. 2016. *Developing Countries and Preferential Services Trade.* Cambridge: Cambridge University Press.

Sieber-Gasser, C. 2021. "Green(er) Trade in Services." In *Trade and Environmental Law, Elgar Encyclopedia of Environmental Law*, edited by P. Delimatsis and L. Reins, pp. 395–399. Cheltenham, UK: Edward Elgar.

Sieber-Gasser, C. 2022. "Services Trade Liberalisation in the Australia-EU FTA: Progress but No Quantum-Leap." In *The Australia-European Union Free Trade Agreement*, edited by M. Bungenberg and A. Mitchell, pp. 59–77. New York: Springer.

United Nations Conference on Trade and Development (UNCTAD). 2021. "e-Handbook of Statistics 2021: Total Trade in Services." https://hbs.unctad.org/total-trade-in-servi ces/#Ref_IEW5B6C5.

van Leeuwen, B. 2018. "Standardisation in the Internal Market for Services: An Effective Alternative to Harmonisation?" *Revue internationale de droit économique* 2018 (3): pp. 319–332.

Wikileaks. 2015. Trade in Services Agreement (TiSA) Annex on Competitive Delivery Services (April 214). June 3. https://wikileaks.org/tisa/document/20140416_Annex-on-Competitive-Delivery/20140416_Annex-on-Competitive-Delivery.pdf.

World Bank. n.d. "Trade in Services (% of GDP)—European Union. https://data.worldb ank.org/indicator/BG.GSR.NFSV.GD.ZS?locations=EU.

World Trade Organization (WTO). n.d. Regional Trade Agreements Database. http:// rtais.wto.org/.

World Trade Organization (WTO). 2000. Canada—Certain Measures Affecting the Automotive Industry. WT/DS 139. February 11. https://www.wto.org/english/tratop_ e/dispu_e/cases_e/ds139_e.htm.

World Trade Organization (WTO). 2021. Declaration on the Conclusion of Negotiations on Services Domestic Regulation. December 2, 2021. WT/L/1129. https://docs.wto. org/dol2fe/Pages/SS/directdoc.aspx?filename=q:/WT/L/1129.pdf&Open=True.

WTO Stats. n.d. WTO Stats Portal. https://stats.wto.org/.

3

Standardization of the Rule of Law and Anti-Corruption Clauses in EU Regional Trade Agreements with Developing Countries

Quo Vadis?

Maryna Rabinovych

Introduction

In the world of increasingly intertwined economies, the need for countries to have common trade standards comes as no surprise. While global economic developments drive the standardization of trade rules, common standards bring about new economic developments that may in turn determine the need for new standards. This process is exemplified by the history of the multilateral trading system that started with the entry into force of the General Agreement on Tariffs and Trade in January 1947 and further expanded, inter alia, to the domains of trade in services, trade facilitation, public procurement, and intellectual property rights under the World Trade Organization (WTO) umbrella. Although multilateral trade negotiations are ongoing under the WTO, their slow pace and the challenge to accommodate various interests have led to the activization of strong economic actors' bilateral and plurilateral trade liberalization policies, such as the European Union (EU) and the United States (US).

More than a decade after, it is of interest to observe that a turn to bilateralism not only enabled the EU to develop a dense network of regional trade agreements (RTAs) with partners worldwide, but also helped

Maryna Rabinovych, *Standardization of the Rule of Law and Anti-Corruption Clauses in EU Regional Trade Agreements with Developing Countries* In: *Standardizing the World*. Edited by: Francesco Duina and Crina Viju-Miljusevic, Oxford University Press. © Oxford University Press 2023. DOI: 10.1093/oso/9780197681886.003.0004 the EU to achieve a significant degree of standardization of definitions, norms, and practices. I argue in this chapter that this phenomenon goes beyond the pragmatist logic pertaining to functionalist cooperation and neo-functionalism: the EU is increasingly inclined to integrate its foreign policy instruments, in general, and use its RTAs as levers to achieve broader objectives in various policy contexts.

Specifically, the contemporary "new-generation" RTAs can be seen as manifesting the EU's "power through trade" that is rooted in both the Market Power Europe (MPE) and Normative Power Europe (NPE) frameworks (Damro 2012; Manners 2002). While the functionalist and neo-functionalist logic underlies the standardization of definitional aspects concerning tangible and intangible objects, processes, and actors, the EU uses its "power through trade" to define the acceptability of specific principles and practices. The latter process signifies "normative standardization."

With the above in mind, this contribution seeks to explore the extent to which the standardization trend has shaped the rule of law (RoL) and anti-corruption provisions under the EU's RTAs with developing countries, and to explain the drivers behind the observable standardization in these domains. Looking particularly at the RoL and anti-corruption clauses is overly important for several reasons. First, the RoL, including the absence of corruption, constitutes an important prerequisite for implementing the provisions of RTAs and developing sustainable business contacts that underlie trade and investment (Egger and Winner 2006; Marjit, Mandel, and Roy 2014). Second, clear and transparent "rules of the game" are of special relevance for "deep" trade liberalization, pursued by the EU, since it envisages a significant degree of regulatory approximation and related day-to-day cooperation by authorities. Third, given member states' varying constitutional traditions and the politicization of the RoL concept, defining and enforcing the RoL at the EU level are not always easy. Subsequently, the RoL and anti-corruption provisions under the RTAs are of interest to look at from the perspective of the EU's efforts to consolidate the RoL concept and enforce it.

The analysis thus demonstrates that, apart from pragmatist concerns about EU businesses entering new markets, the EU RoL and anti-corruption "menu" in its RTAs with developing countries to a considerable extent speaks to the EU's broader value-promotion aspirations. In particular, we see a number of RoL and anti-corruption provisions present in those RTAs: these range from partner countries' broad commitments to the RoL and fight against corruption to detailed definition of procedures aimed to uphold legal certainty and transparency.

How should we account for the EU's ability to promote RoL and anti-corruption principles in RTAs with developing countries? As already noted, in a broader sense, functionalism and neo-functionalism offer valuable perspectives. The same may be said if we consider the "power through trade" paradigm proposed more recently by scholars. Yet, a fuller explanation requires more specificity: numerous factors influence the balance between the bargaining powers of the EU and those of a partner country, such as the latter's economic characteristics, political regime, cultural factors, aid dependence, and the prospects of its single market integration (Rabinovych 2021, ch. 3).

This chapter shows the importance of these specific factors empirically in light of the EU RTAs with developing countries I selected for the purposes of this study. The selection is based on four criteria: (1) an RTA belonging to the "new generation" agreements; (2) a counterpart being a developing country; (3) counterparts representing various regions (i.e., Europe, Latin America, Asia, and African, Caribbean, and Pacific countries); and (4) the varying nature and objectives of the RTAs, ranging from purely commercial arrangements to full-fledged association agreements with a significant EU integration potential. Such a case selection enables the chapter to cover a broad spectrum of the EU's RTAs with developing countries and to map the degree and nature of standardization pertaining to different types of RTAs. Specific cases under consideration include the EU-MERCOSUR Free Trade Agreement (FTA), the EU–Central America Trade Agreement, the EU-CARIFORUM Economic Partnership Agreement (EPA), the EU-Vietnam FTA, and the EU-Ukraine Deep and Comprehensive Free Trade Agreement (DCFTA).

Why RoL and Anti-Corruption Standardization in EU RTAs with Developing Countries?

This section explores two explanations for why standardized RoL and anti-corruption clauses appear in EU RTAs with developing countries: (1) the functionalist and pragmatic neo-functionalist logics, and (2) the EU's use of its "power through trade."

Functionalist and Pragmatic Neo-Functionalist Logics

The functionalist approach to international relations, with its emphasis on cooperation, emerged during the interwar period. It underscored the weakening and obsolescence of nation states. In contrast to realists who viewed states' self-interest as a key driver behind their actions, functionalists emphasized the importance of states' and non-state actors' common interests, and the needs that emerge in processes of international integration. One of the founders of the functionalist approach, David Mitrany (1933), understood international integration as collective governance and economic (material) interdependence between states as they integrate in economic, technical, and functional domains. An important contribution of function-alism was to propose that cooperation in specific public sector–related tasks (e.g., joint air traffic control, the prevention of infectious diseases), rather than cooperation on more sensitive issues (e.g., foreign policy and defense) helps states develop mutual trust (see, e.g., Luard 1983).

Their logic is also applicable to trade liberalization and the issues it raises—such as the rules of origin or trade facilitation—that can promote trust-building and further cooperation in other domains (see, e.g., Christy 1990 with respect to the expansion of multilateral trade liberalization). Here, it is reasonable to assume that cooperation has the potential to boost the parties' trust to the point where they decide to work together on sensitive spheres, such as RoL and anti-corruption. The insight comes, at the same time, with two important limitations. First, we still need to specify *how* exactly the parties come to supplement trade liberalization provisions with RoL and anti-corruption measures: what is the nexus between trade liberalization and cooperation in these areas? Second, in line with the common critique of functionalism, inter alia, in the EU realm (Behr 2021; Weale 1999), such an approach ignores the ideational and political aspects of supplementing the RTAs with RoL and anti-corruption clauses.

Neo-functionalism offers ideas about how such an expansion can occur. In contrast to functionalism's focus on international integration and the opera-tion of specialized international agencies, neo-functionalism was introduced as the EU integration theory. The framework rests on two assumptions which help, to different degrees, explain the standardization of RoL and anti-corruption (Niemann 2006). First, it argues that when countries es-tablish cooperation in a specific sector, the process lays the foundations for, and need to, cooperate in additional sectors. Neo-functionalists use the term "functional spillover" to describe these linkages. Second, neo-functionalists argue that spillovers facilitate the cooperation of subnational actors that eventually themselves become drivers of the integration process through domestic interest groups. Third, and of lesser importance for this chapter, neo-functionalists argue that supranational bodies eventually start pursuing strategies to deepen integration with the support of interest groups.

Importantly, the "functional spillover" logic seems especially relevant when it comes to the substantial "deepening" of the EU trade policy (Niemann 2006, 30). This is clear in areas such as sanitary and phytosanitary standards (SPS) and competition. In the first case, the liberalization of trade in agricultural goods necessarily produces a spillover to the SPS domain because the parties need to agree on quality standards for products. Competition is also crucial for making free trade work since anti-competitive behavior of enterprises in one of the parties to an RTA may negatively affect the other party's enterprises' capacity to enter this party's market. Compared to the SPS, and even competition rules, RoL and anti-corruption issues are even more sensitive and are usually regarded as a part of political cooperation between the EU and partner countries. This chapter, nevertheless, argues that there are important (and insufficiently investigated) links between trade liberalization and the RoL and anti-corruption that eventually lead to comprehensive trade liberalization (i.e., liberalization that incorporates trade in services, public procurement, and financial markets) "spilling over" in those two domains.

Of course, we can note that the challenge one faces when investigating the nexus between trade liberalization and RoL and anti-corruption in the context of EU RTAs is the "essentially contested" nature of the RoL concept itself (Gallie 1956). In the EU context, such contestation stems in part from the member states' divergent legal cultures around RoL (Kochenov 2009). Indeed, the RoL crises in Poland and Hungary that started in 2014–2015 gave an impetus not only to the debate about the intra-EU RoL enforcement, but also to the inevitable consolidation of the EU-wide understanding of the RoL that such enforcement requires (Kochenov and Pech 2016).

Yet, it is possible to identify an emergent EU-wide consensual approach to RoL. The 2014 Commission's RoL Framework was the first element of the EU RoL toolbox articulating a "non-exhaustive list" of principles that constitute the RoL concept under art. 2 of the Treaty of the European Union (TEU). According to the Framework, these principles encompass "legality, which implies a transparent, accountable, democratic and pluralistic process for enacting laws; legal certainty; prohibition of arbitrariness of the executive powers; independent and impartial courts; effective judicial review including respect for fundamental rights; and equality before the law" (European Commission 2014, 4). The emphases on these RoL components were reinforced in numerous subsequent decisions by the Court of Justice of the EU (CJEU) (CJEU 2017, 2018, 2019; Rabinovych 2020; Saenz de Santa Maria 2021). In this regard, corruption, especially in the judiciary and law enforcement agencies, is widely regarded as a threat to the RoL and human rights (see CoE 2021) and is defined by the European Commission as the "abuse of power for private gain" that may take different forms, such as bribery or abuse of functions (European Commission 2022a).

Numerous contributions from development economics and "law and development" literature demonstrate the interplay between the RoL and anti-corruption, on the one hand, and making best use of trade liberalization and doing business, on the other. Functioning RoL is referred to in literature as a prerequisite for business development and economic growth (see Haggard and Tiede 2011; Haggard et al. 2008). Some of the contributions belonging to this literature strand provide an overview of specific RoL components that are most tightly linked to businesses' interactions and economic growth, such as the predictability of laws and policies, the integrity of property, and property rights protection or the "government-business" interface (see Brunetti et al. 1997; Haggard and Tiede 2011). Alongside the security of property rights and judicial independence, low levels of corruption and strong anti-corruption institutions are emphasized in the literature as essential for fostering trade, investment, and economic growth (see Egger and Winner 2006; Marjit et al. 2014). The opposite is also discussed: quickly changing rules, weak institutions, and corruption "scare businesses away" from new markets and prevent the parties from unveiling the whole potential of RTAs.

The above explanation of a strong nexus between RoL and anti-corruption, on the one hand, and unveiling the potential of RTAs, on the other hand, demonstrates why "deep" trade liberalization "spills over" to the RoL and anti-corruption domain. Since "deep" trade liberalization with the EU requires partner countries to introduce numerous legislative and institutional changes, the "depth" of trade liberalization may immediately correlate with an extent to which it "spills over" to the RoL and anti-corruption domains. Moreover, the impact that RoL and anti-corruption exert on doing international business incentivizes businesses from the EU and partner countries to lobby for RoL and anti-corruption reforms in partner countries. This is the *second* key assumption of neo-functionalism, according to which subnational actors may become the drivers of reforms and integration (the implementation of "deep" trade agenda).

The EU's Power through Trade and RTAs as Levers to Promote RoL and Anti-Corruption

The previous subsection has explored how RoL and the fight against corruption are conducive to trade liberalization and investment. There is also evidence that the pursuit of "deep" EU RTAs is conducive to the RoL-oriented changes in partner countries (see Petersmann 2020; Rabinovych 2020, 2021). The way this relationship works is consonant with the functionalist logic, as rather technical transparency and accountability standards are proven to contribute to fostering fundamental values (Freyburg et al. 2011). Nevertheless, the EU also deliberately uses its trade power to advance broader objectives (European Commission 2015).

The EU's use of trade and RTAs as value-promotion tools and the phenomenon of normative standardization are best captured by the concepts of "power through trade" (Meunier and Nicolaïdis 2006) and "normative trade power" or "normative power through trade" (Sicurelli 2015). These concepts are partly rooted in the importance of the EU's identity as "a liberal market order" (Rosamond 2014, 134) and its market power through trade (Damro 2012). Damro (2012, 684) defines the EU as a "power that can and does use its market and regulatory strengths to externalize internal policies." When doing so, it relies on the size of the EU as a single market and trading bloc, its function as a regulatory state, and the active role of competing interest groups in externalizing EU rules (Damro 2012, 687–689). In this way, the MPE portrays the externalization of EU norms and standards as both an implication of the EU's market power and the means of its further strengthening.

While explaining how the EU uses its market power to externalize its norms and standards, the MPE concept does not explain why the EU does so. To do so, we shall stress the normative dimension of the EU's "normative power through trade." The normative aspects of the EU's international role are addressed by Manners (2002) in his NPE concept. According to Manners (2002), the EU constructs its identity, inter alia, through promoting its own norms and values beyond its borders. MPE can be thus seen as an essential prerequisite for the export of values, lying at the heart of the EU's identity as a normative actor. This statement can be confirmed by the recourse to the Commission's "Trade for All Strategy" and its emphasis on "a trade agenda to promote sustainable development, human rights and good governance" (European Commission 2015, 22). Notably, the Strategy refers to specific means the EU shall apply to reach its normative objectives through trade, including the use of RTAs to "monitor domestic reform in relation to the rule of law and governance and set up consultation mechanisms in cases of systemic corruption and weak governance" (European Commission 2015, 26). It also proposes to "negotiate ambitious provisions on anticorruption in all future trade agreements" (European Commission 2015, 26). Taking a stronger stance, the 2021 Trade Policy Review not only rhetorically links trade and values, but also suggests strengthening "the EU's focus on implementation and enforcement of trade agreements and ensur[ing] a level playing field" (European Commission 2021, 11). With this, the 2021 Review seeks enhancing the EU's "power through trade" with a stronger nexus between the EU's normative objectives and its market power.

Ultimately, it is the combination of the EU market and normative powers that lies behind its ability to use RTAs as levers to advance the RoL and anti-corruption, thus reinforcing "functional spillovers" that stem from the tight nexus between trade liberalization, and the RoL and anti-corruption.

Specific Factors That Shape Standardization under the EU RTAs

As noted in the Introduction to the volume, this contribution understands standardization as the phenomenon of including identical definitional and normative provisions pertaining to the RoL and anti-corruption into the EU RTAs with different partners. Definitional standardization encompasses provisions that define specific concepts (e.g., "measures of general application" or "legitimate trade"), institutions and their authorities (e.g., obligations to create institutions entrusted with anti-corruption authorities), or procedures (e.g., public procurement procedures). Normative standardization, in contrast, stipulates the parties' commitment to phenomena and practices, considered as positive (e.g., transparency, accountability), or condemnation of those regarded as negative (corruption). Though in some cases the borderline between normative and definitional standardization may be blurred, the normativity factor is central for distinguishing between normative clauses (conveying the parties' shared attitude toward a phenomenon or practice) and definitional ones (stipulating specific rules).

In practical terms, the application of both normative and definitional standardization not only enables the Commission to capture the key trade-related aspects of the RoL and anti-corruption, but also strengthens its leverage in new RTA negotiations and helps to avoid legal uncertainty and fragmentation (Allee and Elsig 2019, 611). Standardization also makes it easier for the Commission to monitor the RTAs' implementation and conduct cross-country comparisons. Interestingly, "a heavy reliance on models and templates" is overall characteristic for RTAs, even when global agreements (that are believed to be peculiar and distinct) are concerned (Allee and Elsig 2019).

The empirical part of the analysis seeks to illustrate two phenomena. First, it shows that definitional standardization predominantly speaks to the functionalist and neo-functionalist logic, while normative standardization can be better explained with the EU "power through trade" concept. Second, it illustrates that the scope of both normative and definitional standardization in the RoL and anti-corruption domains varies depending on the ratio between the bargaining power of the EU and that of a partner country or countries, which is, in turn, dependent on economic factors and the volume of trade between the parties, aid dependence, political regime in a partner country and domestic veto players, and the prospect of a counterpart's single market integration.

Economic power and capabilities of a state, often linked in the literature to the size of its market, constitute a crucial aspect of its bargaining power (see Saguier and Tussie 2014). The EU's and its counterpart's market powers shall be understood in relative terms and, thus, it is not only market size as such, but also an economy's dependence on imports and exports that affects the parties' bargaining powers in trade negotiations (Saguier and Tussie 2014, 14). Import or export dependence on the EU necessarily lowers a counterpart's bargaining power. A factor that will, however, increase it deals with the counterpart's participation in negotiating coalitions (Lamprecht 2014, 25). This factor is particularly relevant if there is a region-to-region trade deal at stake (e.g., as in the case of the EU-MERCOSUR FTA). Alongside a counterpart's export or import dependence on the EU, there is a factor of aid dependence that lowers developing countries' bargaining power in trade negotiations with the EU, even if they negotiate a trade deal as a coalition (Rabinovych 2021, ch. 3).

A partner country's readiness to accept the RoL and anti-corruption obligations also considerably depends on its current political regime, the regime's declared objectives, and the impact of domestic veto-players (Rabinovych 2021, ch. 3). Coupled with economic factors, these factors deliver various modalities of the EU's trade relations with partner countries, whereby the incorporation of value-related provisions into RTAs with powerful autocracies, such as China or the Gulf Cooperation Council countries (and eventually the negotiations of RTAs as such), are excluded. Weaker autocracies that seek ties with the EU are expected to negotiate concessions when it comes to the RoL and anti-corruption clauses (Rabinovych 2021, ch. 3). An important role, in this vein, can be played by cultural factors and divergencies in understanding the RoL that may require either vaguer formulations or, vice versa, the focus on uncontested technical issues.

Importantly, an extent to which the EU can incorporate RoL and anti-corruption clauses into its RTA with a third country depends on the "depth" of aspired economic relations with the EU and whether or not an RTA with a third country entails a prospect for its membership in the EU or single market integration. This statement will be further illustrated by reference to the strong RoL/anti-corruption dimension of the EU-Ukraine DCFTA, regarded as one of the most ambitious RTAs ever concluded between the EU and a third country (Van der Loo 2016, 1).

An insight into a variety of factors that shape the ratio of the EU's and its counterparts' bargaining powers in trade negotiations testifies to the impossibility for the EU to use a "one-size-fits-all" approach in all RTA negotiations. I argue that the strongest RoL and anti-corruption standardization under an RTA is possible under the confluence of a counterpart's export/import dependence on the EU, dependence on EU aid, domestic orientation on democracy and market economy, and the single market integration prospect of a partner country. Other combinations of respective factors are expected to be associated with weaker RoL and anti-corruption clauses, especially when it comes to the institutions- and process-related norms. These assumptions are further explored in the empirical part of the analysis.

Definitional Standardization in the RoL and Anti-Corruption Domains

I argue that definitional standardization is largely inspired by functionalist and neo-functionalist logic, as it reflects the parties' need for common definitions, institutions, and procedures to make use of the RTAs. Definitional standardization is found to be present across the whole spectrum of RTAs, irrespective of whether they serve solely pragmatic trade objectives (RTAs with Vietnam and MERCOSUR) or aim at building association relations with the EU (RTAs with CARIFORUM and Central America). The single market integration prospect under the EU-Ukraine Association Agreement (AA) is found to correlate with strong definitional standardization of institutions, while definitions and the regulations related to processes are broadly used throughout all the RTAs in question.

Rule of Law

The challenge with exploring definitional standardization in the RoL domain is concerned with the "essentially contested" nature of this concept. The analysis below is, therefore, based on the consensual conceptualization of the RoL, contained in the 2014 Commission's Rule of Law Framework and the relevant Commission's documents and CJEU discussed above.

Hereby it shall be mentioned that definitional standardization may simultaneously concern both the RoL and anti-corruption, more specifically. This statement can be exemplified by "Transparency" chapters, present across all the RTAs in question that are designed to promote the tightly intertwined legal certainty, transparency, and accountability standards, and to counter corruption. Except for the "Transparency" chapters, important sources for definitional standardization include the RTAs' provisions on administrative cooperation, customs cooperation, and trade facilitation, and "deep" disciplines, such as public procurement and competition.

Table 3.1 exemplifies the coverage of the RoL standards by the relevant chapters of the RTAs. This analysis reveals several insights as to definitional standardization under the RTAs. First, as it can be exemplified by detailed and intertwined RoL standards under the "Transparency" chapters of all RTAs in question, definitional standardization follows the functional and pragmatic logic. The inclusion of the entire spectrum of RoL standards, including the right to review and appeal, in the RTAs under study, demonstrates their immediate role in making "deep" RTAs functional. Second, detailed definitional, institutional, and procedural RoL standards complement weak normative standardization (discussed below) in cases when the EU has

Table 3.1 Examples of Definitional Standardization in the RoL Domain

Rule of Law Standards	RTA Provisions		
	"Transparency" chapters	Administrative cooperation, customs cooperation, and trade facilitation	Deep disciplines (public procurement, competition)
Legality	Notions of a measure of general application," "interested person," and "administrative decision" (e.g., EU-MERCOSUR 2019, "Transparency chapter," art. 1; EU-Vietnam 2019, art. 14.3)	Framework rules customs legislation (e.g., EU–Central America 2012, art.118; EU-MERCOSUR 2019, art. 1)	Basic standards as to the publication of intended procurements, award of contracts, and judicial protection (e.g., EU-CARIFORUM 2008, art. 166; EU-Ukraine 2014, art. 151; EU–Central America 2012, art. 209(2); EU-Vietnam, ch. 9, art. 9.1) Definitions of "competition authority" and "competition laws" (e.g., EU-Ukraine 2014, art.253)
Legal certainty	An obligation to administer measures of general application "in a uniform, impartial and reasonable manner" (e.g., EU-Vietnam 2019, art. 14.5; EU-Central America 2014, art. 339(1); EU-CARIFORUM 2008, art. 235)	Defining authorities' rights and obligations concerning information exchange and customs cooperation (e.g., EU-Vietnam 2019, ch.4, art. 4.2)	Detailed procedures as to the award of public procurement contracts (e.g., EU-Ukraine 2014, art. 151(5–14))
Non-discrimination	Providing interested parties with an opportunity to become acquainted with planned measures of general application and the rationale for them (e.g., EU-Central America 2014, art. 339(1); EU-Ukraine AA 2014, art. 283(a))	Requirements as to the transparent and non-discriminatory nature of customs and related trade legislation and procedures (e.g., EU-Ukraine 2014, art. 76; EU-Vietnam 2019, ch.4, art. 4.3)	Transparency of public procurement information and its disclosure to suppliers (e.g., EU–Central America 2012, art. 223–224; EU-MERCOSUR, "Government Procurement," art. 23–24)

Authorities' accountability	An obligation to designate contact points to ensure the effective RTA implementation (e.g., EU–Central America 2012, art. 340; EU–Ukraine 2014, art. 284)	Defining authorities' rights and obligations concerning information exchange and customs cooperation (e.g., EU–Vietnam 2019, ch.4, art. 4.2)	Requirements as to the openness of tender documentation to suppliers (e.g., EU–Vietnam 2019, ch.9, art. 9.11; EU–Ukraine 2014, art. 151(2–4); EU–Central America 2012, art. 223)
Transparency	An obligation to publish the measures of general application and related draft laws (e.g., EU–MERCOSUR 2019, "Transparency chapter," art. 3; EU–Vietnam 2019, art. 14.4; EU–CARIFIORUM 2008, art. 235)	Defining the Parties' obligations concerning information exchange (e.g., EU–Ukraine 2014, art. 80e; EU–CARIFIORUM 2008, art. 31(2))	Limited use of simplified tendering procedures (e.g., EU–Ukraine AA, art. 151(12–13); EU–Central America 2012, art. 221)
Judicial independence and impartiality	An obligation to "establish or maintain courts or other independent tribunals, including, where relevant, quasi-judicial or administrative tribunals" (e.g., EU–Ukraine AA; EU–Ukraine 2014, art. 286) An obligation to ensure independent and impartial review and appeal against administrative decisions (e.g., EU–MERCOSUR 2019, "Transparency chapter," art. 6; EU–Vietnam 2019, art. 14.5)	Requirement to provide effective, prompt and impartial procedures to appeal against customs and other agencies' decisions (e.g., EU–Central America 2012, art. 76(2)(c); EU–CARIFIORUM 2008, art. 118(3)(c))	Ensuring individuals' right to appeal against decisions made by competition authorities (e.g., EU–Ukraine 2014, art. 255(3); EU–Vietnam 2019, ch.10, art. 10(3)) Right of appeal against the decisions of government procurement agencies and the design of domestic review procedures (e.g., EU–Ukraine 2014, art. 151(15); EU–Vietnam 2019, ch. 9, art. 9.19; EU–Central America 2012, art. 225; EU–MERCOSUR, 2019, art. 25)

limited bargaining power in negotiations with partner countries who are interested in solely pragmatic cooperation, rather than taking over EU normative standards (e.g., Vietnam, MERCOSUR). Third, though all the RTAs in question are found to contain RoL standards, the degree of envisaged single market integration significantly influences the scope of standardization. In this vein, the public procurement and competition chapters under the EU-Ukraine AA are marked by the most far-reaching RoL clauses among the RTAs in question that take the form of Ukraine's legislative approximation obligations and detailed substantive standards (EU-Ukraine 2014, Part IV, chs. 8–9). By comparison with other RTAs, definitional standardization of institutions under the EU-Ukraine AA is more nuanced, marked, inter alia, by detailed requirements in the design of relevant institutions in the public procurement and competition domains (EU-Ukraine 2014, art. 150, art. 255).

In a nutshell, definitional RoL standardization under the RTAs follows neo-functionalist pragmatic logic and encompasses multiple intertwined definitions, institutions, and procedures that influence not only the RoL but naturally also nurture the fight against corruption.

Anti-Corruption

As in the case of the RoL, the RTAs in question do not contain separate anti-corruption chapters. Definitional anti-corruption provisions can be hardly distinguished from the RoL clauses analyzed above.

The RTAs' "Transparency" chapters represent the key source of definitional standardization under the "new generation" RTAs (European Parliament 2018, 16–17). As described above, "Transparency" chapters are marked by strong standardization across the RTAs in question, especially when it comes to definitions and procedures. Despite sharing the definitions and many of institutional and procedural requirements, it is only the EU–Central America AA that explicitly stipulates the link between transparency and anti-corruption (EU–Central America 2012, art. 338). The "Transparency" chapters under the RTAs, nonetheless, address corruption in several ways. First, the requirements for publishing the measures of general application and providing access to draft laws make it hardly possible for partner governments to use legal uncertainty as a room for corruption and discriminatory action against the businesses of another party (see EU-MERCOSUR 2019, "Transparency," art. 3). Second, similar effects are envisaged by standardized procedures as to the administration of measures of general application (e.g., EU-MERCOSUR 2019 "Transparency," art. 5). Third, the "Transparency" chapters are marked by the provisions on review and appeal that may help not only foreign but domestic businesses protect their interests (see EU-MERCOSUR 2019, "Transparency," art. 6; EU-Ukraine 2014, art. 286). Going beyond the "Transparency" chapters, definitional standardization of anti-corruption norms may be found in the RTAs' provisions on countering fraud and illicit financial activities. It mainly concerns definitions (e.g., "active corruption," "passive corruption," or "conflict of interest") (EU-Ukraine 2014, Annex XLIII to the Title IV) and cooperation procedures (e.g., EU-Ukraine 2014, Annex XLIII to the Title IV; EU-CARIFORUM 2008, art. 237). In contrast to the neo-functionalism-backed standardization under the "Transparency" chapters, anti-corruption and financial cooperation clauses are strongly linked to the aspired political relations between the parties. The EU-Ukraine AA is thus marked by the most detailed anti-corruption and financial cooperation clauses (EU-Ukraine 2014, Annex XLIII to the Title IV).

With this, the analysis demonstrates a strong nexus between definitional standardization in the RoL and anti-corruption domains, explained by the neo-functionalist dynamics.

Normative Standardization in the RoL and Anti-Corruption Domains

In contrast to definitional standardization, normative standardization encompasses desired practices or outcomes (e.g., fighting corruption) or condemns the unacceptable ones (e.g., corruption). As previously mentioned, normative and definitional standardization may be tightly intertwined. The chapter, therefore, uses the normativity/"desired result" criterion to distinguish between the instances of normative standardization and definitional provisions that concern specific notions, institutions, and procedures.

The selected case studies show that the EU has achieved a significant level of normative standardization in the RoL domain. Nevertheless, in contrast to definitional standardization, the formulations of respective standards

are highly dependent on the extent to which the EU can exercise normative power through trade in each specific case. Different levels of detail and
the ratio between strongly required and aspirational RoL standards are thus
determined by the confluence of factors, underlying the parties' bargaining
powers and making up for the EU's normative power through trade. Norms
as to specific RoL aspects are less prone to such divergencies, though the
single market integration aspirations under an RTA are found to correlate
with additional RoL commitments. Compared to the RoL provisions, normative anti-corruption provisions are marked by stronger variation and context orientation, which can be explained by the sensitive nature of corruption
issues.

Rule of Law

An insight into the RTAs under study demonstrates three key legal avenues
they use to channel normative RoL standards. As demonstrated in Table 3.2,
these are the "essential element" clauses, "hard" or "soft" law commitments
to the RoL as a whole or stipulating it as an objective of cooperation and the
commitments to specific RoL standards. "Essential element" clauses enable
the EU to use trade agreements as levers to safeguard fundamental values,
including the RoL (see Hachez 2015). Declaring the RoL as an "essential element" under an RTA enables the EU to suspend a partner country's benefits
under this RTA if it violates the RoL principle in line with art. 60 of the Vienna
Convention on the Law of Treaties (United Nations 1969). Despite the sound
legal basis, the EU's practice of invoking "essential element" clauses is marked
by selectivity, thus turning this instrument into the gateway for political dialogue, rather than a tool of the EU's automated response to the RoL violations
(Rabinovych 2020, 14–16). General commitments to the RoL as an objective
of cooperation also serve as a way to start political dialogue. Nevertheless, it
is the politicization and contestation of the RoL that determines a considerable variation in the normative RoL standardization throughout the RTAs,
especially when it comes to the first two categories of commitments. By contrast, the RTAs share numerous sector-specific commitments to specific RoL
standards, such as transparency or non-discrimination, often linked to the
parties' commitments under the WTO law, such as the Technical Barriers
to Trade (TBT) Agreement or the Plurilateral Agreement on Government

Table 3.2 Normative RoL Standardization in EU RTAs with Developing Countries

Agreement	Factors Influencing the Ratio of Bargaining Powers	"Essential Element" Clauses	"Hard" and "Soft" Commitments to the RoL	Examples of "Hard" and "Soft" Commitments to Specific RoL Standards
EU–CARIFORUM EPA (2008)	Lower significance of trade with the EU for CARIFORUM than with China and the US (European Commission 2020a) But (1) beneficial access to EU market and the EPA's focus on aid Ambition for closer association relations	Yes RoL and "transparent and accountable governance" are referred to as "integral part of sustainable development" (EU-CARIFORUM 2008, art. 2; EU–ACP 2000, art. 9)	Reference to the RoL in the Preamble	Objective of establishing and implementing "an effective, predictable and transparent regulatory framework for trade and investment" Numerous sectoral legal certainty, transparency, and non-discrimination standards (e.g., ch. 5, art. 168)
EU–Central America AA (2012)	Relatively low trade volumes between the EU and Central America Central American countries' improved access to government procurement, services, and investment markets Ambition for closer association relations, EU's assistance and support for regional integration	Yes Linkage to sustainable development and Millennium Development Goals (art. 1)	RoL as one of the standards EU–Central America association is based on and which the parties shall cooperate toward under the broader governance framework (art. 12, art. 24(2), art. 30)	Numerous sectoral legal certainty, transparency, and non-discrimination standards (e.g., art 118(3), art. 338)
EU-Ukraine AA/DCFTA (2014)	EU as Ukraine's largest trading partner (European Commission 2020b) Ukraine's aspirations for membership and AA's orientation on Ukraine's single market integration	Yes Strong fundamental values-security nexus (art. 2)	Detailed provisions on political dialogue, aimed at strengthening the RoL, and good governance, the reinforcement of institutions at all levels and the administration of justice (art. 4, art. 14)	Numerous sector-specific commitments to transparency, non-discrimination, judicial independence and impartiality, as well as the broad concepts of "regulatory cooperation" and "good administrative behaviour" (see art. 285, 287; Rabinovych 2021, ch.4)

(continued)

Table 3.2 Continued

Agreement	Factors Influencing the Ratio of Bargaining Powers	"Essential Element" Clauses	"Hard" and "Soft" Commitments to the RoL	Examples of "Hard" and "Soft" Commitments to Specific RoL Standards
EU-MERCOSUR FTA (2019)	EU as MERCOSUR's key trading partner (European Commission 2022b) Considerable collective bargaining power of MERCOSUR countries No ambition for closer association relations with the EU Pragmatic nature of cooperation	N/A as the FTA is only published as an agreement in principle	Referred to as an aspirational standard under the EU-MERCOSUR Interregional Framework Cooperation Agreement (EU-MERCOSUR 1999)	Objective of fostering "a transparent and predictable regulatory environment" (art. 2). "Hard law" commitments to the transparency of government procurement and the non-discriminatory, predictable, and transparent nature of customs procedures (art. 1 of the "Government procurement" and "Customs and trade facilitation" chapters)
EU-Vietnam FTA (2019)	Neither is the EU is Vietnam's key trade partner, nor does Vietnam play such a role for the EU Insignificant thematic cooperation (energy) No ambition for closer association relations Pragmatic nature of cooperation	None	"Soft" commitment to the RoL and "general principles of international law" in EU-Vietnam PCA (EU-Vietnam 2016, art. 1)	"Hard" and "soft" commitments to legitimate trade, transparency, and non-discrimination (art. 4.1, 4.3, 5.7)

Procurement (WTO 1995, 2012; see EU–Central America 2012, art. 125–126; EU–Ukraine 2014, art. 53).

With this, we see that normative standardization in the RoL domain is to a considerable extent explained by the EU's aspiration to use trade as a lever to promote normative objectives, rather than pragmatic neo-functionalist logic. In other words, it is the significant normative power through trade that enables the EU to complement trade-related definitional provisions pertaining to the rule of law and anti-corruption with broader normative commitments in these areas. The scope of normative standardization under RTAs is, therefore, considerably influenced by the ratio of the parties' bargaining powers and, particularly, the political regime and aspirations of a partner country or countries. The degree to which norms are detailed and the ratio between required and aspirational standards can be seen as key legal techniques that the parties use to navigate respective differences.

Anti-Corruption

Corruption is widely recognized to endanger trade and doing business (see Bardhan 1997). Given the fact that countering corruption represents an essential aspect of the RoL and the sensitivity of the issue, there is a significant context-related variation of anti-corruption clauses across the RTAs. As illustrated in Table 3.3, the reach of these normative clauses significantly varies across the RTAs in question, dependent on the scope of existing or aspired political ties between the EU and a partner country or countries.

The analysis reveals a considerable variation in the scope and ambition of normative anti-corruption clauses, clearly linked to the parties' bargaining powers and political context. The most ambitious anti-corruption clauses correlate with the prospect of the parties' "deep" association relations, including a strong political component (e.g., EU-Ukraine DCFTA). Directed to pragmatic "trade-only" cooperation, EU FTAs with MERCOSUR and Vietnam contain a considerably weaker normative anti-corruption component. As well as normative standardization in the RoL domain, normative anti-corruption standardization can be explained by the EU power through trade concept rather than the neo-functionalist logic.

Table 3.3 Normative Anti-Corruption Clauses in EU RTAs with Developing Countries

Agreement	Anti-Corruption Clauses
EU-CARIFORUM EPA (2008)	• Commitment to international anti-corruption treaties (e.g., the 2003 UN Convention against Corruption) (art. 237) • Reference to art. 9 of the Cotonou Agreement, which argues that "only serious cases of corruption, including acts of bribery leading to corruption" constitute a violation of that element (EU-ACP 2000, art. 9)
EU–Central America AA (2012)	• Commitment to combating corruption as one of the principles of the AA (art. 1(3)) • Anti-corruption as an area of political dialogue (art. 13) • Recognition of the "importance of preventing and combating corruption in the private and public sphere" (art. 38) • Commitment to specific international anti-corruption treaties (art. 37)
EU-Ukraine AA/ DCFTA (2014)	• Commitment to the fight against corruption and fight to organized crime as "central to enhancing the relationship between the Parties" (art. 3) • Combating corruption as one of the objectives of EU-Ukraine cooperation (art. 14, art. 22(1)) • Commitment to specific international anti-corruption treaties (art. 22(4))
EU-MERCOSUR FTA (2019)	• No immediate reference to fight against corruption both under the FTA itself and the EU-MERCOSUR Interregional Framework Cooperation Agreement (EU-MERCOSUR 1999, art. 4)
EU-Vietnam FTA (2019)	• No immediate reference to fight against corruption in the FTA itself • Affirming the parties' "attachment to the principle of good governance and the fight against corruption" and referring to anti-corruption as one of the cooperation objectives under the EU-Vietnam Framework Agreement (EU-Vietnam 2016, Preamble, art. 23)

Conclusion

The analysis demonstrates that, except for strictly trade-related norms, the EU RTAs with developing countries are marked by a considerable degree of normative and definitional standardization in the RoL and anti-corruption domains. As the RoL and anti-corruption traditionally fall within the scope of the EU's political cooperation with third countries, the RoL and anti-corruption aspects of the EU's trade relations with third countries are seldom explored in academic literature. It is, however, highly interesting to note that the RoL and anti-corruption standardization in RTAs can be explained not only by the EU's aspiration to use trade as a lever to achieve political objectives, but also by the functionalist and neo-functionalist logic under which the RoL and anti-corruption provisions are strictly necessary to unveil the full potential of the RTAs. The functionalist and neo-functionalist line of logic is well suited to explain the phenomenon of definitional standardization in the RoL and anti-corruption domains. An extent and design of normative standardization is, in contrast, shaped by the EU's normative power through trade. In each particular case, the design of the RoL and anti-corruption norms is influenced by a unique combination of factors, such as the parties' bargaining powers, status quo, and aspirations in their relations with the EU.

Notably, researching of the RoL and anti-corruption standardization under the RTAs is marked by two intertwined challenges, namely the lack of the EU-wide definition of the RoL and the tight nexus between the RoL and anti-corruption clauses. Respective research thus requires nuanced operationalization of concepts being used. Overall, the case of the RoL and anti-corruption standardization offers an exciting example of the interplay between economic, normative, and neo-functionalist logic with respect to standardization under the EU's RTAs with third countries.

References

Allee, T., and M. Elsig. 2019. "Are the Contents of International Trade Agreements Copied and Pasted? Evidence from Preferential Trade Agreements." *International Studies Quarterly* 63 (3): pp. 603–613.

Bardhan, P. 1997. "Corruption and Development: A Review of Issues." *Journal of Economic Literature* XXXV: pp.1320–1346.

Behr, D. 2021. "Technocracy and the Tragedy of EU Governance." *Journal of Contemporary European Research* 17 (2): pp. 224–238.

Brunetti, A., G. Kisunko, and B. Weder. 1997. "Institutions in Transition: Reliability of Rules and Economic Performance in Former Socialist Countries." Policy Research Working Paper Series 1809. Washington, DC: World Bank Publications.

Council of Europe (CoE). 2021. "Corruption Undermines Human Rights and the Rule of Law." January 19. https://www.coe.int/en/web/commissioner/blog-2021/-/asset_pu blisher/aa3hyyf8wKBn/content/corruption-undermines-human-rights-and-the-rule-of-law?inheritRedirect=false.

Court of Justice of the European Union (CJEU). 2017. *Case C-64/16 Associação Sindical dos Juízes Portugueses* (Portuguese Judges), EU:C:2018:117.

Court of Justice of the European Union (CJEU). 2018. *Commission v. Poland* (Independence of the Supreme Court), EU:C:2018:1021.

Court of Justice of the European Union (CJEU). 2019. *Case C-192/18 Commission v. Poland* (Independence of Ordinary Courts), EU:C:2019:924.

Damro, C. 2012. "Market Power Europe." *Journal of European Public Policy* 19 (5): pp. 682–699.

Egger, P., and H. Winner. 2006. "How Corruption Influences Foreign Direct Investment: A Panel Data Study." *Economic Development and Cultural Change* 54 (2): pp. 459–486.

EU-CARIFORUM. 2008. "Economic Partnership Agreement between the CARIFORUM States, of the one part, and the European Community and its Member States, of the other." *Official Journal of the European Union*, October 30, L289/1, pp. 3–1955. http://publications.europa.eu/resource/cellar/f5c1c99f-9d19-452b-b0b0-ed690a53d d5f.0006.05/DOC_1.

EU–Central America. 2012. "Agreement Establishing an Association between the European Union, on the one hand, and Central America, on the other." https://eur-lex.europa.eu/legal-content/EN/ALL/?uri=CELEX:22012A1215(01).

EU-MERCOSUR. 1999. "Interregional Framework Cooperation Agreement between the European Community and Mercosur." https://eur-lex.europa.eu/legal-content/EN/TXT/?uri=LEGISSUM:r14013.

EU-MERCOSUR. 2019. "The Agreement in Principle and Texts of the Agreement." https://ec.europa.eu/trade/policy/in-focus/eu-mercosur-association-agreement.

European Commission. 2014. "Communication to the European Parliament and the Council: A New EU Framework to Strengthen the Rule of Law." COM/2014/0158final*.

European Commission. 2015. "Trade for All: Towards a More Responsible Trade and Investment Policy." https://trade.ec.europa.eu/doclib/docs/2015/october/tradoc_153 846.pdf.

European Commission. 2020a. "EU-CARIFORUM Economic Partnership Agreement. Creating Opportunities for EU and Caribbean Businesses." October. https://trade.ec.europa.eu/doclib/docs/2020/october/tradoc_158983.pdf.

European Commission. 2020b. "Ukraine: EU's Trade Relations with Ukraine." https://policy.trade.ec.europa.eu/eu-trade-relationships-country-and-region/countries-and-regions/ukraine_en.

European Commission. 2021. "Communication to the European Parliament, the Council, the European Economic and Social Committee and the Committee of the Regions: Trade Policy Review—An Open, Sustainable and Assertive Trade Policy." COM (2021)66final.

European Commission. 2022a. "Corruption." https://home-affairs.ec.europa.eu/policies/internal-security/corruption_en.

European Commission. 2022b. "Trade Topics: EU-Mercosur Trade Agreement." https://policy.trade.ec.europa.eu/eu-trade-relationships-country-and-region/countries-and-regions/mercosur/eu-mercosur-agreement_en#:~:text=The%20EU%20is%20Mercosur's%20number,%E2%82%AC330%20billion%20in%202020.

European Parliament. 2018. "Anti-Corruption Provisions in EU Free Trade and Investment Agreements: Delivering on Clean Trade." Workshop. April. PE 603.867. https://www.europarl.europa.eu/RegData/etudes/STUD/2018/603867/EXPO_STU(2018)603867_EN.pdf.

European Union–African, Caribbean and Pacific Countries (EU-ACP). 2000. "Cotonou Agreement." https://www.consilium.europa.eu/en/policies/cotonou-agreement/.

EU-Ukraine. 2014. "Association Agreement between the European Union and its Member States, of the one part, and Ukraine, of the other part." *Official Journal of the European Union*, May 29, L161/3, pp. 3–2137. https://trade.ec.europa.eu/doclib/docs/2016/november/tradoc_155103.pdf.

EU-Vietnam. 2016. "Framework Agreement on Comprehensive Partnership and Cooperation between the European Union and its Member States, of the one part, and the Socialist Republic of Vietnam, of the other part." https://eur-lex.europa.eu/legal-content/EN/TXT/?uri=CELEX%3A22016A1203%2802%29.

EU-Vietnam. 2019. "Trade and Investment Agreements." https://policy.trade.ec.europa.eu/eu-trade-relationships-country-and-region/countries-and-regions/vietnam/eu-vietnam-agreement/texts-agreements_en.

Freyburg, T., S. Lavenex, F. Schimmelfennig, T. Skripka, and A. Wetzel. 2015. "Democracy Promotion through Functional Cooperation? The Case of the European Neighbourhood Policy." *Democratization* 18 (4): pp. 1026–1054.

Gallie, W. B. 1955–56. "Essentially Contested Concepts." *Proceedings of the Aristotelean Society* 56: pp. 167–198.

Hachez, N. 2015. "'Essential Element' Clauses in EU Trade Agreements Making Trade Work in a Way That Helps Human Rights?" KU Leuven Working Paper No. 158. https://ghum.kuleuven.be/ggs/publications/working_papers/2015/158hachez.

Haggard, S., and L. Tiede. 2011. "The Rule of Law and Economic Growth: Where Are We?" *World Development* 39 (5): pp. 673–685.

Haggard, S., A. MacIntyre, and L. Tiede. 2008. "The Rule of Law and Economic Development." *Annual Review of Political Science* 11: pp. 205–234.

Kochenov, D. 2009. "The EU Rule of Law: Cutting Paths Through Confusion." *Erasmus Law Review* 2 (1): pp. 1–24.

Kochenov, D., and L. Pech. 2016. "Better Later than Never? On the European Commission's Rule of Law Framework and Its First Activation." *Journal of Common Market Studies* 54 (5): pp. 1062–1074. doi: https://doi.org/10.1111/jcms.12401.

Lamprecht, J. 2014. "Bargaining Power in Multilateral Trade Negotiations: Canada and Japan in the Uruguay Round and Doha Development Agenda." PhD thesis, London School of Economics. http://etheses.lse.ac.uk/903/.

Luard, E. 1983. "Functionalism Revisited: The UN Family in the 1980s." *International Affairs* 59 (4): pp. 677–692.

Manners, I. 2002. "Normative Power Europe: A Contradiction in Terms?" *Journal of Common Market Studies* 40 (2): pp. 235–258.

Marjit, S., B. Mandal, and S. Roy. 2014. "Trade Openness, Corruption and Factor Abundance: Evidence from a Dynamic Panel." *Review of Development Economics* 18 (1): pp. 45–58.

Meunier, S., and K. Nicolaïdis. 2006. "The European Union as a Conflicted Trade Power." *Journal of European Public Policy* 13 (6): pp. 906–925.

Mitrany, D. 1933. *The Progress of International Government*. London: Allen and Unwin.

Niemann, A. 2006. *Explaining Decisions in the European Union*. Cambridge: Cambridge University Press.

Petersman, E. U. 2020. "Rule-of-Law in International Trade and Investments? Between Multilevel Arbitration, Adjudication and 'Judicial Overreach.'" Working Paper, EUI Law 2020/10. https://cadmus.eui.eu/handle/1814/67990.

Rabinovych, M. 2020. "The Rule of Law as Non-Trade Policy Objective in EU Preferential Trade Agreements with Developing Countries." *Hague Journal on the Rule of Law* 12: pp. 485–509. doi: http://dx.doi.org/10.1007/s40803-020-00145-z.

Rabinovych, M. 2021. *EU Regional Trade Agreements: An Instrument of Promoting the Rule of Law to Third States*. London: Routledge.

Rosamond, B. 2014. "Three Ways of Speaking Europe to the World: Markets, Peace, Cosmopolitan Duty and the EU's Normative Power." *The British Journal of Politics and International Relations* 16: pp. 133–148.

Saenz de Santa Maria, P. 2021. "Rule of Law and Judicial Independence in the Light of CJEU and ECtHR Case Law." In *Fundamental Rights Challenges: Horizontal Effectiveness, Rule of Law and Margin of National Appreciation*, edited by C. Izquierdo-Sans, C. Martínez-Capdevila, and M. Nogueira-Guastavino, pp. 167–187. London: Routledge.

Saguier, M., and D. Tussie. 2014. "Emerging Trade Politics: The Continuous Pendulum From Multilateralism to Asymmetric Trade Negotiations." *Estudios Internacionalis* 2 (1): pp. 9–26.

Sicurelli, D. 2015. "The EU as a Promoter of Human Rights in Bilateral Trade Agreements: The Case of the Negotiations with Vietnam." *Journal of Contemporary European Research* 11 (2): pp. 230–245.

United Nations. 1969. "Vienna Convention on the Law of the Treaties." *United Nations Treaty Series*, vol. 1155, p. 331. https://treaties.un.org/pages/ViewDetailsIII.aspx?src=TREATY&mtdsg_no=XXIII-1&chapter=23&Temp=mtdsg3&clang=_en.

Weale, A. 1999. "European Environmental Policy by Stealth: The Dysfunctionality of Functionalism?" *Environment and Planning C: Government and Policy* 17(1): pp. 37–51. doi: https://doi.org/10.1068/c170037.

World Trade Organization (WTO). 1995. "Agreement on Technical Barriers to Trade." https://www.wto.org/english/docs_e/legal_e/17-tbt_e.htm.

World Trade Organization (WTO). 2012. "Agreement on Government Procurement." https://www.wto.org/english/tratop_e/gproc_e/gp_gpa_e.htm.

Van der Loo, G. 2016. *The EU-Ukraine Association Agreement and Deep and Comprehensive Free Trade Area*. Leiden: Brill.

4

EU Investment Policy

Regional Convergence or International Standards?

Rodrigo Polanco[*]

Introduction

Investment treaties were born in Europe. The first bilateral investment treaty (BIT) was signed between Germany and Pakistan in 1959. Similar agreements followed, concluded mainly by European countries. In contrast, the United States (US) signed its first BIT only in 1982 (with Panama).[1]

Today, the international investment agreements (IIAs) concluded by European countries represent around 42 percent of the total of these treaties (31 percent currently in force), including BITs and free trade agreements (FTAs) with investment chapters (Alschner et al. 2021). Likewise, the majority of claimants and arbitrators in investor-state dispute settlement (ISDS) come from European countries (Behn et al. 2021).

Yet, the international regulation of foreign investments at the European level has been characterized by fragmentation. Although similar, European BITs have several differences, and a complex division of investment competences has existed among the member states and the European Union (EU) and its predecessors.

During the different phases of the EU investment policy, we distinguish between two types of standardization: definitional and normative (Duina 2006), having in mind that some treaty passages do not clearly fall in any of these categories (or sometimes they do in both).

Definitional standardization relates to the issue of how foreign investment is defined (just foreign direct investment [FDI] or also portfolio?) as well as the model/approach undertaken by the EU to regulate it (e.g., a "dual approach" of distinguishing between establishment and movement of capital, a standalone investment chapter or lumped in with services?). Normative

Rodrigo Polanco, *EU Investment Policy* In: *Standardizing the World*. Edited by: Francesco Duina and Crina Viju-Miljusevic, Oxford University Press. © Oxford University Press 2023. DOI: 10.1093/oso/9780197681886.003.0005

standardization refers to how investments should be promoted (cooperation, information, capacity-building), protected (standards of protection and
dispute settlement mechanisms, like ISDS or an investment court system,
that interpret or define the actual content of those standards), or liberalized
(positive or negative list—more control over what is liberalized vs. default
liberalization).

When possible, we also highlight the causal pathways for the various
standardization outcomes (e.g., borrowing, spillover), keeping in mind the
difference between explaining a pattern of standardization output and the
ability or competence to standardize. In that sense, this chapter also explores
how the EU increasingly gained the competence to standardize investment
policies for its member states and the tensions such process created and
continues to create.

We also point out the limitations of standardization, highlighting the internal divergences between the EU and its member states (and also among
the member states) in respect to investment policy and the general challenges
faced by the existing international investment regime. Examples of these
differences are reflected in the complex evolution of the common commercial policy to include investment and in the continuing signature of member
state BITs. This chapter aims to explain the underlying worldviews that these
approaches embody, from a Keynesian (control capital flows) to a neoliberal
policy (liberalize capital flows), with differing attitudes toward the desirability of short-term or long-term investment.

Together with providing some basic description of the pertinent EU primary law, we trace the evolution of the most relevant investment provisions
included in the trade and investment agreements concluded by the EU over
three phases, each identified by its main treaty (Rome, Maastricht, and
Lisbon). Finally, the chapter examines whether the EU investment policy has
created convergence for the EU and its member states and if IIAs concluded
by the EU have influenced investment treaty-making in other regions of
the world.

First Phase: Treaty of Rome

On March 25, 1957, the treaty establishing the European Economic
Community (EEC) was signed in Rome (the Treaty of Rome, hereafter also

the EEC Treaty). The agreement entered into force on January 1, 1958, and did not provide the EEC with legal competences in regulating international investment flows (Basedow 2016, 745).[2] The notion of "investment" was, in principle, alien to the EEC (Fernández-Pons et al. 2017, 1328). Instead, the Treaty of Rome distinguished between "right of establishment" (ch. 2, arts. 52–58) and "movement of capital" (ch. 4, arts. 67–73).

In parallel, EEC member states were signing BITs on their own. Those agreements granted strong protections to foreign investors, sharing remarkable similarities (Calamita 2012, 323), such as broad-based definitions for investors and investment; full compensation for direct and indirect expropriation; unqualified most-favored-nation (MFN), national treatment (NT), and fair and equitable treatment (FET) standards; broad umbrella clauses; no exceptions for specific sectors; no filter mechanisms; and a broad choice of ISDS mechanisms as well as free choice of arbitrators (Lavranos 2013). Between 1957 and 1991, EEC member states concluded 212 BITs.

According to the Treaty of Rome's approach, the notions of establishment and movement of capital are different, even if there is a link between them. The establishment in a host state of a third-country national or company supposes the formation of a subsidiary, branch, or agency, or the total or partial acquisition of an existing entity. The capital needed for that purpose does not necessarily come from a third country and may be obtained in the host state's national financial market. In contrast, international capital movements involve transfers of monetary or financial assets between countries. They are not necessarily connected with the establishment in a different country from where the transfer originated. The rationale underlying the regulation of these two notions is distinct and is generally managed by different governmental authorities. Right of establishment's regulation is a matter of sectoral policies (e.g., banking, telecommunications, energy) and the domain of their respective ministries. Capital movements' regulation depends on macroeconomic policy, including balance of payments, exchange rate, monetary stability, and inflation control, among other factors. It is the domain of the ministries of economy, finance, and central banks. Macroeconomic and sectoral policies do not always go in the same direction. For example, several countries have significantly liberalized access to capital from third countries. Still, they have not always entirely liberalized the establishment of foreign companies or the domestic companies' control by foreign capital in important sectors (e.g., air transport, audiovisual, or energy) (Fernández-Pons et al. 2017, 1229–1330).

On the other hand, in art. 69, the EEC stated that the free movement of capital was only a subordinated treaty freedom. The liberalization of capital movements should only proceed through secondary legislation and to the extent necessary. Only in the 1980s, when EEC policymakers shifted from Keynesian to neoliberal policies, were they willing to liberalize intra-EU capital (Basedow 2016, 746).

When the EEC started to develop its external economic relations primarily through Association Agreements, either alone or accompanied by its member states (in the so-called mixed agreements),[3] it was inspired by the EEC Treaty itself. Such agreements mirrored the Treaty of Rome and adopted the same "dual" definitional standardization of including provisions on the right of establishment and the movement of capital, together with the setting up of mechanisms to enact secondary law, which created new substantive legal rules within the framework of the treaty (Fernández-Pons et al. 2017, 1334). The legal basis for establishing an association with the Community was already present in the original version of the Treaty of Rome. While art. 113 foresaw the conclusion of trade agreements,[4] art. 238 considered the establishment of an association,[5] being an early and rare example of express external power granted to the Community (Bast 2009).

But this development was not automatic. In fact, the first association agreement (signed with Greece on July 9, 1961) did not include provisions on the right of establishment or movement of capital. This treaty only had a "best efforts" provision to encourage all means of investment in Greece of capital from EEC countries likely to contribute to the development of the Greek economy (EEC 1961, art. 62).

The Convention between the EEC and the eighteen Associated African States and Madagascar, signed on July 20, 1963, in Yaoundé (Cameroon), was the first EEC Agreement that contained provisions on establishment, services, payments, and capital movements (Title III, arts. 29–38). These notably included NT and MFN treatment concerning establishment (art. 30) and the commitment to not introduce restrictions to capital movements or make them more restrictive (art. 37).[6] The treaty was later followed by the second Yaoundé Convention, signed on July 29, 1969, and the First and Second Lomé Conventions, signed, respectively, on February 28, 1975, and October 31, 1979, which kept the same scheme as the First Yaoundé Convention.

A third EEC agreement was signed with Turkey in Ankara on September 12, 1963, and entered into force on December 1, 1964 (European Parliament, n.d.-b). This treaty did not include provisions on the establishment or movement of capital in its initial text, but it did in its additional financial protocol, signed in Brussels on November 23, 1970. The protocol is one of the earliest examples of mechanisms to enact secondary law, establishing that a council of association shall determine the timetable and rules for the progressive abolition of restrictions on freedom of establishment (art. 41). A similar mechanism had already been established in the 1969 Second Yaoundé Convention (art. 34).

A temporary change in investment policies took place after the Ankara Agreement and throughout the 1980s, which can be seen as an early manifestation of normative standardization. During that time, the EEC essentially concluded Cooperation Agreements merely including the encouragement of investment as one of several cooperative activities, with the Association of Southeast Asian Nations (1980), Yugoslavia (1980), China (1985), Pakistan (1985), and Central America (1985). The same pattern was followed in cooperation agreements concluded even in the early 1990s with Uruguay (1991) and Paraguay (1992).

Exceptions in this regard are the Third and Fourth Lomé Convention. The Third Lomé Convention, signed on December 8, 1984, is the first EEC Agreement, including an investment chapter in Title IV ("Investment, Capital Movements, Establishment and Services"). Yet, a closer examination of those provisions (arts. 240–247) reveals that the abovementioned EEC model focused on the right of establishment and movement of capital had not changed, as the investment provisions are largely about cooperation, promotion, and information, and not centered on investment protection, as the large majority of European BITs did at that time.

In contrast, the Fourth Lomé Convention does not contain provisions on the right of establishment. Instead, it includes an investment chapter (ch. 3, strangely as part of Title III "Development Finance Cooperation"). Besides a section on investment promotion (arts. 258 and 259), the chapter has sections on investment financing (arts. 263–266), investment support (art. 267–272), and, notably, investment protection (arts. 260–262). However, the latter section essentially affirms the importance of concluding investment promotion and protection agreements between the Africa, Caribbean, and Pacific Group of States and the EEC member states, providing some guidelines about their content, like the principle of non-discrimination. The only direct obligation concerning investment protection is to accord FET to private investors, surprisingly found in the investment promotion section (art. 258b). But again, this did not mean the complete abandonment of the EEC model described before, as this agreement also includes a dedicated section on capital movements (arts. 273 and 274).

It is important to note that if we examine other agreements concluded in this period (1957–1991), the definitional standardization of including provisions on the right of establishment and movement of capital in trade or investment agreements was largely not followed outside the EEC. Compared to 511 BITs with binding clauses on investment protection concluded during the same period, provisions on the right of establishment are found in only nine agreements: Iran–United Kingdom Treaty of Commerce, Establishment and Navigation (1959); Japan–United Kingdom Treaty of Commerce, Establishment and Navigation (1962); Germany-Spain Treaty of Establishment (1970), which also includes provisions on expropriation, NT, and MFN; Central African Economic and Monetary Community Convention on Liberalization (1973); the Caribbean Community and Common Market (CARICOM) Treaty (1973); France-Senegal Agreement on Establishment (1974); Economic Community of West African States Protocol on Movement of Persons and Establishment (1979); Economic Community of Central African States Treaty (1983); and African Economic Community Treaty (1991). Except for the latter, these agreements did not include provisions on capital movements. In contrast, clauses guaranteeing the transfer of funds, including capital but also profits, payments, and compensation, were commonplace in the BITs concluded at that time. Such a provision is found at least in 447 BITs (Alschner et al. 2021).

The causal pathway of the divide between BITs and EEC Agreements concerning investment persisted, mainly due to the EEC's lack of competency in this matter. This was not for the lack of trying from the side of the European Commission (EC). In 1972 and 1975, the Commission published two draft regulations, one of which foresaw the creation of a European investment guarantee agency, insuring European investors against non-commercial investment risks in third countries. Access to those investment guarantees would be conditional on the existence or conclusion of BITs between the EU and the concerned third countries, which was seen as an indirect push for a European BITs program. The Commission's draft regulation was met with hesitation and rejection based on the lack of competence of the EEC in these matters and was finally unsuccessful (Basedow 2016, 746–747).

Second Phase: The Maastricht Treaty

The Treaty on European Union (TEU), also known as the Maastricht Treaty, was signed on February 7, 1992 (in force since November 1, 1993), and formally created the EU. At the same time, the EEC Treaty was incorporated into the EU and was renamed the Treaty establishing the European Community (TEC).

Previously, in March 1991, the European Commission published a report on the functioning of the EU, discussing advisable modifications to the European treaties. The Commission proposed a far-ranging reform to the common commercial policy (CCP), including, among others, the regulation of trade in services, intellectual property rights, capital movements, establishment, investment protection, and liberalization, through trade agreements and autonomous measures. Advancing a broad interpretation, the Commission held that the CCP already encompassed the regulation of these issues and merely sought to "clarify" but not to broaden the scope of the EU's competences. The member states did not receive the Commission's investment recommendations well and rejected them. However, the Maastricht Treaty established a common external regime governing capital flows between the member states and third countries, which had a spillover effect. It unintentionally provided the EU with a shared competence to regulate investment market access, as cross-border capital movements constitute an essential component of foreign affiliates' establishment and subsequent operation (Basedow 2016, 749).

Following the EEC Treaty's approach, TEC provisions on the movement of capital differed from those on establishment.[7] The latter were mainly rules on NT and MFN treatment, guaranteeing that any treatment more favorable than that granted to nationals or third countries would also be extended to EC companies and subsidiaries. These obligations were subject to a negative list of exemptions. However, one of the new provisions (art. 73c, later art. 57 TEC, and now art. 64 Treaty on the Functioning of the European Union [TFEU]) made a very tangential insertion of the terms "direct investment" concerning possible exceptions to the general principle of free movement of capital (Fernández-Pons et al. 2017, 1334).

The Maastricht Treaty also replaced articles 113 and 228 of the EEC Treaty, which, as discussed, were the legal basis for establishing an association with the European Community. Yet, the treaty repeated that the CCP should be based on uniform principles, particularly regarding the conclusion of trade agreements, but it did not mention investment.

According to Basedow, the Commission remained determined to have the member states recognize, under the CCP, the EU's exclusive competence to regulate all new issues of the Uruguay Round, including international investment (Basedow 2016, 751). In Opinions 1/94 and 2/92, the Court of Justice of the European Union (CJEU) ascribed neither an exclusive explicit nor implicit investment competence to the EU as part of the CCP and held that the European Community retained competences regarding single issues of FDI regulation related to the internal market (Herrmann and Hoffmann 2021, 2229).

Opinion 1/94 was the result of the disagreement between the Commission and the member states over whether the CCP's scope enabled the European Community to conclude the World Trade Organization (WTO) Agreement and its annexes alone—a position supported by the Commission and firmly rejected by the member states—or if it had to be concluded as a mixed agreement (CJEU 1994). The Court sided with the member states and found that the WTO Agreement had to be concluded as a mixed one since the Union did not hold all necessary competences. Furthermore, it held that where it is apparent that the subject matter of an international agreement or convention falls partly within the competence of the Community and of the member states, the requirement of unity in the European Community's international representation calls for close cooperation between the member states and the Community institutions, both in the process of negotiation and conclusion and in the fulfilment of the commitments entered into.

Opinion 2/92 (CJEU 1995) resulted from another discrepancy concerning the European Community's participation in the Organisation for Economic Co-operation and Development (OECD) Third Revised Decision on National Treatment (OECD 1991), a legal instrument stipulating that OECD countries should grant NT to established investors from other OECD countries. The Commission claimed that the European Community had exclusive competence to adhere to such a decision, based again on a broad interpretation of the CCP. As expected, several member states refused the Commission's position. Recognizing that the competence of the Community in this regard did not cover all the matters to which that decision relates, the CJEU held that the member states and the European Community were jointly competent to adhere to it.

Not until the Treaty of Amsterdam (signed on October 2, 1997, and in force since May 1, 1999) was a provision included that EC international negotiations may extend to agreements on intellectual property and services—which tangentially could also affect investment (e.g., "market presence" or mode 3 of trade in services), through a modification of TEC art. 113. In 1995, in an internal report, the Commission had advised extending the scope of the CCP to include trade in services, intellectual property, and FDI, for the latter was not retained (Basedow 2016, 755).

Even though the Maastricht Treaty (or the Treaty of Amsterdam) did not imply a fundamental change from the European Community policy on trade agreements concerning investments, two distinctive patterns appeared in this period (1992–2009). One is keeping the definitional standardization of a "dual" model of agreements with provisions on establishment and capital movements, and another is the normative standardization of cooperation agreements with non-binding provisions on investment promotion and protection. Some agreements include both types of standardization.

The first example of EC agreements keeping the "dual" model is the 1992 European Economic Area Agreement, between the EU and three European Free Trade Association (EFTA) states (Iceland, Liechtenstein, and Norway), which included sections on the right of establishment (arts. 31–35) and movement of capital (arts. 40–45), and did not include provisions concerning investment, besides some exceptions allowing the EFTA states to continue applying domestic legislation regulating foreign ownership and/or ownership by non-residents (Annex XIII).

In the early 1990s, macro-political changes led to changes in the EU's approach. In the context of the disintegration of the Soviet bloc, the issue of foreign investment became particularly relevant. Detailed provisions concerning establishment and treatment after establishment (sometimes called "operation") appeared in the so-called "Europe Agreements": association agreements concluded between 1991 and 1995 with Central and Eastern European countries that formed the legal framework for their EU accession process in 2004–2007.[8] The same definitional standardization was used in the partnership and cooperation agreements with some of the former Soviet Union states, like the Russian Federation (1994), Ukraine (1994), Moldova (1994), Kazakhstan (1995), Kyrgzstan (1995), Belarus (1995), Georgia (1996), Armenia (1996), Azerbaijan (1996), and Uzbekistan (1996). These treaties also included normative standardization provisions on cooperation for investment promotion and protection (e.g., information on investment opportunities and improvement of investment climate), without binding investment protection standards, as European BITs did then. The same format was followed in the agreement with North Macedonia (2001).

A similar template was followed in the association agreement with Chile (2002) and the "Euro-Mediterranean" agreements concluded by the EU with its so-called Southern Neighborhood countries: Tunisia (1995), Israel (1995), Morocco (1996), Jordan (1997), Egypt (2001), Algeria (2002), and Lebanon (2002) (European Commission, n.d.-a).

A partial exception among the Euro-Mediterranean agreements is the one with Palestine (1997), which only includes provisions on payments and capital movements as well as cooperation on investment promotion, but not on the right of establishment. The same model was followed in the association agreement with Mexico (1997). Along the same lines, the agreement with South Africa (1999) includes provisions on capital movements and investment promotion, but concerning the right of establishment only reconfirms the obligations undertaken by the parties in the General Agreement on Trade in Services (GATS).

Another partial exception to this model is the Cotonou Agreement (2000), which replaced the Lomé Conventions. This agreement does not have sections on the "right of establishment" and "movement of capital" as the other treaties mentioned above. Instead, it includes provisions for the promotion of private investment, primarily considering cooperation activities (arts. 21, 22, 23, 24, 29, 34, 37, 74) but also concrete investment promotion commitments (see art. 75, e.g., support capacity-building for investment promotion agencies, disseminate investment information, and maintain a predictable and secure investment climate), investment finance and support (art. 76, including loans and advisory services), and investment guarantees (art. 77, including insurance and reinsurance schemes).[9] The agreement also includes provisions on investment protection (art. 78), essentially promoting the conclusion of BITs, which could also provide the basis for insurance and guarantee schemes, and agreements related to specific investment projects.

It is important to note that all the agreements mentioned also shared an important feature found in the association agreements concluded under the EEC Treaty: they all set up joint councils and committees endowed with extensive competences to produce secondary law. Certain agreements were notably expanded using this technique (e.g., with Mexico and Chile).

However, in parallel, during the same period, several agreements concluded by the EU did not follow the described "dual" definitional standardization. Such treaties, largely cooperation agreements,[10] only consider provisions to promote investments and improve the investment climate, without including the right of establishment or capital transfers. In one of these agreements—with Sri Lanka—the competence of member states to conclude BITs with substantive standards of protection is explicitly recognized, with both parties acknowledging existing agreements between Sri Lanka and some EC member states and supporting further BITs with others based on the principles of non-discrimination and reciprocity (art. 5).

The Treaty of Nice, signed on February 26, 2001 (in force since February 1, 2003), amended the TEU and the TEC. According to art. 310 of the consolidated text of the agreement, the Community may conclude with one or more states or international organizations agreements establishing an association involving reciprocal rights and obligations, common action, and special procedure. The new version of TEC art. 133 brought the regulation of trade in services and intellectual property under the scope of the CCP.

However, this change in the treaty text did not mean a departure from the two policy standards described before. Some agreements followed the "dual" model with detailed provisions on the right of establishment/capital movements and some basic clauses on cooperation for investment promotion and protection,[11] and others the "cooperation" model, only including provisions on investment promotion and improvement of the investment climate.[12]

As in the first phase, the relation between EC trade agreements and BITs concluded by the member states is virtually nonexistent. Just a handful of agreements acknowledge some connection between these two different levels of investment policy.

For example, the association agreement with Mexico includes, as part of investment promotion, the support for the conclusion of agreements to promote and protect investments (and also of the agreements to avoid dual taxation). The same provision is also found in the 2002 agreement with Chile[13] (which also has detailed provisions on exceptions to national treatment in Annex X) and the 2003 agreement with the Andean Community.

The Cotonou Agreement notably fosters the conclusion of investment promotion and protection agreements (Annex II, art. 15). This normative approach considers the principles of irretroactivity and non-discrimination between contracting states or against each other concerning third countries.

Likewise, it promotes the study clauses for a model protection agreement, including legal guarantees to ensure FET and protection of foreign investors, MFN clause, protection against expropriation and nationalization, transfer of capital and profits, and international arbitration in the event of disputes between investor and host state.

As in the first phase, if we examine other agreements concluded in this period (1992–2009), neither the dual nor cooperation models were largely followed in trade or investment agreements outside the EU. Provisions on the right of establishment are only found in nineteen treaties: CARICOM-Venezuela Trade and Investment Agreement (1992); Common Market for Eastern and Southern Africa (COMESA) Treaty (1993); West African Economic and Monetary Union Treaty (1994); Colombia, Mexico, and Venezuela FTA (1994); Canada-Chile FTA (1996); Mexico-Nicaragua FTA (1997); North Macedonia–Turkey FTA (1999); East African Community Treaty (1999); France-Senegal Agreement on Establishment (2000); revised Treaty of Chaguaramas establishing CARICOM (2001); European Free Trade (EFTA) Convention (2001); Central American Common Market (CACM) Agreement on Trade and Services (2002) and its Protocol (2007); Chile-US FTA (2003); Morocco-Turkey FTA (2004); Faroe Islands–Iceland FTA (2005); EFTA-Egypt FTA (2007); Canada-Peru FTA (2008); and the Canada-Colombia FTA (2008). However, several of these agreements only recognize the right of establishment for specific sectors (e.g., financial services or insurance providers) and include binding investment protection provisions (e.g., the COMESA Treaty) or chapters.[14]

In contrast, 2,433 BITs concluded in the same period had binding investment protection provisions. Of these, 1,114 involved the EU member states. Among them, 2,304 treaties included provisions guaranteeing the transfer of funds (1,084 by the EU member states), including not only capital but also profits, payments, and compensations (Alschner et al. 2021). More importantly, during this period, several "intra-EU BITs" were still in force, meaning agreements concluded between the original EU member states and countries that later became part of the Union but were not terminated at the moment of their accession.

The cause behind this persistent divide between BITs and EC Agreements regarding investment is again a spillover effect of the European Community's lack of competency in this matter. As CJEU's Opinions 1/94 and 1/92 attest, the European Commission unsuccessfully intended to change this pattern; the Commission's efforts would finally be rewarded in the next phase.

Third Phase: Treaty of Lisbon

The Treaty of Lisbon, signed on December 13, 2007 (in force since December 1, 2009), amended the TEU and the TEC, renaming the latter the TFEU. As a result, the European Community formally ceased to exist, and its institutions were directly absorbed by the EU. This made the Union the formal successor institution of the Community.

This treaty expanded the EU's influence on investment policies by transferring the exclusive competence for the regulation of FDI within the matters covered by the CCP fully into the EU's hands. Until then, the European Community did not have exclusive competence, but rather shared competence, in international investment matters. The reasons behind this change are not completely clear. As we have seen, the member states had shown great keenness to retain national control over foreign investment rather than see it move into EU competence (Chaisse 2012, 56). When preparing the European Constitution, no discussion was held on the extension of the CCP to investment. Only a passing comment was made in a 300-page impact assessment on the Treaty of Lisbon by the House of Lords (Shan and Zhang 2010, 1049–1050). It is also unclear why the term "FDI" was used instead of "international investment" (Basedow 2016, 761).

Regardless of this critical change, the TFEU kept distinguishing between "Capital and payment" (ch. 4, arts. 63–66) and the "Right of establishment" (ch. 2, arts. 49–55). The main focus of the latter is not market access liberalization but guaranteeing national treatment. Article 49 TFEU states that "[...] restrictions on the freedom of establishment of nationals of a Member State in the territory of another Member State shall be prohibited. [...] Freedom of establishment shall include the right to take up and pursue activities as self-employed persons and to set up and manage undertakings, in particular companies or firms [...], under the conditions laid down for its own nationals by the law of the country where such establishment is effected [...]."

Article 50 confers the EU extensive competence to produce uniform law through secondary law, stipulating: "In order to attain freedom of establishment as regards a particular activity, the European Parliament and the Council, acting in accordance with the ordinary legislative procedure and after consulting the Economic and Social Committee, shall act by means of directives [...]."

Chapter 4 on Capital and Payments follows an entirely different approach from the chapter on the right of establishment. Article 63 TFEU imposes a general obligation to liberalize market access (both to and from the EU member states and to and from third countries). The following articles introduce specific exceptions and confer on the EU some competences to enact secondary law, limited mainly to movements of capital from and to third countries.

Alongside the conclusion of trade agreements, as foreseen in TFEU art. 207 (ex art. 133 TEC), a legal basis to establish association agreements with the EU is found in TFEU art. 217 (ex art. 238 TEC), complemented by arts. 216, 218, and 219, mainly using modified provisions of the preceding treaties.

But this time, the change led to a new definitional standardization in the treatment of establishment and investment in EU trade agreements. The primary examples of this approach are the Comprehensive Economic and Trade Agreement with Canada (CETA) (2016) and the agreements with Singapore (2018) and Vietnam (2019). In July 2020, a Commission's communication mentioned broader policy objectives for future negotiations, like promoting the rule of law, human rights, sustainable development, and the OECD guidelines for multinationals (Calamita 2012, 62–63).

The new EU investment competency is the cause of this important change in the Union's investment standardization. However, the "old" EU standard did not wholly vanish and was still clearly perceptible in the first wave of association agreements negotiated after the Treaty of Lisbon. In fact, the first agreement concluded under the Treaty of Lisbon, with the Republic of Korea FTA (2010), kept the "classic" dual distinction between the right of establishment, and payments and capital movements.[15] The same happened in the EU-Iraq Partnership and Cooperation Agreement (2012), EU-Colombia-Peru FTA (2012), and EU–Central America Association Agreement (2012). In these two last agreements, investment protection, including ISDS, was explicitly excluded from the treaty. In the EU-Ukraine Association Agreement (2014), its central provision on establishment (art. 88, in ch. 6, section 2) envisages only national treatment and MFN treatment, and no article on "market access" is included. The same model was followed in the agreements with Georgia (2014), Moldova (2014), Kosovo (2015), Kazakhstan (2015),[16] and Armenia (2017). Finally, the Economic Partnership Agreement (EPA) with the Southern African Development Community (2016) includes a section on payments and capital movements but not on the right of establishment. According to art. 74, parties merely agree to cooperate on investment and may in the future consider negotiating an agreement on investment in economic sectors other than services.

The significant definitional change in the EU external investment policy took place during the failed negotiations of the Transatlantic Trade and Investment Partnership (TTIP) between the EU and the US, which started in 2013 and met with strong opposition from civil society, particularly in Europe. After the US halted the negotiations in 2018, the EC declared the negotiations obsolete and no longer relevant in 2019. The EU Proposal for the TTIP included an investment chapter for the first time (European Commission, n.d.-b).

The new approach has two distinctive features. First, unlike member state BITs that did not contain provisions liberalizing investment, a key feature of the new EU investment agreements is their emphasis on investment liberalization together with investment protection (Dimopoulos 2020, 2272). It clearly separates the international exchanges of services (or cross-border supply of services), defined as modes 1 and 2 of GATS, and that on investment/establishment, applicable to all sectors. Therefore, establishment (GATS mode 3) is no longer treated differently according to whether it relates to services sectors or other sectors. Second, a separate chapter on investment includes the typical provisions found in BITs, but with several clarifications about standards of treatment or protection that had been subject to ISDS cases, like FET and indirect expropriation. By the time the Treaty of Lisbon entered into force, the EU member states had concluded more than 1,100 BITs, but the majority did not include such clarifications.

In these two features, the EU agreements partially borrowed the model mainly developed by the US after the early North American Free Trade Agreement (NAFTA) ISDS arbitrations, found in the US Model BITs of 2008 and 2012, but most importantly in treaties like the Central America–Dominican Republic Free Trade Agreement and the Trans-Pacific Partnership. Indeed, in a 2011 Resolution, the European Parliament explicitly recalled the experience of Canada and the US under NAFTA, noting that these states "have adapted their model BITs in order to restrict the breadth of interpretation by the arbitration and ensure better protection of their public intervention domain" (European Parliament 2011, 2).

Likewise, CETA introduced a significant change to EU agreements' scope of obligations: the "positive list" method was replaced by that of the "negative list" in both the services and investment/establishment chapters. This is also a feature traditionally present in agreements concluded by the US. It means that foreign investors are treated like domestic investors, as the treaty's terms apply to all sectors except those expressly listed as exclusions, and not only if a sector is included in the schedule of commitments. This change is particularly relevant when applied to market access in the investment/establishment chapter. Due to the negative list method, the agreement must include extremely long annexes/schedules of reservations and exceptions and a list of carved-out sectors.

A third distinctive feature—this time a pure European creation—also appeared during the failed TTIP negotiations: the replacement of the most common ISDS mechanism—investor-state arbitration—with a new investment court system (ICS), including standing tribunals of first instance and an appellate tribunal. It was then added to the negotiations with Vietnam and included in its initially agreed text. The Commission advanced the idea of an ICS as a solution to several disadvantages of investor-state arbitration (conflict of interests and lack of consistency, among others). But some have criticized this policy as a rebranding of ISDS, which keeps the central tenets of a system that empowers corporations to sue states (Eberhardt 2016).

CETA originally only included several provisions to "improve" ISDS similar to those provided in the initial text of the EU-Singapore FTA (2014). However, an important change was made in the "scrubbed" version of the agreement on February 29, 2016. Now, the investment chapter includes the establishment of an investment tribunal and an appellate tribunal for resolving disputes between investors and states, abandoning the investor-state arbitration system. Until now, the only other EU agreements that contain ICS are the EU-Vietnam and EU-Singapore Investment Protection Agreements (IPAs). Earlier versions of both treaties considered that feature in the same text of the FTAs. The removal of their investment chapters was a consequence of CJEU Opinion 2/15 of May 16, 2017, concerning the competence of the EU to conclude the FTA with Singapore and the additional ratification by the member states' parliaments. According to the CJEU, all subject matters of that agreement fall within the scope of the CCP, with the crucial exceptions of non-direct forms of investments and ISDS. Although the Court granted much leeway to the EU in exercising exclusive treaty-making powers, it still required that the agreement be ratified at a national level, which is something that CETA's ratification process has proven to be challenging to achieve. The segregation of investment issues from trade agreements to improve the chances of their ratification[17] negatively impacts the EU's ability to use its unitary political weight to shape the standardization of investment rules and discontinue the EU's short-lived policy of including trade and investment jointly together in one comprehensive economic agreement (Hainbach 2018). The inclusion of the ICS is also being considered in the process of the modernization of the EU FTAs with Mexico and Chile (which also include the features of investment liberalization and investment protection), but are not signed yet.

However, the EU definitional standard concerning external investment has not been wholly consistent. Even an intermediate third model has appeared between the classic "dual" model and the most recent liberalization model. For example, in the EU-Japan EPA (2018), there is a chapter on capital movements, payments, and transfers, and a section exclusively devoted to investment liberalization. Still, there are no provisions on investment protection or dispute settlement, and both topics have been left for later negotiations, even though the EC declared that for the EU, "ISDS is dead" (European Commission—Trade 2018). A similar format has been followed in the post-Brexit EU-UK Trade and Cooperation Agreement (2020).

In contrast, the text of the future replacement of the Cotonou Agreement, the EU-Organisation of African, Caribbean and Pacific States Partnership Agreement (initialed on April 15, 2021) only includes clauses on investment facilitation and mobilization of sustainable and responsible investment. No provisions on establishment, capital movements, investment protection, liberalization, or dispute settlement are included, which is an important departure from earlier agreements with these countries. Furthermore, the Comprehensive Agreement on Investment with China (text "in principle" made public on January 22, 2021) has sections on investment liberalization, domestic regulatory framework, and sustainable development. Notably, dispute settlement provisions include neither investor-state arbitration nor ICS but a state-to-state mechanism (including both mediation and arbitration).

However, the EU has been consistent in the rejection of investor-state arbitration as a normative standard and has not concluded any agreement with this feature in recent years (the latest was the earliest version of CETA). At the same, the EU has been able to install the idea of the ICS as a feasible alternative, and the proposal of a multilateral investment court is now part of the discussions taking place since November 2017 in the UN Commission on International Trade Law Working Group III on Investor-State Dispute Settlement Reform (UNCITRAL 2022). This is nothing short of remarkable, considering that none of the EU treaties that include ICS is currently in force. (The provisional application of CETA does not include investment disputes [OJEU 2017], and the IPAs with Vietnam and Singapore have not been ratified.) Also, outside the abovementioned three concluded by the EU, no other investment agreements currently include ICS (besides the modernization of EU agreements with Mexico and Chile currently in progress).

The EU has also been relatively successful in "putting the house in order" concerning intra-EU BITs. After years of asking the member states to terminate them, the fervent opposition of some member states was met with the CJEU ruling in the *Achmea* case, where the Court decided that the arbitration clause contained in art. 8 of the 1991 Netherlands-Slovakia BIT has an adverse effect on the autonomy of EU law and was incompatible with it (CJEU 2018). In a subsequent decision, the CJEU declared that the individual rights deriving from EU law must be protected within the framework of the judicial system of the member states (CJEU 2021b). Furthermore, the Court also held that the Energy Charter Treaty (ECT)—an agreement establishing a multilateral framework for cross-border cooperation and protection in the energy industry and the basis of more than 150 ISDS cases—must be interpreted as not being applicable to disputes between an EU member state and an investor of another member state concerning an investment made by the latter in the first member state (CJEU 2021a).

In contrast, a couple of years before *Achmea*, in a "non-paper" of April 2016, Austria, Finland, France, Germany, and the Netherlands acknowledged that, in parallel to terminating intra-EU BITs, it was necessary to afford European investors with modern guarantees on substantive and procedural investment protection to maintain a level playing field vis-à-vis their foreign competitors (Council of the European Union, Trade Policy Committee, Services and Investment 2016).

Following the declarations of January 15–16, 2019, on the legal consequences of the judgment of the CJEU in *Achmea* and on investment protection in the EU, on October 24, 2019, EU member states agreed on a plurilateral treaty for the termination of intra-EU BITs. The agreement was signed by twenty-three member states on May 5, 2020, and entered into force on August 29, 2020 (OJEU 2020). Yet, some signatories (Lithuania, Luxembourg, and Portugal) have expressed their concern that such termination may have a negative impact on the protection of investor's rights and investment climante in the EU. Four member states have not signed the agreement (Austria, Finland, Sweden, and Ireland—although the latter has no intra-EU BITs).

The CJEU efforts to assert EU dominance over IIAs—when the dispute concerns EU member states—have been recently reaffirmed by a decision of an ISDS arbitral tribunal in a dispute against Spain under the ECT. On June 16, 2002, the tribunal in *Green Power v. Spain* declined jurisdiction over claims brought by two Danish claimants against Spain. It decided that the case could not proceed due to its intra-EU nature, upholding the primacy of EU Law, described as "lex superior" overriding the ECT with respect to the relevant states (Denmark, Spain, and Sweden—the latter being the seat of the arbitration) (SCC 2022).

Consolidating the triumph of this approach, on June 24, 2022, the Energy Charter Conference agreed, among other issues, to introduce an article to the ECT clarifying that investment dispute settlement shall not apply among contracting parties' members of the same Regional Economic Integration Organisation, explicitly mentioning the EU (Energy Charter Secretariat 2022).

Yet, the EU's competence to regulate foreign investment is still not absolute. While it is true that the EU is now exclusively competent to regulate FDI, and member states have largely lost the necessary competences to pursue their own international investment policies (Basedow 2016, 744), they still retain a key competence for non-FDI investment.

The notion of "investment" has been traditionally used, including the distinction between "portfolio" and direct investment. However, differentiating between these two types is not easy. Portfolio investment is defined as "cross-border transactions and positions involving equity or debt securities, other than those included in direct investment or reserve assets" (IMF 2009, 110), which, unsatisfactorily, makes the definition circular and dependent on what is defined as direct investment. Furthermore, the distinction is often described as depending on imprecise distinctions like short term/long term or the existence or absence of "a lasting interest" (Galeza and Chan 2015, 34–35).

Regulation 1219/2012 addresses the status of the member states' BITs under EU law and establishes the terms, conditions, and procedures under which they are authorized to amend or conclude such agreements. It stipulates that BITs concluded by the member states before their EU accession can still be maintained until the EU concludes an investment agreement with the respective counterparts. The Commission may authorize member states to open new negotiations to amend or sign a BIT with third countries if the EU has not yet concluded an agreement with them (European Parliament 2012).

This has left a door open for the member states willing to pursue independent investment treaty-making (and not as part of trade or association agreements). As a result, recent years have seen the development of Model BITs from the Czech Republic (2016), Slovakia (2016, 2019), Belgium-Luxembourg Economic Union (2019), Netherlands (2019), and Italy (2020, 2022). Since the entry into force of the Treaty of Lisbon, 98 BITs have been concluded by the EU member states.[18]

Conclusion

Although investment treaties were first created in Europe, for a long time, the agreements concluded by the EEC, the European Community, and the EU treated investment as an alien notion, which was largely part of the regulatory domain of member states. Several causal pathways explain the evolution of EU investment policy, with some borrowing and some creation. But the evolution of the definitional European investment standards in the past decades is mainly the reaction to the changes in competency between the member states and the Community/Union.

Under the aegis of the Treaty of Rome, the investment competence of the Community was limited, and EEC agreements with "dual" provisions on the right of establishment and movement of capital coexisted with hundreds of BITs concluded by the member states, with binding provisions on investment protection and ISDS. These treaties—and not the ones concluded by the EEC—created a de facto "gold standard" of investment treaties which was followed around the world, particularly in the 1990s, after the success of the Washington Consensus.

After some changes introduced by the Treaties of Maastricht, Amsterdam, and Nice, the European Community's investment competence expanded slightly. However, this did not imply a fundamental change in the external investment policy. In fact, besides continuing with the negotiation and conclusion of agreements following the "dual" approach, a second model arose, only including cooperation commitments on investment promotion.

During these periods, the European Commission's entrepreneurship was decisive in extending the EU's competences in international investment policy (Basedow 2016, 767). After finally succeeding with the inclusion of

FDI as part of the common commercial policy in the Treaty of Lisbon, the Commission could implement a new policy of EU agreements which included investment liberalization, updated standards of investment promotion, and a new dispute settlement mechanism (the ICS) born as a response to the intensive backlash against investor-state arbitration. However, after more than a decade of these new competences, there is still some lack of consistency in EU agreements, which do not always follow the same model.

Yet, in recent years, the EU has been successful in two key normative standards: presenting the ICS as a feasible alternative to investor-state arbitration and in the termination of intra-EU BITs that have been decided incompatible with EU law—a position that the Commission had held for several years.

However, there is still some room for inconsistency, because of the remaining competences of member states to conclude investment treaties (separated from trade or association agreements), which involve non-FDI (or portfolio) investment, a possibility that has been used several times in the last decade.

Notes

* I am grateful to Francesco Duina, Gabriel Siles-Brügge, and Crina Viju-Miljusevic for their useful comments on a preliminary version of this chapter. All errors and omissions are mine.

1. However, since the end of World War II, the US started a program of Friendship, Commerce, and Navigation agreements, which also included investment provisions quite similar to early BITs (Vandevelde 2017).

2. The only mentions of investment are the establishment of a "European Investment Bank" (Title IV), and the prohibition of agreements between enterprises consisting in the limitation or control of investment, which was deemed incompatible with the common market (EEC Treaty art. 85b).

3. Mixed agreements are international treaties where the EU and the member states act together because the competence is shared, concurrent, or there is an exclusive competence of the member states. As a result, these agreements must additionally be ratified through the domestic procedure of established by each member state (European Parliament 2016).

4. EEC art. 113:

> "1. [. . .] the common commercial policy shall be based on uniform principles, particularly in regard to tariff amendments, the conclusion of tariff or trade agreements, the alignment of measures of liberalisation, export policy and

protective commercial measures including measures to be taken in cases of dumping or subsidies.

2. The Commission shall submit proposals to the Council for the putting into effect of this common commercial policy.

3. Where agreements with third countries require to be negotiated, the Commission shall make recommendations to the Council, which will authorise the Commission to open the necessary negotiations.

The Commission shall conduct these negotiations in consultation with a special Committee appointed by the Council to assist the Commission in this task and within the framework of such directives as the Council may issue to it.

4. The Council shall, when exercising the powers conferred upon it by this Article, act by means of a qualified majority vote."

5. EEC art. 238:

"The Community may conclude with a third country, a union of States or an international organization, agreements creating an association embodying reciprocal rights and obligations, joint actions and special procedures.

Such agreements shall be concluded by the Council acting by means of a unanimous vote and after consulting the Assembly.

Where such agreements involve amendments to this Treaty, such amendments shall be subject to prior adoption in accordance with the procedure laid down in Article 236."

6. Unless mentioned otherwise, the agreements cited in this chapter are accessible at the Electronic Database of Investment Treaties (EDIT): https://edit.wti.org/.

7. However, the Chapter "Capital" was renamed "Capital and payments," and art. 67–73 were substituted for art. 73b–73g.

8. Agreements signed bilaterally with Hungary (1991), Poland (1991), Romania (1993), Czech Republic (1993), Slovakia (1993), Bulgaria (1993), Latvia (1995), Estonia (1995), Lithuania (1995), and Slovenia (1995).

9. We find a similar scheme in the Overseas Association Decision of 2001, between the EU and the Overseas Countries and Territories, which included provisions on investment promotion, investment support and financing. Council Decision of 27 November 2001 on the association of the overseas countries and territories with the European Community (European Council 2001). Interestingly, the most recent decision of 2021 reverts to the traditional format, including provisions on payments and capital movements and right to establishment, and does not include investment provisions (European Council 2021).

10. These are the agreements with Macao (1992), Mongolia (1992), Brazil (1992), India (1993), Sri Lanka (1994), Vietnam (1995), Nepal (1995), and the Southern Common Market, which includes Argentina, Brazil (again), Paraguay and Uruguay (1995), South Korea (1996), Cambodia (1997), Laos (1997), Yemen (1997), and Pakistan (2001).

11. See, for example, the Agreement with Tajikistan (2004); the Interim Agreement with Cameroon (2009), which only include provisions on capital movements and reiterates GATS commitments concerning establishment; and the Stabilisation and

Association Agreement between the EU and the Western Balkan countries (Albania [2006], Montenegro [2007], Serbia [2008], and Bosnia [2008]).

12. See, for example, the agreements with the Andean Community (2003), which includes Bolivia, Colombia, Ecuador, and Peru; the Stepping Stone Economic Partnership Agreement with Côte d'Ivoire (2008); and the Interim Agreement with the Southern African Development Community (2009), which includes Botswana, Lesotho, Mozambique, Namibia, and Eswatini; and the Interim Agreement with Eastern and South African States (2009), which includes Comoros, Madagascar, Mauritius, Seychelles, Zambia, and Zimbabwe.

13. Under art. 134, parties to the EU-Chile Association Agreement confirm their rights and obligations existing under any bilateral or multilateral agreements to which they are parties.

14. See, for example, the Colombia, Mexico, and Venezuela FTA, Canada-Chile FTA, Mexico-Nicaragua FTA, Chile-US FTA, the CACM Agreement and Protocol, Canada-Peru FTA, and the Canada-Colombia FTA.

15. A provision on improving the investment environment is included in the establishment Chapter Seven (art. 7.10).

16. Art. 56 of this agreement considers the possibility of future negotiations, including general principles of investment protection, after a review to identify joint barriers to investment.

17. The EU-Singapore FTA entered into force on November 21, 2019, and the EU-Vietnam FTA entered into force on August 1, 2020. However, both IPAs will enter into force after it has been ratified by all EU member states. As of February 2022, only twelve member states have ratified it. The IPA with Vietnam has already been ratified by that country.

18. See, for example, the Colombia-Spain BIT (2021), Hungary-Kyrgyzstan BIT (2020), Belarus-Hungary BIT (2019), Lithuania-Turkey BIT (2018), Iran-Luxembourg BIT (2017), Slovakia–United Arab Emirates BIT (2016), Denmark–North Macedonia BIT (2015), Colombia-France BIT (2014), Austria-Nigeria BIT (2013), Haiti-Spain BIT (2012), India-Slovenia BIT (2011), and Austria-Tajikistan BIT (2010).

References

Alschner, W., M. Elsig, and R. Polanco. 2021. "Introducing the Electronic Database of Investment Treaties (EDIT): The Genesis of a New Database and Its Use." *World Trade Review* 20 (1): pp. 73–94.

Basedow, R. 2016. "A Legal History of the EU's International Investment Policy." *Journal of World Investment & Trade* 17 (5): pp. 743–772.

Bast, J. 2009. "European Community and Union, Association Agreements." *Oxford Public International Law.* https://opil.ouplaw.com/view/10.1093/law:epil/9780199231690/law-9780199231690-e625?prd=OPIL.

Behn, D., M. Langford, L. Létourneau-Tremblay, and R. Hilleren Lie. 2021. "Evidence-Guided Reform: Surveying the Empirical Research on Arbitrator Bias and Diversity in Investor–State Arbitration." In *International Economic Dispute Settlement: Demise or*

Transformation?, edited by M. Elsig, R. Polanco, and P. van den Bossche, pp. 264–294. Cambridge: Cambridge University Press.

Calamita, N. J. 2012. "The Making of Europe's International Investment Policy: Uncertain First Steps." *Legal Issues of Economic Integration* 39 (3): pp. 301–330.

Chaisse, J. 2012. "Promises and Pitfalls of the European Union Policy on Foreign Investment—How Will the New EU Competence on FDI Affect the Emerging Global Regime?" *Journal of International Economic Law* 15 (1): pp. 51–84.

Council of the European Union. 2016. "Trade Policy Committee (Services and Investment). Intra-EU Investment Treaties." Non-paper from Austria, Finland, France, Germany and the Netherlands. Herbert Smith Freehills Public International Law Notes.

Court of Justice of the European Union (CJEU). 1994. Opinion of the Court of 15 November 1994. Competence of the Community to conclude international agreements concerning services and the protection of intellectual property—Article 228 (6) of the EC Treaty. *European Court Reports. 1994 I-05267.* https://eur-lex.europa.eu/legal-cont ent/EN/TXT/?uri=CELEX%3A61994CV0001.

Court of Justice of the European Union (CJEU). 1995. Opinion 2/92 pursuant to the second subparagraph of Article 228(1) of the EC Treaty, 24 March 1995. I-525. https://eur-lex.europa.eu/legal-content/EN/TXT/PDF/?uri=CELEX:61992CV0 002_SUM&from=FR.

Court of Justice of the European Union (CJEU). 2018. Judgment of the Court (Grand Chamber) of 6 March 2018, *Slovak Republic v. Achmea B.V.* (Case C-284/16), §21, 59.

Court of Justice of the European Union (CJEU). 2021a. Judgment of the Court (Grand Chamber) of 2 September 2021, *République de Moldavie v Komstroy LLC,* § 65.

Court of Justice of the European Union (CJEU). 2021b. Judgment of the Court (Grand Chamber) of 26 October 2021, *Republiken Polen v PL Holdings Sàrl,* §68.

Dimopoulos, A. 2020. "EU Investment Agreements: A New Model for the Future." In *Handbook of International Investment Law and Policy,* edited by J. Chaisse, L. Choukroune, and S. Jusoh, pp. 2263–2284. Singapore: Springer.

Duina, F. 2006. *The Social Construction of Free Trade.* Princeton, NJ: Princeton University Press.

Eberhardt, P. 2016. *The Zombie ISDS.* Brussels: Corporate Europe Observatory.

Energy Charter Secretariat. 2022. Decision of the Energy Charter Conference. CCDEC 2022, 10 GEN. June 24. Brussels. https://www.energycharter.org/fileadmin/Documen tsMedia/CCDECS/2022/CCDEC202210.pdf.

European Commission. n.d.-a. "Trade: Southern Neighbourhood." https://policy.trade. ec.europa.eu/eu-trade-relationships-country-and-region/countries-and-regions/ southern-neighbourhood_en.

European Commission. n.d.-b. "Transatlantic Trade and Investment Partnership. Chapter II—Investment." Commission Draft Text TTIP—investment. https://trade.ec.europa. eu/doclib/docs/2015/september/tradoc_153807.pdf.

European Commission—Trade. 2018. "A New EU Trade Agreement with Japan." https:// trade.ec.europa.eu/doclib/docs/2017/july/tradoc_155684.pdf.

European Council. 2001. Council Decision of 27 November 2001 on the association of the overseas countries and territories with the European Community (Overseas Association Decision) 2001/822/EC. https://eur-lex.europa.eu/legal-content/EN/ TXT/?uri=CELEX%3A02001D0822-20130701.

European Council. 2021. Council Decision (EU) 2021/1764 of 5 October 2021 on the association of the Overseas Countries and Territories with the European Union including relations between the European Union on the one hand, and Greenland and the Kingdom of Denmark on the other (Decision on the Overseas Association, including Greenland). https://eur-lex.europa.eu/legal-content/EN/TXT/?uri=uriserv:OJ.L_.2021.355.01.0006.01.ENG&toc=OJ:L:2021:355:TOC.

European Economic Agreement (EEC). Agreement Establishing an Association Between the European Economic Community and Greece. 1961. https://www.cvce.eu/en/obj/agreement_establishing_an_association_between_the_european_economic_community_and_greece_9_july_1961-en-ea36b530-f7ee-46f3-a26b-5dc4ea1a5508.html.

European Parliament. n.d.-a. Treaty of Rome (EEC Treaty). https://www.europarl.europa.eu/about-parliament/en/in-the-past/the-parliament-and-the-treaties/treaty-of-rome.

European Parliament. n.d.-b. EU-Turkey Association Agreement (the "Ankara Agreement"). https://www.europarl.europa.eu/delegations/en/d-tr/documents/eu-texts.

European Parliament. 2011. European Parliament Resolution of 6 April 2011 on the future of European international investment policy. Strasbourg. https://www.europarl.europa.eu/doceo/document/TA-7-2011-0141_EN.html.

European Parliament. 2012. Regulation (EU) No. 1219/2012 of the European Parliament and the Council of 12 December 2012 establishing transitional arrangements for bilateral investment agreements between Member States and third countries [2012] OJ L351/40. https://eur-lex.europa.eu/legal-content/EN/TXT/?uri=celex%3A32012R1219.

European Parliament. 2016. "A Guide to EU Procedures for the Conclusion of International Trade Agreements." Briefing. https://www.europarl.europa.eu/thinktank/da/document/EPRS_BRI(2016)593489.

Fernández-Pons, X., R. Polanco, and R. Torrent. 2017. "CETA on Investment: The Definitive Surrender of EU Law to GATS and NAFTA/BITs." *Common Market Law Review* 54 (5): pp. 1319–1358.

Galeza, T., and J. Chan. 2015. "What Is Direct Investment?: Investors Often Seek Profits from a Long-Term Stake in a Foreign Operation." *Finance & Development* 52: pp. 34–35.

Hainbach, P. 2018. "The CJEU's Opinion 2/15 and the Future of EU Investment Policy and Law-Making." *Legal Issues of Economic Integration* 45 (2): pp. 199–209.

Herrmann, C., and M. Hoffmann. 2021. "Investment in the European Union: Competences, Structures, Responsibility and Policy." In *Handbook of International Investment Law and Policy*, edited by J. Chaisse, L. Choukroune, and S. Jusoh, pp. 2213–2261. Singapore: Springer.

International Monetary Fund (IMF). 2009. *Balance of Payments and International Investment Position Manual*. 6th ed. Washington, DC: International Monetary Fund, 2009.

Lavranos, N. 2013. *The New EU Investment Treaties: Convergence towards the NAFTA Model as the New Plurilateral Model BIT Text?* Rochester, NY: Social Science Research Network.

Official Journal of the European Union (OJEU). 2017. Notice concerning the provisional application of the Comprehensive Economic and Trade Agreement (CETA) between Canada, of the one part, and the European Union and its Member States, of the other part. September 16. L 238/9. https://eur-lex.europa.eu/legal-content/EN/TXT/PDF/?uri=CELEX:22017X0916(02)&rid=1.

Official Journal of the European Union (OJEU). 2020. Agreement for the termination of Bilateral Investment Treaties between the Member States of the European Union. Vol. 63. May 29. https://eur-lex.europa.eu/legal-content/EN/TXT/?uri=OJ:L:2020:169:TOC.

Organisation for Economic Co-operation and Development (OECD). 1991. *Third Revised Decision of the OECD Legal Instruments Council concerning National Treatment*. December 12. https://legalinstruments.oecd.org/public/doc/232/232.en.pdf.

Shan, W., and S. Zhang. 2010. "The Treaty of Lisbon: Half Way toward a Common Investment Policy." *European Journal of International Law* 21 (4): pp. 1049–1073.

Stockholm Chamber of Commerce (SCC). 2022. *Green Power Partners K/S and SCE Solar don Benito APS v. Spain (SCC)*. Award. June 16. §469–470.

United Nations Commission on International Trade Law (UNCITRAL). 2022. Working Group III: Investor-State Dispute Settlement Reform. https://uncitral.un.org/en/working_groups/3/investor-state.

Vandevelde, K. 2017. *The First Bilateral Investment Treaties: U.S. Postwar Friendship, Commerce, and Navigation Treaties*. New York: Oxford University Press.

5

Sustainable Development Standards in EU Preferential Trade Agreements

Evgeny Postnikov

Introduction

The European Union (EU) has championed the linkage between trade and labor and environmental issues in its numerous preferential trade agreements (PTAs) signed with multiple partners in the developed and developing world over the past two decades. This linkage occurs through the so-called sustainable development (SD) provisions (or standards) which are incorporated into all EU PTAs. They constitute one of the most distinctive features of EU trade agreements and represent the wider EU approach toward global trade. Over the years, the specificity and volume of what they include have increased, as SD provisions become better articulated and more legalized. Yet the EU's PTA template has shown, until recently, remarkable stability when it comes to SD clauses. In particular, the EU's template has eschewed the use of coercive means of enforcement, relying instead on a range of institutional mechanisms aimed at fostering dialogue between the trading partners.

The EU's attempts to link trade with SD are by no means unique. Trade is thought to generate negative externalities for labor and the environment, leading to a "race to the bottom," or social dumping and erosion of environmental protection, particularly in the developing world. Countries have explored linking trade to both labor and environmental issues for many years, starting with the General Agreement on Tariffs and Trade (GATT) agenda in the 1980s (Charnovitz 1987). At the World Trade Organization's (WTO) inception in the 1990s, the EU and the US attempted to create a social clause that was vehemently rejected by developing countries. Thus, labor and environmental standards, collectively known as SD, appeared in bilateral PTAs with developing countries where the EU enjoys a bargaining leverage.

Evgeny Postnikov, *Sustainable Development Standards in EU Preferential Trade Agreements* In: *Standardizing the World*. Edited by: Francesco Duina and Crina Viju-Miljusevic, Oxford University Press. © Oxford University Press 2023.
DOI: 10.1093/oso/9780197681886.003.0006

Significant literature has been devoted to explaining the inclusion, design, and effects of these standards (Harrison et al. 2019; Oehri 2014; Orbie et al. 2016; Postnikov 2020; Postnikov and Bastiaens 2014). Many of these studies compare and contrast the EU's approach with that advanced by the US—which has also pursued this linkage, albeit through somewhat different policy instruments. However, scholars have not yet examined the sociological dimension of this linkage (i.e., a particular idea of trade articulated through it by the EU). As argued by scholars, trade policy not only is an outcome of aggregation of material interests of domestic groups (a conventional international political economy approach), but also is socially constructed (Duina 2006). Thus, it is embedded in larger foreign policy and social relations and cannot be viewed in isolation from values, norms, and identities of political actors that imbue trade relations with particular meaning. Global actors take on certain foreign policy roles consistent with those, and trade policy is no exception (Aggestam 2006). This chapter takes this holistic view of trade: it will explain the nature of the linkage and what its growing standardization means in terms of the worldview projected by the EU in the global trade system.

This chapter examines the evolution of SD standards and attempts to explain the drivers for both their stability and change over the years, paying particular attention to international and institutional factors. It looks at both definitional and normative components of SD standards. The chapter argues that the EU's desire to project a certain idea of trade globally and institutional path-dependence in EU trade policymaking explains the evolution and particular design of social standards in EU PTAs. It also discusses how the EU's approach has attracted followers across the globe, leading to the diffusion of its template and shaping of the global trade agenda. The chapter first describes the growing standardization of social provisions in EU PTAs. It then explores the drivers behind it and looks at the diffusion of the EU template globally through the networks of PTAs.

Standardizing Sustainable Development in EU PTAs

The emphasis on SD provisions in EU PTAs has grown over time, resulting in an increase in definitional and normative standardizing content. Labor and environmental standards in EU PTAs were first mentioned in the so-called first generation of EU PTAs concluded in the late 1990s and the following decade. In those earlier agreements, labor and environment were treated separately in distinct chapters (in addition to more disjointed general references throughout PTA texts). The parties to an agreement were only required to adhere to their own domestic standards and not violate them for trade purposes. This means that the definition of labor and environmental standards was left to the interpretation of the parties, while the normative focus was largely on trade objectives. These standards were also part of the political cooperation agreement, outside the trade agreement proper.[1] This meant that they were excluded from standard dispute-resolution mechanisms and the implementation was referred to the civil society dialogues (CSD), not to be confused with the EU's internal advocacy mechanism within the Directorate-General for Trade (DG Trade) comprising government and civil society representatives from the EU and the partner state. Thus, legalization was lacking, and both labor and environmental standards were best described as a form of soft conditionality. Substantively, the focus had been mainly on the commercial clauses of the agreements, which makes social standards rather declaratory and de-linked from trade.

The EU's approach toward labor and environmental standards changed in 2006 with the publication of the Global Europe Strategy and the resulting shift toward more aggressive trade bilateralism. In the new PTA template that emerges, both provisions are included in the same chapter focused on trade and SD.[2] Thus, the position on labor and environment has changed significantly, with both now seen as contributing to making trade more sustainable, in accordance with the EU's own growing focus on sustainability in its internal policies. The relevant standards become, therefore, more stringent and holistic.

SD standards in the new template also become more specific and wider reaching in explicit fashion. The requirement is to adhere not only to the domestic but also to international standards (i.e., not EU-specific standards as such). The latter contain a mix of both normative and definitional components which are often hard to distinguish as they are framed quite broadly.

Specifically, when it comes to labor, these are defined as the International Labour Organization's (ILO) core labor standards (CLS) outlined in the 1998 Declaration on Fundamental Rights and Principles at Work. EU trading partners are expected to "respect and implement" four key principles in their laws and practices: (1) freedom of association and the right to collective bargaining (e.g., forming trade unions); (2) getting rid of all forms

of forced or compulsory labor; (3) abolishing child labor; and (4) ending discrimination in the workplace. These principles entail combinations of definitional and normative principles, especially given the relevant supporting
materials.

Additionally, the definition of labor standards is further elaborated in
more recent EU PTAs with Global North partners. For example, in the EU's
Comprehensive Trade and Economic Agreement with Canada (North-North
PTA), labor standards, in particular, became a contentious issue during
negotiations, given Canada's own strong emphasis on labor rights and conditionality in its own PTAs. Thus, the trade and sustainable development (TSD)
chapter (ch. 22) is supplemented with a separate chapter dealing with labor
issues (ch. 23). While the main architecture of these clauses remains largely
unchanged, mostly centered on international norms, the chapters reaffirm
the parties' right to maintain their respective levels of regulation and domestic legislation, ensuring regulatory autonomy. This is further guaranteed
through the so-called Joint Interpretive Instrument, an accompanying document aimed at the domestic critics weary of the potential dampening of social regulations. It remains unlikely that this distinct approach, owing to the
strength of both sides' negotiating teams and a common denominator built
around their respective preferences, will be replicated in future agreements
between the EU and developing countries.

On the environmental front, in turn, the EU expects its partners to adhere
to the multilateral environmental agreements (MEAs) they joined, including
(1) the Convention on International Trade in Endangered Species of Wild
Fauna and Flora; (2) the 1992 Framework Convention on Climate Change;
(3) the 2015 Paris Agreement; (4) the Kyoto Protocol on climate change;
(5) the Montreal Protocol on ozone layer protection; (6) the Convention on
Biological Diversity; (7) the Stockholm Convention on Persistent Organic
Pollutants; (8) the Rotterdam Convention on international trade in hazardous chemicals and pesticides; and (9) the Basel Convention on hazardous
waste movement and disposal (DG Trade 2019). The wider focus on climate
change is evident. And, of course, these agreements contain a wide array of
definitional and normative principles transposed into PTAs.

While the fundamentals of this template have remained unchanged since
2006, SD standards have also undergone a greater definitional elaboration,
driven by the specific circumstances of a trade partner (i.e., their domestic
environmental conditions). As such, there have been steady increases and
precision in the number of MEAs incorporated into EU TSD chapters, with a
greater emphasis on fisheries, forestry, and biodiversity. Morin and Rochette

(2017) discuss the convergence between the European and US environmental standards on substantive matters. For example, while the EU–South Korea agreement refers to only three MEAs, the EU-Indonesia agreement already mentions eight (Nessel and Orbie 2022).

While implementation is beyond the scope of this volume, we can note here that the EU still envisions consultations through CSD but also develops new institutional mechanisms. This includes the Committee on Trade and Sustainable Development and Domestic Advisory Group in each party to an agreement, composed of relevant stakeholders from government and civil society. They are expected to hold regular meetings to oversee the implementation of the agreement's SD standards.

Moreover, and of course crucially for our discussion of standardization, the SD standards in new generation agreements are fully legally binding and are part of the full-fledged dispute settlement mechanism on par with commercial issues. This makes the relevant standards mandatory. This mechanism starts with government consultations if a dispute arises. If consultations fail, the Committee on Trade and Sustainable Development is convened and can further decide to create a panel of experts to investigate a matter further and issue a recommendation that is open to feedback from stakeholders. The panel outlines measures to implement its report in line with the feedback. Thus, the panel can only issue recommendations, and parties cannot be sanctioned for failure to implement its rulings. This means that the EU continued with its non-coercive approach toward enforcing SD standards that started with the old generation PTAs, despite the growing legalization of these provisions. Scholars have written extensively on how this soft approach, based on dialogue and cooperation, is replicated throughout all subsequent PTAs, becoming the EU's signature way of linking trade with SD. Its effectiveness is widely debated in the literature (Bastiaens and Postnikov 2017; Harrison et al. 2019; Postnikov and Bastiaens 2014).

In addition, there has been further elaboration of the mandatory aspect of TSD chapters in EU PTAs, as the level of obligation (i.e., legalization) has varied across some agreements. For instance, while some PTAs require parties to "*commit to/reaffirm the commitment* [emphasis added]" to ILO CLS, others mention that they "*shall promote and implement* [emphasis added]" these standards. This variation could be driven by specific partner characteristics, such as the number of ratified ILO conventions and/or weakness of domestic standards (Nessel and Orbie 2022).

Overall, there has been not only growing standardization of SD in EU PTAs, resulting in stronger definitional and normative articulation, but also a remarkable stability of the EU's template. In terms of definition, at the broadest level, the EU's approach has been to group labor and the environment jointly under the banner of SD, making it its signature approach, unlike its major competitor in the policy space, the US. This reflects a deeply entrenched view of managed globalization, where social dumping resulting from trade needs to be tackled holistically, unlike the more conventional race-to-the-bottom approach that views different negative externalities of trade in isolation from one another.

At the same time, it is also the case that the EU has pursued a largely neoliberal, trade-first approach in which social goals are subjugated to the economic interest and trade is also viewed as a way to address social and developmental issues. The EU's overarching preference has been to rely on international norms, not exporting its own rules (Young 2015). This indicates the adherence to the spirit of multilateralism and cooperation as opposed to the coercive unilateral approach, even in situations of power disparity favoring the EU, in many bilateral negotiations. At the same time, the focus on civil society inclusion in monitoring trade agreement implementation reflects the EU's own values and echoes its approach toward the enlargement.

Importantly, in June 2022, the EU opted for the new approach to trade to promote green and just growth which, remarkably, includes hard enforcement of SD chapters through the use of trade sanctions, mimicking the US approach (European Commission 2022). There will be also greater focus on partner-specific implementation through the use of road maps and support for civil society. This further underscores the mandatory nature of the standards in play: violation of principles will be followed by punitive action, which suggests a greater institutionalization of sustainability as a norm governing trade. Explaining this shift in the long-term EU approach is beyond the scope of this chapter but can be related to both the changing views of the European Commission (normative change from within, related to its embrace of the European Green Deal) and changes in the political environment and the continuing politicization of trade (De Bièvre and Poletti 2020).

The Drivers of Standardization

What accounts for the growing standardization of SD in EU PTAs over time, and what factors can explain the particular design of these provisions? It is argued here that, in order to understand the drivers of SD standards, one needs to look at both international and EU-level institutional factors. At the systemic level, the EU competes with other major players for its own unique vision of the global trade order and the norms and rules underpinning it. This vision is advanced by the European Commission acting as the defender of the EU's interests and shaping the EU's international identity, playing a distinct foreign policy role. At the same time, institutional constraints preclude certain societal actors from uploading their preferences to the EU level to influence SD standards in PTAs. This means that the Commission has a unique institutional advantage to promote its own definitional and normative preferences in the design of PTAs.

Institutional path-dependence in EU trade policymaking enables this further. In essence, the EU's approach is built on diplomacy and eschews coercion as a means of ensuring compliance in order to assert its foreign policy role and international identity vis-à-vis the US with its more punitive, coercive approach. Different actors within the EU try to influence the trade agreement design and advance their own policy preferences with regard to SD, and it is important to understand their positions and the extent to which they shape PTA standards. These actors include societal entities (i.e., labor and environmental constituencies), organized business, as well as political entities (i.e., the Commission, the Council, and the European Parliament, which all have a say over trade policy). The opposition of the Union of Industrial and Employers' Confederations of Europe (UNICE) toward labor standards has been long-standing (UNICE 2006). Both labor and environmental activists have long demanded stronger SD clauses in EU PTAs. For example, the European Trade Union Confederation (ETUC) wanted the inclusion of EU rules, such as the Decent Work agenda, as well as requiring the ratification of specific ILO conventions, in addition to the CLS. In terms of enforcement, both environmental non-governmental organizations (NGOs) and the ETUC have long advocated the full use of dispute settlement and sanctions to strengthen SD standards and have perceived the EU's approach as lacking the binding framework (see, for example, Blot and Kettunen 2021). Similarly, the European Parliament has been persistent in its calls to strengthen SD chapters, along with greater legal enforcement. For example, on the eve of signing the EU–South Korea Free Trade Agreement, the Parliament's Committee on International Trade advocated for the establishment of a comprehensive social development chapter and complained about the lack of enforcement of labor standards in the agreement, simultaneously referring to the example of US PTAs and their sanctioning mechanisms as a model for this chapter (European Parliament 2010).

The preferences of the European Commission, and DG Trade in particular, can be derived from its institutional role as the enforcer of EU rules internally and in projecting a certain image of Europe externally. The Commission's preferences toward the new generation of FTAs stem from the Global Europe approach advanced in 2006. EU Trade Commissioner Peter Mandelson (2006) has nicely summarized this approach in the following way:

> The EU has always rejected a sanctions-based approach to labour standards—and that will continue. But equally, we can do more to encourage countries to enforce basic labour rights, such as the ILO core conventions, along with environmental standards—not simply in principle, but in practice. Cooperation and social dialogue are certainly important. Transparency, through an independent mechanism, will also help us highlight areas where governments should take action against violations of basic rights.

As such, the calls of civic groups in the EU for expanding the definitional and normative component of SD standards have remained unheeded while the Commission's views have largely dictated policy outcomes. It is puzzling as to why those voices are not translated into the design of labor and environmental clauses in EU PTAs despite the relative openness of the EU toward including civil society in its trade policymaking. To understand this remarkable stability of the EU's template, one needs to examine the institutional makeup of the EU's trade policy and its evolution.

The EU's trade policy has a supranational setup: the Commission acts as the agenda-setter, negotiating trade deals on the EU's behalf, and member states delegate their authority to DG Trade (Meunier 2005). The EU trade policymaking process has traditionally favored business interests and has given little representation to other civil society actors, such as various NGOs. The weakness has been well described in the literature (e.g., Dür and De Bièvre 2007). In 1998, to address the deficiency of interest groups' input in the trade policymaking process, the Commission created a novel multi-stakeholder institutional mechanism, known as the CSD,[3] which allowed civil society groups to formally participate in the making of EU trade policy. It includes various civil society actors, such as public and private actors' associations, NGOs, and businesses, that regularly meet with Commission officials and receive updates about the course of trade negotiations and that can bring their concerns directly to the attention of DG Trade officials. Interest groups are encouraged to use this mechanism to provide their input in the negotiation process. However, the CSD plays only a consultative role, and societal actors are not able to directly influence the course of negotiations and are not given access to the negotiation texts, which makes it largely ineffective in terms of civil society lobbying (Jarman 2011). Furthermore, through the CSD, the Commission can give preferential access to various groups, which only enhances further its role of the agenda-setter in EU trade policy. Thus, unsurprisingly, Dür and De Bièvre (2007) found that despite their inclusion in the policymaking process, NGOs have largely failed to influence EU trade policy outcomes.

As described above, EU PTAs' now also include the CSD mechanism, which could potentially augment the effectiveness of societal demands by creating transnational links between various civil society groups in the EU and its trading partners. Civil society actors on both sides establish links during the negotiation stage of FTAs and work together even more during the implementation stage when formal meetings begin to be held. The existence of such a mechanism and its growing institutionalization since 2000 should have given civil society actors enough time to organize and learn how to use it most successfully, especially since the pace at which EU FTAs are signed has been accelerating and social issues have been ever more prominent on the new trade agenda. As civil society actors learn from their previous interactions with their counterparts in partner states, one could expect that the effectiveness of EU interest groups should increase in the new generation of PTAs. Furthermore, the Dialogue mechanism has been augmented quite significantly in the new generation of EU FTAs, potentially providing even more opportunities for civil society groups concerned with the PTAs agenda and the implementation of social standards. Yet, recent studies of this mechanism show that it is far from being effective, owing to the weakness of civil society actors in EU trading partners (Harrison et al. 2019).[4] Additionally, this rise of institutional platforms for agreement implementation forces them to focus their resources on the implementation stage rather than the agenda-setting and negotiation process during which agreement SD clauses are designed. Civic groups have already invested substantial efforts in the CSD, cultivating a direct relationship with Commission officials from DG Trade. Adding another venue can make their efforts more diffuse, potentially exacerbating the collective action problem and undermining their lobbying effectiveness, as argued by the scholars of EU lobbying (Coen 2009; Klüver 2013).

Overall, the Commission has been able to successfully co-opt civil society while pursuing its own institutional preferences toward the design of SD standards. By doing so, it has managed to legitimize a certain idea of trade that links it with SD, responding to civil society concerns. However, it has done this using a particular definition of SD as part of PTA template that achieves this issue linkage in a manner reflecting its own values, prioritizing international norms and dialogue.

Civil society has long been critical of EU trade policy and has tried to influence the agenda. The Commission's response has been the proliferation of consultative mechanisms both within the EU and through PTAs for civil society actors wanting to influence the SD agenda and its implementation. This has created the illusion of inclusivity and influence (Drieghe et al. 2022). Yet, such proliferation of lobbying venues is problematic for civic actors with limited resources, diluting their efforts to influence the trade agenda. Overall, the EU's trade policymaking has exhibited a path-dependent dynamic locking in the Commission's role as the agenda-setter that uses various legitimation techniques to solidify its role. It is able to strategically select civil society inputs when those suit its own institutional agenda.

With the Lisbon Treaty, the EU trade policy is characterized by a greater involvement of the European Parliament that now has the power to ratify all EU FTAs, using the consent procedure, akin to the US Congress.[5] The Parliament now acts as an additional veto player in EU trade policymaking, according to many observers, and has been able to exercise its influence over trade politics in some instances (e.g., defeating the Anti-Counterfeiting Trade Agreement). The ratification by the Parliament should have provided interest groups with more influence, which, in turn, should have led to more politicization of the PTAs' agenda and stricter labor standards. Indeed, the definitional scope of social standards in, for example, EU agreements with South Korea, Peru, and Columbia has broadened. There are provisions for more civil society participation, such as domestic advisory groups, with the goal to oversee agreement implementation that could provide new institutional space for governments and civil society actors to speak with each other where previously such opportunities might have been absent. However, in terms of both normative and definitional components, SD standards still largely reflect the Commission's views.

Overall, making the European Parliament a co-ratifier should have increased the opportunities for civic actors to influence the Commission. However, this perspective obscures its internal politics, and in order to assess the potential effectiveness of the Parliament as an institutional channel for societal actors, one must look into the patterns of societal interest representation within it. Unlike national legislators who are linked very tightly with their key constituents through a direct electoral relationship, legislators come to the European Parliament from a variety of ideologically similar national parties, forming the so-called party groupings. These groupings aggregate a much wider range of societal interests across the member states, which means that members of the European Parliament in Brussels are further removed from their constituents, diminishing the potential impact of the latter's preferences over policy outputs.

Additionally, the veto players' theory (Tsebelis 2002) can further shed light on the new institutional dynamic of EU trade policymaking and help us understand why civil society actors did not have better success, despite a greater involvement of the European Parliament in the making of EU trade deals. The EU policymaking system has been notorious for its stability and tendency toward incrementalism, and the number of party veto players is larger in the European Parliament than in the US Congress. According to the veto players' theory, this should make policy change even less likely. Party groupings have to adopt the lowest common denominator decisions, reflecting various societal interests, including those of organized businesses, which do not view strict labor standards very favorably. In this institutional environment, any PTA becomes a package deal, opening up a possibility for negotiation among the diverse set of interests and various side payments to placate those. Furthermore, the uncertainty among European Parliament legislators allows the executives in the Commission to act strategically in shaping the agreement agenda, especially when the agenda-setting rules are already conducive to it, as anticipated by the veto players' theory.[6] Thus, it is not surprising that the new generation of EU FTAs still largely reflects the preferences of the Commission, and to a lesser extent of organized businesses, rather than those of civic groups. This dominance of executive preferences and business interests has been noted by previous studies (Dür and Mateo 2012).

In sum, the addition of the European Parliament's consent to the EU trade policymaking process had a potential to open new lobbying venues for societal interests. However, surprisingly, it did not. The nature of interest representation in the EU trade policymaking process is not conducive to big policy changes and allows the executive with the power of agenda-setter to shape policy outcomes. Overall, in accordance with the veto players' theory expectations, the policymaking system of the EU tends to prioritize stability and incremental adjustment over large-scale policy change, and labor standards in EU FTAs are a further case in point. Thus, the EU trade policymaking system exhibits a strong path-dependent dynamic, despite important institutional changes that have been introduced. The persistent absence of sanctions until recently, despite the continued calls to introduce them expressed by societal actors, highlights the Commission's role of a policy entrepreneur who sets the agenda for the EU external trade policy. It is likely that the recent shift in the EU's approach toward SD standards is also primarily driven by executive preferences that evolve in line with larger institutional developments within the EU, such as embedding green policies more systematically across all policy domains.

As the Commission remains institutionally insulated from societal interests due to its supranational authority, the EU's SD agenda in trade therefore is captured by executive preferences. The multiplicity of positions among the member states also means that the Commission is prone to pursue the lowest common denominator approach that would satisfy all the governments and not create disagreements among them over the shape of SD standards. It is acting as a powerful institutional broker despite the changing role of various actors in the trade policy process.

The persistence of the EU's approach across multiple PTAs over time indicates the stability of the template and a particular normative worldview enshrined in a foreign policy role that the EU tries to play within the global rules-based order, making its trading partners submit to the same idea of trade/sustainable development linkage. Thus, it is largely irrelevant whether PTA standards are sufficiently strong to advance the sustainability agenda the EU subscribes to. The template is as much about how exactly the EU wants to be seen by its interlocutors (i.e., both trading partners and systemic rivals who try to shape the trading system in their own image—notably the US and Canadian templates have also remained quite stable since the ne-gotiation of the North American Free Trade Agreement (NAFTA) in the 1990s). The strength of enforcement demands has grown with greater insti-tutionalization of SD over time, eventually culminating in a more expansive and coercive approach, suggesting that the worldview projected outward is strongly influenced by the institutional and normative evolution within the EU. Importantly, the US is seen as a different role model by the Commission when defining its own foreign policy role aimed at constructing the EU's international identity in the global trade system via PTAs and their SD standards. Interviews with DG Trade officials suggest that they specifically want to draw a distinction between the EU and US approaches, emphasizing that the former is built on cooperation and persuasion (Postnikov 2020).

The EU's template also reflects its own values by prioritizing institution-building over enforcing contracts. This is highly visible in the open-ended nature of SD implementation through CSD, the creation of domestic advisory groups, and setting up TSD committees that try to foster transnational links. Growing legalization of standards, on the other hand, is also reflective of the EU's strong norm for the respect of the rule of law. Being an exercise in cooperation and multilateralism itself, the EU is promoting its own foundational norms through its SD clauses. Soft conditionality works through the attraction of the EU's internal market and gradual socialization through internalizing its norms in a cumulative way, triggering domestic reforms (Postnikov and Bastiaens 2014). This has been the hallmark EU approach toward its enlargement, and it is projected further outward. Thus, in addition to being a policy tool for making international trade greener and more equitable, the design of SD chapters in EU PTAs should be seen as a foreign policy role and identity-building exercise. The recent change toward greater enforceability outlined in June 2022 might indicate the evolution of normative views of the Commission and its institutionally derived preferences informed by the European Green Deal but could be also a strategic response to the politicization of trade in the EU and the desire to win public approval for further trade deals.

In summary, the institutional path-dependencies in EU trade policymaking endow the Commission with the privileged position of the agenda-setter on trade/sustainable development linkage, relegating civil society and the European Parliament to secondary roles. This allows officials in DG Trade to play the role of policy entrepreneurs and to assert their institutional preferences, which explains the particular design of the EU's labor and environmental standards and the evolution, definitional and normative, of the EU's template.

The Diffusion of the EU Template

The effectiveness of EU SD standards in terms of their potential to trigger policy change in trading partners and improve social conditions has been hotly debated by the scholars. Statistical analyses have shown the net positive result through gradual socialization and policy learning (Bastiaens and Postnikov 2017; Postnikov and Bastiaens 2014) while qualitative case studies have been less supportive, identifying multiple implementation pathologies (Harrison et al. 2019). Leaving aside the question of effectiveness, one important consequence of the EU's SD standards stands out: the EU's template has been diffusing throughout the large universe of PTAs, suggesting the influence of the EU's worldview through socialization and policy learning among trading partners owing to the EU's agreement design.

The literature on PTA design finds that copy-pasting of templates occurs through PTAs networks, triggered by the inclusion of certain non-trade issues by the Global North (Allee and Elsig 2019; Milewicz et al. 2018). Low institutional costs and bargaining efficiency are some of the mechanisms identified behind this diffusion. Others find that socialization of trade policy officials is the predominant mode of the diffusion of non-trade issues from North-South to South-South PTAs (Gamso and Postnikov 2021). Given the notorious opposition of the developing countries to linking trade with both labor and environmental issues, it is likely that deeper internalization of norms promoted by the EU is responsible for reshaping their preferences toward trade agreement design.[7]

Traditionally, developing countries have not been in favor of linking trade with SD, viewing it as protectionism in disguise by the Global North. Collectively, they have resisted the inclusion of social clauses in the WTO in the 1990s, strongly favored by both the EU and the US. However, in bilateral negotiations with the EU they often play a role of policy-taker attracted by the market access a PTA provides and agreeing to a host of trade-plus rules they previously opposed at the multilateral level. This logic has been well examined with regard to the inclusion of SD standards (Postnikov 2020). Yet, surprisingly, over time developing countries have begun incorporating similar provisions to their own trade agreements, the so-called South-South PTAs. For example, Chile has been one of the first and most ardent proponents of the trade-labor linkage, replicating it through its multiple PTAs with developing nations since the negotiation of EU and US agreements, pointing at their compound effect. More recently, Peru and South Korea have adopted EU-style labor provisions in their bilateral PTA. This has generally occurred after having the experience of negotiating trade deals with the EU and other states in the North who demand such provisions. In the absence of strong societal pressure to include social issues in PTAs in developing countries, it is plausible that the socialization of trade officials negotiating trade agreements into the norms of trade advocated by the EU and its like-minded partners is responsible for the emergence of trade/sustainable development linkage in South-South PTAs. Thus, the EU, together with the US, has been able to mainstream the linkage between trade and SD across multiple PTAs, including in the Global South (Postnikov 2022).

The attractiveness of the EU template vis-à-vis the US template might depend on the range of factors that lead to a particular style of PTA adopted—the NAFTA-style or the EU-style (Milewicz et al. 2018). At the same time, multiple South-South agreements now include SD provisions, in the same way the EU does, albeit in a weaker fashion (e.g., the PTA between the Eurasian Economic Union and Vietnam). This suggests that the soft rather than punitive approach is more palatable to the countries interested in pursuing the trade/sustainable development linkage. This diffusion indicates that the EU model resonates across the PTA universe, and the values underpinning it are attractive and internalized. This can be seen as another example of the EU's normative power manifesting itself globally (Manners 2002).

In essence, the EU has played a role of a global norm entrepreneur on linking trade with SD. It remains to be seen whether the EU's efforts might lead to the larger norm cascade through the universe of PTAs. The true indication of the internalization of EU norms would be the willingness to negotiate a social clause at the multilateral level, multilateralizing SD standards under the aegis of the WTO, as tried by the EU in the 1990s. At the same time, the growing acceptance of the linkage at the bilateral level can be seen as a real success of EU leadership in terms of its ability to shape the trade agenda across the globe, including in the Global South.

Conclusion

This chapter has examined the growing standardization of SD provisions in EU PTAs. Both labor and environmental standards in EU PTAs have become better defined, relying on a set of well-articulated international rules. The extent to which the relevant principles are made mandatory has grown. Attention has also increasingly gone to creating new institutional mechanisms to make the provisions work.

Yet the EU has stubbornly resisted using punitive tools to enforce these provisions until a recent shift in June 2022. The chapter has attributed these trends to institutional path-dependence in the EU's trade policymaking and attempts by the European Commission, institutionally insulated from societal actors, to advance a particular worldview to solidify the EU's international identity. This worldview has taken hold in the larger PTA universe as trading partners, previously opposed to the trade/sustainable development linkage, began including similar clauses in their subsequent PTAs. SD standards have become emblematic of the EU's larger successful attempts to standardize world trade through its PTAs. The new focus on enforceability will further test the attractiveness of EU model.

Notes

1. For example, the 1999 EU PTA with South Africa, known officially as the Trade and Development Cooperation Agreement, refers to labor and standards in non-trade chapters dealing with social and environmental cooperation (under Title VI devoted to cooperation on other matters). The other old-generation agreements with Egypt, Israel, Jordan, Lebanon, Tunisia, and Morocco, signed in the first decade of the twenty-first century and collectively known as the Euro-Mediterranean Association Agreements, include similar provisions with respect to social cooperation. The EU-Mexico Global Agreement, signed in 2000, has no special reference to labor issues. The EU-Chile Association Agreement, signed in 2002, follows a similar path with regard to labor and environmental standards.
2. The 2009 EU-Korea PTA has been the first one signed under the new strategy and has been seen as a model for the agreements that followed. Chapter 13 is fully devoted to trade and SD.
3. The CSD created by the Commission to manage the trade policymaking process in the EU should not be confused with the implementation mechanism in PTAs analyzed in the proceeding sections, also called the CSD.
4. Orbie et al. (2016) point out that the discussions between officials and NGOs participating in civil society meetings became more constructive, focusing more on making concrete recommendations and less on debating the pros and cons of free trade.
5. Previously, EU PTAs had to be ratified only by the member states in the Council, acting through the Art. 133 Committee.
6. In trade policy, the Commission drafts the negotiating mandate that then has to be approved by the Art. 133 Committee, which makes it effectively the agenda-setter, including on FTAs social provisions.
7. It must be noted that it is notoriously difficult to separate the effect of EU PTAs from other developed nations who have signed agreements with the same partners. Various quantitative and qualitative techniques have been used in empirical studies but, ultimately, the effect is likely to be interactive and cumulative.

References

Aggestam, L. 2006. *Role Theory and European Foreign Policy: A Framework for Analysis.* London: Routledge.

Allee, T., and M. Elsig. 2019. "Are the Contents of International Treaties Copied and Pasted? Evidence from Preferential Trade Agreements." *International Studies Quarterly* 63 (3): pp. 603–613.

Blot, E., and M. Kettunen. 2021. *Environmental Credentials of EU Trade Policy: A Comparative Analysis of EU Trade Agreements.* London and Brussels: Institute for European Environmental Policy.

Charnovitz, S. 1987. "The Influence of International Labor Standards on the World Trading Regime: A Historical Overview." *International Labour Review* 126 (5): pp. 565–584.

Bastiaens, I., and E. Postnikov. 2017. "Greening Up: The Effects of Environmental Standards in EU and US Trade Agreements." *Environmental Politics* 26 (5): pp. 847–869.

Coen, D. 2009. "Business Lobbying in the European Union." In *Lobbying the European Union: Institutions, Actors, and Issues*, edited by D. Coen and J. Richardson, pp. 145–168. Oxford: Oxford University Press.

De Bièvre, D., and A. Poletti. 2020. "Towards Explaining Varying Degrees of Politicization of EU Trade Agreement Negotiations." *Politics and Governance* 8 (1): pp. 243–253.

Directorate-General for Trade (DG Trade). 2019. "Sustainable Development." https://policy.trade.ec.europa.eu/development-and-sustainability/sustainable-development_en.

Drieghe, L., J. Orbie, D. Potjomkina, and J. Shahin. 2022. "Participation of Civil Society in EU Trade Policy Making: How Inclusive is Inclusion?" *New Political Economy* 27 (4): pp. 581–596.

Duina, F. 2006. *The Social Construction of Free Trade.* Princeton, NJ: Princeton University Press.

Dür, A., and D. De Bièvre. 2007. "Inclusion Without Influence? NGOs in European Trade Policy." *Journal of Public Policy* 27 (1): pp. 79–101.

Dür, A., and G. Mateo. 2012. "Who Lobbies the European Union? National Interest Groups in a Multilevel Polity." *Journal of European Public Policy* 19 (7): pp. 969–987.

European Commission. 2022. Commission Unveils New Approach to Trade Agreements to Promote Green and Just Growth. Press Release. June 22. https://ec.europa.eu/commission/presscorner/detail/en/ip_22_3921.

European Parliament. 2010. "Human Rights, Social and Environmental Standards in International Trade Agreements." November 25. 2009/2219 (INI). https://www.europarl.europa.eu/doceo/document/TA-7-2010-0434_EN.html.

Gamso, J., and E. Postnikov. 2021. "Leveling-up: Explaining the Depth of South-South Trade Agreements." *Review of International Political Economy* 29 (5): pp. 1601–1624. doi: 10.1080/09692290.2021.1939762.

Harrison, J., M. Barbu, L. Campling, B. Richardson, and A. Smith. 2019. "Governing Labour Standards Through Free Trade Agreements: Limits of the European Union's Trade and Sustainable Development Chapters." *Journal of Common Market Studies* 57 (2): pp. 260–277.

Jarman, H. 2011. "Collaboration and Consultation: Functional Representation in EU Stakeholder Dialogue." *Journal of European Public Policy* 33 (4): pp. 385–399.

Klüver, H. 2013. *Lobbying in the European Union: Interest Groups, Lobbying Coalitions and Policy Change.* Oxford: Oxford University Press.

Mandelson, P. 2006. "Trade Policy and Decent Work." Speech at the EU Decent Work Conference on Globalisation. December 5. Brussels. http://europa.eu/rapid/press-rel ease_SPEECH-06-779_en.htm?locale=en.

Manners, I. 2002. "Normative Power Europe: A Contradiction in Terms?" *Journal of Common Market Studies* 40 (2): pp. 235–258.

Meunier, S. 2005. *Trading Voices: The European Union in International Commercial Negotiations*. Princeton, NJ: Princeton University Press.

Milewicz, K., J. Holloway, C. Peacock, and D. Snidal. 2018. "Beyond Trade: The Expanding Scope of the Nontrade Agenda in Trade Agreements." *Journal of Conflict Resolution* 62 (4): pp. 743–773.

Morin, J.-F., and M. Rochette. 2017. "Transatlantic Convergence of Preferential Trade Agreements Environmental Clauses." *Business and Politics* 19 (4): pp. 621–658.

Nessel, C., and J. Orbie. 2022. "Sustainable Development in EU–Asia Trade Relations." In *A Geo-Economic Turn in Trade Policy? EU Trade Agreements in the Asia-Pacific*, edited by J. Adriaensen and E. Postnikov, pp. 197–221. London: Palgrave Macmillan.

Oehri, M. 2014. "Comparing US and EU Labour Governance 'Near and Far'—Hierarchy vs Network?" *Journal of European Pubic Policy* 17 (3): pp. 368–382.

Orbie, J., D. Martens, M. Oehri, and L. Van den Putte. 2016. "Promoting Sustainable Development or Legitimising Free Trade? Civil Society Mechanisms in EU Trade Agreements." *Third World Thematics: A TWQ Journal* 1 (4): pp. 526–546.

Postnikov, E. 2020. *Social Standards in EU and US Trade Agreements*. New York: Routledge.

Postnikov, E. 2022. "Labour Standards in EU and US Preferential Trade Agreements: Mainstreaming the Trade-Labour Linkage." In *Handbook on Globalisation and Labour Standards*, edited by K. Elliott, pp. 244–257. Cheltenham, UK: Edward Elgar.

Postnikov, E., and I. Bastiaens. 2014. "Does Dialogue Work? The Effectiveness of Labor Standards in EU Preferential Trade Agreements." *Journal of European Public Policy* 21 (6): pp. 923–940.

Tsebelis, G. 2002. *Veto Players: How Political Institutions Work*. Princeton, NJ: Princeton University Press.

UNICE. 2006. "UNICE Strategy on an EU Approach to Free Trade Agreements." December 7. http://trade.ec.europa.eu/doclib/docs/2007/january/tradoc_133068.pdf.

Young, A.R. 2015. "Liberalizing Trade, Not Exporting Rules: The Limits to Regulatory Co-ordination in the EU's 'New Generation' Preferential Trade Agreements." *Journal of European Public Policy* 22 (9): pp. 1253–1275.

PART II
MAJOR TRADING PARTNERS

6

Regulatory Convergence in Transatlantic Trade Agreements

Lessons Learned

Ferdi De Ville

Introduction

Claims about how the European Union (EU), as a power in and through trade (Meunier and Nicolaïdis 2006), uses free trade agreements (FTAs) to export its standards to the rest of the world are often based on examples of agreements with smaller countries in its near proximity. Indeed, the EU has successfully exported its enormous acquis to neighboring countries that pursue either accession to the EU or maximum integration into the EU's single market. In these integration-driven agreements, as well as in development-driven agreements between the EU and its former colonies in Africa, the Caribbean, and Pacific (ACP), there is a clear asymmetric dependency relationship. These countries strongly depend on the EU as an export destination and source of imports and investment, and this makes them willing rule-takers vis-à-vis the EU. Regulatory convergence—the reduction of differences in rules that may impede trade—in these instances implies the one-directional acceptance of EU rules by these partner countries. Since the 2006 Global Europe Strategy, the EU has also been pursuing trade agreements with larger, more advanced, and distant partners. This strategy stated that "new competitiveness-driven FTAs would need to be comprehensive and ambitious in coverage [. . .] FTAs should also tackle non-tariff barriers (NTBs) through regulatory convergence wherever possible" (European Commission 2006, 9), although analysis of some of these

Ferdi De Ville, *Regulatory Convergence in Transatlantic Trade Agreements* In: *Standardizing the World.* Edited by: Francesco Duina and Crina Viju-Miljusevic, Oxford University Press. © Oxford University Press 2023. DOI: 10.1093/oso/9780197681886.003.0007 "new generation" FTAs, as with Singapore, Central America, and South Korea, has shown that export of EU regulations through these agreements has been limited (Young 2015).

In this chapter, I discuss regulatory convergence—a specific instance of standardization, defined in this volume as "the production of agreed-upon definitional and normative principles"[1]—in transatlantic trade negotiations between the EU and the United States (US) and Canada. The failed negotiations on a Transatlantic Trade and Investment Partnership (TTIP) between the EU and the US provide a fascinating case study for this volume. Obviously, the EU could not expect to simply export its standards unidirectionally to the US through TTIP. The EU and the US both aspire to be global rule-makers and to use trade to promote their own regulatory approaches and worldviews in the rest of the world. The EU and the US are often seen as having distinct regulatory approaches and even cultures, with EU regulation rooted in the precautionary principle, while US rules are based on scientific risk assessment, although the significance of these differences is debated (see Morag-Levine 2014; Vogel 2012; Wiener et al. 2010). Notwithstanding these predictable challenges, regulatory convergence was the central objective of the TTIP negotiations. As I will show, rather than trying to export its own standards, as in agreements with smaller countries, the EU was willing to pursue the mutual recognition of rules with the US.

Consistent with this volume's constructivist approach (Duina and Viju in this volume; see also Duina 2006), the EU adapted its justifying discourse to the different approach to regulatory convergence it was willing to pursue in TTIP. Negotiators stressed the similarities between EU and US worldviews, values, and regulatory approaches and downplayed the differences. They hoped that this would reduce concerns about mutual recognition leading to lower levels of protection in the EU. And they argued that regulatory cooperation in TTIP would allow the EU and the US to—together—set "global standards." Rather than exporting its standards *across the Atlantic*, advocates stated that TTIP would allow the EU to remain a *global* rule-maker jointly with the US. Instead of trying to remake the US through TTIP "in the EU's image," EU policymakers claimed that they would build a transatlantic market in the image of the EU's own single market. However, these arguments failed to convince TTIP skeptics. Negotiations, facing strong civil society contestation and inherent difficulties in agreeing about the equivalence of different rules, failed to make significant progress until they were aborted after the election of Donald J. Trump as US president.

TTIP thus presents an interesting negative case, whereby the way in which the EU approached standardization can be seen as a crucial factor in the failure of the negotiations. Under certain conditions, (the ambition of) regulatory convergence can be an obstacle to, rather than an outcome of, a trade agreement. In contrast, the Comprehensive Economic and Trade Agreement (CETA) between the EU and Canada was successfully concluded, although in 2016 the deal became embroiled in the contestation of TTIP and was passed with great difficulty in Europe (and still awaits ratification by some member states). As I will show, regulatory convergence in CETA was less ambitious (in terms of the scope and depth of the regulatory cooperation that was being pursued) than in TTIP and therefore also less controversial. Provisions in the agreement about regulatory cooperation are mainly forward-looking and prepare the ground for future regulatory convergence, rather than eliminating existing differences. Hence, the content of the negotiations and approach to regulatory convergence that was followed helps explain why TTIP is a negative and CETA a positive case of standardization through trade negotiations. Finally, I discuss the latest initiative launched by the EU and the US to pursue regulatory convergence: the Trade and Technology Council (TTC). I analyze how and to what extent the parties have learned lessons from the failure of TTIP, and the success of CETA, in structuring and framing the TTC.

The remainder of this chapter proceeds as follows. In the next section, I discuss why regulatory convergence has become an important dimension of trade agreements, how it can be achieved, and how the EU has pursued it in the past. The third section discusses regulatory cooperation in TTIP, how it was approached and justified, and why it failed. The fourth section turns to the successful conclusion of CETA and discusses the approach to regulatory convergence in the agreement, and how this helps explain the negotiations' success. The fifth section then reviews the TTC launched by the EU and the US in 2021, compares it to regulatory cooperation in TTIP and CETA, and discusses its prospects. The final section concludes and reflects on the issue of standardization between powers that equally aspire to be rule-makers.

Regulatory Convergence and (EU) Trade Agreements

Differences in domestic regulations for goods and services have become an increasingly important topic in international trade. In the second half of the twentieth century, simultaneously, the volume of international trade grew spectacularly, the levels of import tariffs were reduced, and, as a consequence of the increase in both welfare and negative externalities from growth in industrialized societies, the quantity and stringency of domestic regulations increased. Therefore, regulatory differences became viewed more and more as "non-tariff barriers" to trade (cf. Lang 2011). When international firms must adapt their products to comply with different national regulations and/or must have their products tested multiple times to prove conformity with prescriptions, this is seen to increase costs (equal to the effect of a tariff) or even to prohibit international trade. Eliminating regulatory divergence through regulatory cooperation is, therefore, seen to bring significant trade and economic benefits. International regulatory cooperation is also promoted to pursue global public goods and prevent or mitigate global public bads and to achieve efficiency gains in the public sector. However, regulatory cooperation may undesirably restrain the sovereignty or policy space of governments or may prohibit governments from responding to public preferences that are substantially different from the public preferences present in trading partners.

Eliminating or reducing regulatory differences can be pursued through different forms of regulatory cooperation between states. The Organisation for Economic Co-operation and Development (OECD) has identified eleven different categories of regulatory cooperation mechanisms[2] that are not mutually exclusive and may overlap (OECD 2014). I distinguish here, for the sake of clarity and parsimony, between three different objects of cooperation—*processes* (how rules are made and implemented), *regulations* (the rules themselves), and *conformity assessment* (how compliance with rules is tested)—and two different modes of eliminating regulatory differences—*harmonization* and *mutual recognition*. In the case of harmonization, parties agree to apply the same process, rule, or conformity assessment, while under mutual recognition, parties agree to accept as equivalent each other's process, rule, or conformity assessment.[3] Harmonization is the clearest and most far-reaching form of regulatory convergence. It eliminates regulatory divergence with little room for interpretation. But it is therefore also the most intrusive into the regulatory autonomy of states. Moreover, harmonization may be difficult to achieve because of its political economy consequences. Harmonization may come with asymmetric adjustment costs if it is achieved through one party adopting the existing regulation or conformity assessment procedure of the other party. Mutual recognition does not have this asymmetric adjustment characteristic and leaves national autonomy de jure intact. But, in turn, it requires a sufficient level of trust in the equivalence of regulations and/or test procedures of the other party. Moreover, mutual recognition may lead to concerns about de facto race-to-the-bottom dynamics if rules or conformity assessment procedures are accepted while not being completely equivalent. Cooperation on the domestic processes of adopting and implementing rules often implies that parties commit to applying certain practices that limit the probability that (new) regulations are more trade-restrictive than necessary. This is often called "good regulatory practices" and includes commitments on early notification of regulatory initiatives and considering the trade impact when contemplating the introduction of new regulations.

The ambition and mode of regulatory cooperation in EU trade agreements is dependent on the status of the FTA partner. In general terms, a differentiation can be made between EU trade agreements with an integration or development focus and EU trade agreements with a commercial focus (cf. Golberg 2019). EU trade agreements with an integration focus refer to agreements between the EU and (former) neighboring countries that prepare these countries for full accession to the EU (such as the Europe Agreements with Central and Eastern European countries from the 1990s or the stabilization and association agreements with western Balkan countries from the following decade) or for integration into the single market without accession to the EU (the deep and comprehensive free trade agreements with the EU's current eastern and southern neighbors, like Ukraine or Georgia). In these cases, the EU partner countries agree to fully align their regulations to the EU acquis. In development-driven FTAs, such as the Economic Partnership Agreements between the EU and former colonies in the ACP region, partner countries agree to implement EU regulations and get EU technical and financial assistance and better market access in return. Hence, the mode of regulatory cooperation in these cases is harmonization of partner countries' regulations with the EU's existing regulations. The burden of adjustment is fully with these partner countries. But because the prize is so rewarding and the EU often represents a very large share of their total exports, imports, and inward investment, governments and firms in these countries are happy—or have no alternative than—to incur these adjustment costs. In other words, standardization works when the relationship between the EU and partner countries is so asymmetrical that the division between the EU as a rule-maker and these other countries as rule-takers is uncontested (see Sicurelli,

Chapter 8 in this volume, for contested EU trade negotiations with developing and emerging economies where these conditions for one-directional standardization are absent). The EU encounters little to no disadvantages from harmonization toward its rules: It does not have to concede any sovereignty, does not have to make any adjustment costs, and does not risk race-to-the-bottom effects.

Naturally, regulatory convergence with an equal partner and (aspiring) rule-maker such as the US could not be pursued in the same way. In the next section, I discuss how regulatory convergence was approached in TTIP, how this was justified, and why it failed.

The Failure of Standardization through TTIP

TTIP has often been characterized as the most ambitious attempt ever at regulatory convergence through an FTA. But before analyzing how standardization was pursued, it is important to note that TTIP was not the first attempt at transatlantic regulatory cooperation. Then, I explain why regulatory convergence was so important in TTIP and how it was pursued. Next, I discuss how negotiators tried to neutralize opposition to standardization in TTIP through two framing strategies: emphasizing the commonality of worldviews and values on both sides of the Atlantic, and promising that the agreement would lead to "global standards."

The Eternal Quest for Transatlantic Regulatory Convergence

The proposal for a transatlantic free trade area has been raised multiple times since the start of the European integration process itself (cf. Sapir 2011). In the late 1960s, there was some talk about a North Atlantic Free Trade Area (NAFTA, not to be confused with the 1994 North *American* Free Trade Agreement between the US, Canada, and Mexico) between the US, Canada, the European Free Trade Area, and the European Economic Communities (the EU's predecessor). After the end of the Cold War, the idea reappeared as supporters of Atlanticism wanted to reinforce the EU-US relationship now that the common enemy of communism had disappeared. As the proposal of what was then called a Transatlantic Free Trade Area (TAFTA) met with considerable opposition, in 1995 a more modest New Transatlantic Agenda

(NTA) was adopted. This "bold yet limited experiment in international governance [. . . aiming for . . .] deep integration in the absence of deep institutionalization" (Pollack 2005, 901) established a structure of regular dialogue between EU and US institutions and civil society (including transatlantic business, labor, and consumer dialogues).

The economic pillar of the NTA was focused on removing NTBs through regulatory cooperation and dialogue. This led to the adoption of a series of regulatory cooperation agreements, including six mutual recognition agreements (MRAs) (see Pollack 2005). In 1998, a new comprehensive agreement was added, the Transatlantic Economic Partnership, leading to additional agreements on regulatory cooperation, dialogue, and convergence. However, the implementation of these agreements, and the MRAs, in particular, was difficult because regulators were wary about conceding responsibility to their colleagues on the other side of the Atlantic by recognizing as equivalent their regulations or conformity assessment. As Pollack (2005, 912) put it, "domestic regulators can be resistant to co-operation that they perceive to be a distraction from their core regulatory mandates." Another reason why regulatory cooperation proved difficult is that it is a much more political exercise than is sometimes assumed by scholars and politicians. Pollack (2005, 912) has again summarized it succinctly:

> transatlantic regulatory cooperation is not a purely technical exercise but poses important questions about the distributive consequences of different regulatory standards and the role of power in determining outcomes of regulatory conflicts [. . .] in many instances, however, the setting of international standards more closely resembles a "battle of the sexes" game, in which the various parties agree on the desirability of establishing a common standard, but disagree on the content, which can have important distributional consequences, creating winners and losers among producers in different jurisdictions.

The latest iteration before the launch of the TTIP negotiations was a new "framework for advancing transatlantic economic integration" between the EU and the US that would establish a high-level Transatlantic Economic Council (TEC) to pursue closer economic integration. As this new idea was promoted by Chancellor Angela Merkel during Germany's 2007 EU presidency, it is also known as the "Merkel Initiative." But the TEC would also produce few tangible results. Instead of giving up on transatlantic regulatory cooperation after this series of frustrating attempts, the EU and the US would double down and launch negotiations on a transatlantic trade and investment partnership in 2013.

Regulatory Cooperation in TTIP

As with the older proposals from the 1990s, the idea of TTIP was floated to cement the transatlantic relationship at a time when there were concerns in the EU that the US was losing interest in Europe, in this case because it was making a "pivot to Asia." The proponents of stronger transatlantic economic integration seemed to have concluded from the failures of pursuing regulatory convergence through separate regulatory cooperation agreements that a better strategy was to pursue a comprehensive free trade agreement. A comprehensive trade agreement supported at the highest political level, in which both sides invest significant political capital, and allowing for package deals and diffuse reciprocity across issue areas, would put more pressure on regulators to constructively engage in cooperation. From the onset, leaders at both sides of the Atlantic made clear that far-reaching regulatory convergence would be the key objective of the talks. When US president Barack Obama, United Kingdom prime minister David Cameron, European Commission president José Manuel Barroso, and European Council president Herman Van Rompuy announced the launch of the TTIP negotiations at Lough Erne in Northern Ireland in the margins of a June 2013 G8 meeting, each stressed that regulatory cooperation was the sine qua non to reach significant benefits from a deal (The White House 2013, all following quotes from this source). "Our regulators need to build bridges faster and more systematically," Barroso said. "What is at stake with the transatlantic free trade area is to enshrine Europe and America's role as the world's standard-setters," Van Rompuy added. According to Cameron, TTIP would be "a once-in-a-generation prize and we are determined to seize it." Obama realized that this would require "resisting the temptation to downsize our ambitious or avoid tough issues just for the sake of getting a deal."

Trade negotiations between the US and the EU were always going to be difficult. Trade and investment flows between both sides of the Atlantic were already relatively free thanks to earlier rounds of multilateral and unilateral liberalization, so there was little low-hanging fruit to pick. Tariffs represented only a minor nuisance to transatlantic trade, and remaining pockets of tariff protection were concentrated on sensitive products such as food and agriculture that would be politically delicate to reduce. In the two decades preceding the launch of TTIP, EU-US trade relations had regularly soured over widely publicized conflicts on issues such as bananas, genetically modified organisms, the use of hormones in beef, chlorinated chicken, geographical indications, public procurement, steel tariffs, aircraft subsidies, and data privacy. Proponents of an EU-US trade agreement seemed to reason that overcoming resistance to eliminating remaining and sensitive barriers to trade required presenting the rewards of making such concessions as too good to miss. Impact assessments (CEPR 2013; ECORYS 2009) done before the launch of the negotiations had shown that less ambitious tariff-only, services-only, or procurement-only agreements would bring very limited economic benefits (a higher EU GDP of 0.1, 0.01, and 0.02 percent, respectively). An ambitious comprehensive trade agreement, eliminating 100 percent of tariffs, 25 percent of goods and services NTBs, and 50 percent of barriers to public procurement access, would lead to a more significant addition to the EU's GDP of 0.48 percent. Of this, more than half (0.26 percent) would have to come from eliminating NTBs to trade in goods or, in other words, from regulatory convergence, with automotive and chemicals as the main sectors in which regulatory convergence would contribute to growth. Promoting transatlantic trade negotiations as economically meaningful, therefore, required setting the ambitions for regulatory convergence high.

Regulatory convergence therefore became the crux of the TTIP negotiations, necessary to achieve significant economic gains. How would regulatory convergence be achieved through TTIP? Negotiations were organized along three pillars and twenty-four working groups (the agreement's structure would be based on this organization). One of these pillars was called "regulatory cooperation." It covered a horizontal chapter on regulatory cooperation, chapters on technical barriers to trade (TBT), sanitary and phytosanitary (SPS) measures (building on the WTO's TBT and SPS Agreements), and nine sectoral annexes.[4] The horizontal chapter would commit both parties to good regulatory practices, including to inform and consult each other (and incorporating private actors in this) about new regulatory initiatives and to cooperate on new rules or revisions of existing rules as much as possible. To encourage transparency, consultation, and cooperation, a regulatory cooperation body would be set up. The sectoral annexes aimed at the elimination of existing regulatory divergences. It became clear at an early stage that, for the political economy reasons discussed above, harmonization would not be on the table. The high ambitions that leaders set for TTIP meant that regulatory cooperation would have to go beyond mutual recognition of conformity assessment and would include mutual recognition of rules themselves. In the early phase of the talks, negotiators hinted that mutual recognition of rules would be the approach that they would be pursuing. Karel De Gucht, the EU's commissioner for trade at that time, stated ahead of the second round of negotiations that he would "be pressing for an ambitious outcome [. . .] and what I mean by this is we should ultimately strive for *mutual recognition of our regulations across a broad range of sectors* [emphasis added]" (De Gucht 2013b). De Gucht presented European integration as the model for how NTBs could be eliminated: "I know we can achieve this because in many ways Europe has 'been there, seen that and done that' in its early preparations during the 1980s for a Single Market. Of course, neither side has the ambition to go that far but our aim should still be to progressively build a more integrated transatlantic marketplace" (De Gucht 2013b). Hence, the European Commission's aim was to make a transatlantic market "in the EU's image." The trade commissioner assumed that the analogy between regulatory cooperation in TTIP and the completion of the EU's own single market would "reassure critics who claim TTIP will water down Europe's current set of rules and regulations" (De Gucht 2013b) because the EU's single market had resulted in higher rather than lower levels of consumer, health, or environmental protection.

But skeptics were not reassured—to the contrary. The prospect of significant regulatory convergence, necessary to credibly predict significant economic gains from TTIP, and the way it was being pursued would backfire. Rather than creating enthusiasm for the talks, the prospect of regulatory cooperation provoked anger among a wide spectrum of civil society organizations (CSOs) concerned about the consequences for EU levels of consumer, health, environmental, or labor protection (De Ville and Siles-Brügge 2016; Duina 2019). They feared that lowering regulatory barriers to trade, often referred to by TTIP negotiators as "red tape," would imply lowering levels of protection in the EU. Again, this shows how language affects politics. TTIP negotiators used terms like "red tape" to portray a set of regulatory differences as not contributing anything to levels of protection while having trade-reducing protectionist effects. But CSOs interpreted this differently and feared that negotiators held a deregulatory perspective and saw all regulations through the lens of negative effects on trade, rather than seeing their positive effects for public policy goals. That regulatory convergence was pursued in a comprehensive trade negotiation, which was seen by proponents of TTIP as necessary to ensure sufficient political pressure on regulators to make compromises, added to CSOs' worries. Trade negotiations are characterized by reciprocal exchange of market access concessions. Reciprocity does not need to be strictly equal for specific products; liberalization can be maximized by issue-linkages and package deals, where commitments by one party on one issue are reciprocated by the other party on another issue. In the TTIP negotiations, CSOs feared that EU regulations would become a bargaining chip that could be offered in exchange for better access to, for example, American procurement markets.

To justify its approach in the face of contestation, the European Commission developed two framing strategies: stressing common values and setting global standards.

Stressing Common Values and Setting Global Standards

To counter the concern that regulatory cooperation in TTIP would lead to lower levels of protection in the EU, the European Commission tried to debase the image that "our European model is much better than the American one" (De Gucht 2014; see also Duina 2019). While earlier there used to be a tendency among EU policymakers to stress the unique qualities of the European social model (often, at least implicitly, juxtaposed against the American "cowboy capitalism" model), in the context of TTIP policymakers emphasized the commonality of European and American values, standards, and cultures: "[O]ur values and concerns are much more similar than with any other part of the world" (De Gucht 2014). While the Commission made sure to underline that in some very sensitive areas where EU regulations differed substantially from those in the US—such as on genetically modified organisms (GMOs) or the use of hormones in beef—no convergence would be pursued, it argued that these irreconcilable differences are the exception rather than the rule.

Another line of argument for promoting regulatory cooperation in TTIP that the advocates of the deal used is that it would allow the EU and the US to set global standards. Rather than abandoning regulatory sovereignty through TTIP, the deal would allow the EU to remain a rule-maker by joining hands with the US: "[T]oday our combined weight in the global economy means that many who wish to sell into our markets will have an interest in moving towards whatever rules we can achieve. That effect cannot be guaranteed in the longer term" (De Gucht 2013a). While this aspect would be emphasized more prominently and forcefully over the course of the negotiations, the EU would frame this strategic dimension of TTIP in less explicit geopolitical terms than the US would do. The EU was careful not to frame the deal as an alliance against China (or Russia), while the US exercised less restraint in calling TTIP an "economic NATO."

However, the selling point that TTIP would allow the EU and the US to "standardize the world" together suffered from a logical inconsistency with how negotiators were approaching regulatory convergence (cf. De Ville and Siles-Brügge 2016). If transatlantic regulatory convergence is pursued through harmonization, this can indeed be projected to lead to global standards. At the time of negotiations, the combined EU and US share of global imports exceeded 50 percent. This made it likely that if the EU and the US would adopt common regulations, firms and governments would automatically align their products and legislation, through what could be called a "Brussels-Washington effect" (cf. Bradford 2020). But as we have seen, harmonization was not on the table in TTIP because of the difficult political economy of achieving it. Mutual recognition of rules, which was being pursued, may also lead to global standards, but under a specific condition, that is, if firms located outside of the EU and the US can also profit from mutual recognition agreed in TTIP (meaning that approval of their product by either the EU or the US is recognized by the other party), called *erga omnes* mutual recognition. This then provides an incentive to these foreign firms to align their products with either EU or US regulations and to lobby their government to change domestic rules accordingly. But analysis of EU documents has shown that negotiators in TTIP wanted to limit mutual recognition to firms located in the EU or the US rather than extending this *erga omnes* (see European Commission 2013, 41–43). The preference for bilateral rather than *erga omnes* mutual recognition flows from a combination of reasons: *erga omnes* mutual recognition requires an even further leap of faith in the rules and conformity assessment of third countries; it increases competition for domestic firms without resulting in reciprocal increased market access in countries that are not a party of the FTA; and it reinforces race-to-the-bottom concerns.

Under pressure from unprecedented outside contestation, negotiators failed to make sufficient progress in the TTIP negotiations. In mid-2016, after fourteen rounds of negotiations, in almost half of the working groups negotiators had not succeeded in agreeing on a consolidated text as the basis for seeking a compromise. This included negotiations on sectoral regulatory convergence, where negotiators had been forced to continuously lower the level of ambitions in response to CSO contestation. Eventually, the election of Donald J. Trump as the 45th US president in November 2016 provided the final blow to TTIP's fate, and it was put (indefinitely) officially in the deep freeze. But the German vice-chancellor at the time, Sigmar Gabriel, had already called TTIP "dead in the water" in the summer of 2016.

Lessons from TTIP's Failure

Regulatory convergence was a central objective in TTIP, but it was also central to the negotiation's failure. With hindsight, it can be said that the goal set for regulatory convergence in TTIP—eliminating a large chunk of existing regulatory differences between the EU and the US—constituted an own goal. Especially in combination with proposing mutual recognition as the approach to eliminate regulatory differences, this evoked concerns among CSOs, regulators, and parliamentarians that TTIP would undermine levels of social, environmental, consumer, or health protection.[5] Pursuing across-the-board regulatory convergence through a trade agreement added to these fears because skeptics reasonably worried that regulations would become a bargaining chip in a broad package deal.

Building a transatlantic market to the image of the EU's single market based on the mutual recognition principle not only evoked alarm among actors concerned about levels of EU protection but was probably unrealistic from the start. As the EU's former lead negotiator on TTIP, Ignacio Garcia Bercero, wrote (in a paper with Kalypso Nicolaïdis), "without the 'eco system' that comes along with it [mutual recognition] is an extremely ambitious exercise" (Garcia Bercero and Nicolaïdis 2021, 17). Mutual recognition in the EU's single market is embedded in a supranational governance structure where legislative bodies (the European Parliament and the Council of the European Union) can introduce minimum standards that put a floor under regulatory competition. Judicial bodies (the Court of Justice of the European Union) can adjudicate disputes over the equivalence of regulations and standards, and weigh competing objectives of free trade and consumer, health, or environmental protection. Obviously, TTIP would not establish a transatlantic parliament or a transatlantic court with broad powers. Even the less ambitious and intrusive goal of mutual recognition of conformity assessment is complicated when it is not embedded in a context of political integration. Outsourcing inspection and enforcement of one's regulations requires a certain degree of trust in the other side's regulatory culture and administration, which cannot be taken for granted.

In the next two sections, I discuss CETA as a successful agreement, and the EU-US TTC as a new attempt at transatlantic regulatory cooperation. Did CETA succeed because the approach to regulatory cooperation was different from TTIP? And which lessons did the EU and the US take from TTIP when launching the TTC?

Regulatory Cooperation in CETA

CETA became embroiled in the contestation of TTIP years after the EU and Canada had concluded the negotiations, when member states and the European Parliament had to give their consent to the agreement (cf. Hübner et al. 2017). While some civil society groups had tried to politicize CETA in an earlier phase, this only really took off after CETA could be depicted as a "Trojan horse" that would allow American firms with affiliates in Canada to sue EU governments or enter the EU market under lower conditions even in the absence of TTIP. It can be reasonably assumed that without the contamination of politicization of TTIP, CETA would have been smoothly approved in the EU. A trade agreement with Canada is easier to pursue for the EU than one with the US. Canada is an advanced but much smaller economy than the US, giving the EU more asymmetric bargaining power, especially as it has been a key objective of Canadian foreign economic policy to diversify away from the US. This can, for example, be seen in the acceptance by Canada of over 170 EU geographical indications in CETA. Moreover, the EU had other offensive interests in CETA that did not require regulatory convergence, like the inclusion of Canadian provinces and territories to improve the market access for EU firms at the sub-federal level, especially in government procurement. Moreover, Canada is often considered a more social democratic, European-like country on the other side of the Atlantic, with similar concerns, for example, regarding cultural diversity as a reason to treat audiovisual products differently in the global trading system (but cf. Duina 2019, who stresses cultural differences between the EU and Canada to understand opposition to CETA). Consequently, CETA was an agreement in which the

EU had significant offensive interests beyond regulatory convergence, had asymmetric interdependence advantages, and negotiated with a country seen as more culturally similar.

These circumstances made regulatory convergence not only less of a necessity to make a deal worthwhile, but also, where it was pursued, less controversial. This is also evidenced by the fact that once CETA became politicized in the wake of the protests against TTIP, activists took aim at the investment protection provisions and the hybrid list approach to services liberalization rather than at regulatory cooperation. All this does not mean that CETA has no regulatory cooperation provisions. CETA contains a separate chapter (ch. 21) on regulatory cooperation.[6] As summarized on the European Commission's webpage outlining the agreement, "[t]his chapter encourages regulators to exchange experiences and information and identify areas where they could cooperate. All cooperation is voluntary and regulators in the EU and Canada retain their power to adopt legislation" (European Commission, n.d.). The chapter establishes a "regulatory cooperation forum," which will provide a platform for the parties to discuss regulatory policy issues of mutual interest, review regulatory initiatives that may provide potential for cooperation, encourage bilateral regulatory cooperation, and review the progress, achievements, and best practices of such cooperation. The chapter is cloaked with aspirational language and contains no real binding commitments. It sets up an institutional structure that may allow for increased ambition in achieving regulatory convergence over time.

Besides this horizontal chapter, CETA contains just one regulatory sectoral annex on "cooperation in the field of motor vehicle regulations" (Annex 4-A). This annex contains commitments on cooperation like the horizontal chapter, but these are formulated more specifically and are compulsory. The annex commits Canada to incorporate into domestic law United Nations (UN) technical regulations on motor vehicles, "unless doing so would provide for a lower level of safety [. . .] or would compromise North American integration." In addition, CETA also contains a "protocol on the mutual acceptance of the results of conformity assessment" and a "protocol on the mutual recognition of the compliance and enforcement programme regarding good manufacturing practices for pharmaceutical products" to reduce duplicative testing for certain non-agricultural products and medicinal products and drugs.

To sum up, the ambition of regulatory cooperation in CETA has been limited compared to the objectives set for TTIP. Commitments on good regulatory practices are formulated in an aspirational and voluntary way, while setting up a structure that may allow for more intensified cooperation in the future. The agreement foresees mutual recognition of conformity assessment in a few product categories. In only one sector is harmonization of regulations foreseen, and that is for motor vehicle regulations where Canada has committed to adopt relevant UN regulations.

The EU-US Trade and Technology Council

After Trump became US president, EU-US transatlantic trade relations deteriorated significantly beyond the termination of the TTIP talks. Trump imposed tariffs on the imports of aluminum and steel, including from the EU, leading to retaliatory tariffs by the latter. Similarly, Trump threatened the EU with tariffs on cars, which would have dealt an even harder economic blow. Eventually, the EU avoided a further worsening of trade relations with the US when President Trump and European Commission president Jean-Claude Juncker agreed on a joint statement in July 2018 (European Commission 2018). In this statement, they agreed, inter alia, to pursue "zero tariffs, zero non-tariff barriers, and zero subsidies on non-auto industrial goods," including through "close dialogue on standards in order to ease trade, reduce bureaucratic obstacles, and slash costs." This agenda was dubbed a TTIP-lite by some, but would lead to no real results. Instead, very quickly after Joseph R. Biden, Jr., won the 2020 US presidential elections, the European Commission proposed a "Transatlantic Trade and Technology Council" to set joint standards on new technologies. This council would resuscitate the parts of TTIP that focused on cooperation on new regulations. An EU official declared that "it's very hard to align rules on products that already exist, but it is fairly easy to do it on emerging technologies" (Hanke Vela and Herszenhorn 2020). Eventually, the TTC would be launched in June 2021 and would hold its first meeting in Pittsburgh in September 2021. The inaugural joint statement declared that its central objectives are to "coordinate approaches to key global technology, economic, and trade issues; and to deepen transatlantic trade and economic relations, basing policies on shared democratic values" (European Commission 2021).

Regulatory cooperation in the TTC differs from regulatory cooperation in TTIP in several important respects. First, cooperation is focused on future regulations for new technologies, rather than pursuing harmonization or mutual recognition of existing regulations. Second, the TTC is framed more in terms of geopolitical than economic goals. There has been no mention of concrete economic benefits, like with TTIP. This has the advantage that it evokes less concern that high levels of protection will be sacrificed at the altar of economic growth. Moreover, this time the EU uses clearer antagonistic language to highlight the geostrategic dimension of the cooperation. The inaugural statement, for example, mentions that "we stand together in continuing to protect our businesses, consumers and workers from unfair trade practices, in particular those posed by non-market economies that are undermining the world trading system" (European Commission 2021). By juxtaposing more explicitly the EU and the US as democratic market economies versus other countries (China, in particular) as autocratic state-led economies, transatlantic similarities are highlighted while differences become seen as marginal.

To achieve its objectives, the TTC is composed of ten working groups, focusing on the following: technology standards cooperation, climate and clean tech, secure supply chains, information and technology security and competitiveness, data governance and technology platform, misuse of technology threatening security and human rights, export controls cooperation, investment screening cooperation, promoting small and medium-sized enterprise access to and use of digital technologies, and global trade challenges. During the second meeting of the TTC, in May 2022 in Paris, a geopolitical outlook was even more present due to the war in Ukraine, with the EU and the US coordinating their export controls to Russia. As current EU trade commissioner Valdis Dombrovskis put it: "[t]hese advances show that the TTC really is becoming our problem-solving platform to equip our economies in a fast-changing world" (Dombrovskis 2022).

Conclusion

The EU and the US have, over the past three decades, tried to achieve significant regulatory convergence through different initiatives. In the 1990s, separate low-profile mutual recognition agreements for a limited number of sectors were pursued. Outside of the public spotlights, regulators felt insufficient incentives to give up their autonomy, and the implementation of these agreements failed. Proponents of intensified transatlantic economic integration hoped that negotiating regulatory convergence in the context of a comprehensive trade agreement would generate sufficient political pressure on regulators on both sides of the Atlantic to cooperate. But, instead, TTIP generated unprecedented contestation on the side of civil society, who feared that transatlantic regulatory convergence would lower EU levels of environ- mental, social, health, or consumer protection. When pursuing regulatory convergence with an economic equal and fellow global rule-maker like the US, the EU could not hope to export its own rules as in trade agreements with smaller economies that seek integration with the EU's market. Instead, EU policymakers stated that TTIP would establish over time a transatlantic market in the image of the EU's single market, based on the mutual recog- nition principle. But this approach only added fuel to the flames of skeptics' concerns, especially in the absence of transatlantic political and judicial institutions. Discursive strategies stressing the similarities between EU and US regulatory goals, values, and cultures and arguing that TTIP would allow the transatlantic alliance to remain global rule-setters rang hollow, espe- cially as negotiators were aiming for bilateral rather than *erga omnes* mutual recognition.

Regulatory cooperation in CETA was more modest and less ambitious but, therefore, also less contested and more feasible. It focuses on establishing structures that facilitate cooperation on future regulations in new sectors, as well as deliberation on reducing existing divergences. Being volun- tary and forward-looking in nature, these provisions did not provoke the same concerns as in TTIP, while they allow for trust-building as a prereq- uisite for regulatory cooperation. Sectoral regulatory convergence is lim- ited to vehicles, where Canada has committed to adopting UN Economic Commission for Europe standards, de facto harmonizing toward EU rules. If future regulatory convergence through the procedural and institutional provisions of CETA happens, it is likely that it will follow the same pattern, with Canada adopting EU (proposed) rules. This is due to the asymmetric dependency relationship between the two, as well as Canada's eagerness to diversify away from the US. At the same time, Canada will always have to be careful not to let regulatory cooperation with the EU jeopardize market ac- cess to the US, a condition explicitly included in the provisions on vehicles.

Given the difficult history of EU-US regulatory cooperation, one would have low expectations of the recently launched Transatlantic Trade and Technology Council as well. But the TTC differs from earlier attempts at transatlantic regulatory convergence in several important respects. First, the TTC is focused exclusively on cooperation on future rules in new sectors. This is a much more feasible objective than pursuing regulatory convergence of current regulations, as regulators do not have to abandon autonomy over existing rules, no party must incur adjustment costs, and civil society cannot fear lowering levels of protection if no level has been set yet. Second, advocates of the TTC refrain from making claims about the economic gains from the initiative, which were central to the justification of TTIP. This has the advantage that it evokes less concerns that regulatory objectives will be sacrificed at the altar of economic growth. Instead, and third, the initiative is couched in geopolitical terms. Indeed, the discourse that the TTC may result in global standards is much more plausible than it was in TTIP, if regulators succeed in agreeing to new common standards. This is now framed much more explicitly to counter China's rise in critical new technologies, which are important from not only an economic but often also a security perspective. So far, this does not raise much contestation from civil society, perhaps because geopolitically driven standardization may lead to high levels of (privacy, security, etc.) protection, as well as transatlantic trade facilitation.

What does this review of TTIP, CETA, and the TTC teach us about the prospect of standardization through EU trade agreements? First, and quite straightforward, is the observation that pursuing regulatory convergence with an equal economic power and rule-maker is difficult. The absence of asymmetric interdependence and political economy dynamics make harmonization toward EU rules implausible. The alternative of mutual recognition might be easier to negotiate and more attractive to business, but evokes concerns among CSOs who fear that this will lead to a race to the bottom. Second, therefore, it is more productive to focus efforts on regulatory convergence on future rules. This can be stimulated by establishing procedures and institutions that encourage exchange of information, deliberation, and cooperation and result in trust-building. This is what the TTC is about. Third, in terms of building support for regulatory convergence, a geopolitical framing may be more convincing than an economic rationale.

Notes

1. For the sake of simplicity and readability, in the remainder of this chapter, I will mostly use the terms "standardization" and "regulatory cooperation/convergence" interchangeably.
2. On a continuum from most to least legally binding: integration/harmonization through supranational institutions, specific negotiated agreements (treaties/conventions), formal regulatory cooperation partnerships, joint standard setting through intergovernmental organizations, trade agreements with regulatory provisions, mutual

recognition agreements, trans-governmental networks of regulators, unilateral convergence through good regulatory practices and adoption of relevant frameworks in other jurisdictions, recognition and incorporation of international standards, and soft law (principles, codes of conducts; dialogue/informal exchange of information).

3. A similar approach to mutual recognition is a decision of equivalence, whereby one party accepts as equivalent another party's regulation or test procedure. While mutual recognition implies a reciprocal agreement, equivalence is a unilateral decision.

4. Annexes on chemicals, cosmetics, engineering products, information, and communication technologies, medical devices, pesticides, pharmaceutical, textiles, and vehicles.

5. The general public was probably not aware of the intricacies of regulatory convergence pursued in TTIP (see Spilker et al. 2020), and CSOs tried to simplify their message about race-to-the-bottom concerns by focusing on specific products, such as "chlorinated chicken," for which regulatory convergence was actually not seriously considered.

6. Besides this dedicated chapter, CETA contains other chapters relevant to regulatory convergence, such as chapters on technical barriers to trade (ch. 4), SPS measures (ch. 5), and domestic regulation (ch. 12).

References

Bradford, A. 2020. *The Brussels Effect: How the European Union Rules the World.* Oxford: Oxford University Press.

Centre for Economic Policy Research (CEPR). 2013. *Reducing Transatlantic Barriers to Trade and Investment: An Economic Assessment.* London: Centre for Economic Policy Research.

De Gucht, K. 2013a. Speech: A European Perspective on Transatlantic Free Trade. March 2. European Conference, Harvard Kennedy School. https://ec.europa.eu/commission/presscorner/detail/en/SPEECH_13_178.

De Gucht, K. 2013b. Statement by EU Trade Commissioner Karel De Gucht on the Transatlantic Trade and Investment Partnership (TTIP) ahead of the Second Round of Negotiations. September 30. Brussels: European Commission. https://ec.europa.eu/commission/presscorner/detail/en/MEMO_13_835.

De Gucht, K. 2014. Statement by Commissioner Karel De Gucht on TTIP at European Parliament Plenary Debate. July 15. Strasbourg: European Commission. https://ec.europa.eu/commission/presscorner/detail/en/SPEECH_14_549.

De Ville, F., and G. Siles-Brügge. 2016. *TTIP: The Truth about the Transatlantic Trade and Investment Partnership.* Cambridge: Polity Press.

Dombrovskis, V. 2022. Debrief by Executive Vice-President Valdis Dombrovskis on the Trade and Technology Council at European Parliament Committee for International Trade. May 17. https://ec.europa.eu/commission/commissioners/2019-2024/dombrovskis/announcements/debrief-executive-vice-president-valdis-dombrovskis-trade-and-technology-council-european-parliament_en.

Duina, F. 2006. *The Social Construction of Free Trade: The European Union, NAFTA, and MERCOSUR.* Princeton, NJ: Princeton University Press.

Duina, F. 2019. "Why the Excitement? Values, Identities, and the Politicization of EU Trade Policy With North America." *Journal of European Public Policy* 26 (12): pp. 1866–1882.

ECORYS. 2009. *Non-Tariff Measures in EU-US Trade and Investment: An Economic Analysis*. Rotterdam: ECORYS.

European Commission. n.d. "CETA Chapter by Chapter." Brussels: European Commission. https://policy.trade.ec.europa.eu/eu-trade-relationships-country-and-region/countries-and-regions/canada/eu-canada-agreement/ceta-chapter-chapter_en.

European Commission. 2006. *Global Europe: Competing in the World. A Contribution to the EU's Growth and Jobs Strategy*. Brussels: European Commission.

European Commission. 2013. *European Commission Staff Working Document: Impact Assessment Report on the Future of EU-US Trade Relations*. SWD(2013) 68 final. Brussels: European Commission.

European Commission. 2018. Joint U.S.-EU Statement following President Juncker's Visit to the White House. July 25. https://ec.europa.eu/commission/presscorner/detail/en/STATEMENT_18_4687.

European Commission. 2021. EU-US Trade and Technology Council Inaugural Joint Statement. September 29. https://ec.europa.eu/commission/presscorner/detail/en/STATEMENT_21_4951.

Garcia Bercero, I., and K. Nicolaïdis. 2021. "The Power Surplus: Brussels Calling, Legal Empathy and the Trade-Regulation Nexus." *CEPS Policy Insights*, No. PI2021-05.

Golberg, E. 2019. "Regulatory Cooperation—A Reality Check." M-RCBG Working Paper No. 115. https://www.hks.harvard.edu/sites/default/files/centers/mrcbg/img/115_final.pdf.

Hanke Vela, J., and D. M. Herszenhorn. 2020. "EU Seeks Anti-China Alliance on Tech with Biden." *Politico*, November 30. https://www.politico.eu/article/eu-seeks-anti-china-alliance-on-tech-with-joe-biden/.

Hübner, K, A.-S. Deman, and T. Balik. 2017. "EU and Trade Policy-Making: The Contentious Case of CETA." *Journal of European Integration* 39 (7): pp. 843–857.

Lang, A. 2011. *World Trade Law after Neoliberalism: Reimagining the Global Economic Order*. Oxford: Oxford University Press.

Meunier, S., and K. Nicolaïdis. 2006. "The European Union as a Conflicted Trade Power." *Journal of European Public Policy* 13 (6): pp. 906–925.

Morag-Levine, N. 2014. "The History of Precaution." *The American Journal of Comparative Law* 62 (4): pp. 1095–1132.

Organisation for Economic Co-operation and Development (OECD). 2014. *International Regulatory Co-operation: Addressing Global Challenges*. Paris: OECD Publishing.

Pollack, M. A. 2005. "The New Transatlantic Agenda at Ten: Reflections on an Experiment in International Governance." *Journal of Common Market Studies* 43 (5): pp. 899–919.

Sapir, A. 2011. "The Political Economy of Transatlantic Regulatory Cooperation and Competition: A (Unofficial) View from Europe." In S. J. Evenett and R. M. Stern (eds.), *Systemic Implications of Transatlantic Regulatory Cooperation and Competition*, pp. 47–61. London: World Scientific.

Spilker, G., Q. Nguyen, and T. Bernauer. 2020. "Trading Arguments: Opinion Updating in the Context of International Trade Agreements." *International Studies Quarterly* 64 (4): pp. 929–938.

The White House. 2013. Remarks by President Obama, U.K. Prime Minister Cameron, European Commission President Barroso, and European Council President Van

Rompuy on the Transatlantic Trade and Investment Partnership. June 17. https://obam awhitehouse.archives.gov/the-press-office/2013/06/17/remarks-president-obama-uk-prime-minister-cameron-european-commission-pr.

Vogel, D. 2012. *The Politics of Precaution*. Princeton, NJ: Princeton University Press.

Wiener, B., M. D. Rogers, J. K. Hammitt, and P. H. Sand (eds). 2010. *The Reality of Precaution: Comparing Risk Regulation in the United States and Europe*. London: Routledge.

Young, A. R. 2015. "Liberalizing Trade, Not Exporting Rules: The Limits to Regulatory Co-ordination in the EU's 'New Generation' Preferential Trade Agreements." *Journal of European Public Policy* 22 (9), pp. 1253–1275.

7

Interregionalism, Trade, and Standardization

The Long Road to the EU-MERCOSUR Trade Agreement and the Uncertainties Ahead

Andrea C. Bianculli

Introduction

In June 2019, the European Union (EU) and the Common Market of the South (MERCOSUR) reached a political accord for a comprehensive free trade deal as part of the wider interregional Association Agreement, which also includes a pact on political dialogue and cooperation.[1] This political consensus came after twenty years of on-off negotiations as these had to be suspended at different times because of major discrepancies between the parties. More than three years later, however, the agreement has not been signed, and there is still considerable doubt about its future given that it faces a difficult ratification process. In both regions, but to a greater extent in Europe, resistance and opposition to the approval of the agreement have increased.

Taken as "region-to-region relations," interregionalism has imbued the EU's external policies since the 1990s (Söderbaum and Van Langenhove 2005) and has been a key element of EU trade policy. As noted by Aggarwal and Fogarty (2005, 327), the EU has been the "patron saint of interregionalism in international economic relations." Thus, the EU has encouraged and supported regional integration beyond its borders and actively promoted its own model of regionalism (Börzel and Risse 2012; De Lombaerde and Schulz 2009; Farrell 2009). Moreover, the EU's interregional strategy has reflected its specific commitment to economic liberalization and market-building, which

Andrea C. Bianculli, *Interregionalism, Trade, and Standardization* In: *Standardizing the World*. Edited by: Francesco Duina and Crina Viju-Miljusevic, Oxford University Press. © Oxford University Press 2023. DOI: 10.1093/oso/9780197681886.003.0008 have bestowed the EU with relevant regulatory capacity based on inclusive and extensive norms and combining national and supranational regulations (Majone 1994). Consequently, and from an international perspective, the EU has been an active promoter of "a 'deep' trade agenda: seeking multilateral agreements on the making of domestic rules" in different policy areas, including competition policy, environment, labor and investment, among others (Young and Peterson 2006, 795). Within this strong advocacy of trade rules and regulations, interregionalism thus worked as a tool to push for regulatory standards and governance, though showing mixed results (Bianculli 2016, 2021).

The EU-MERCOSUR partnership stood out as one of the most developed cases of interregionalism. However, it has also been the most difficult to reach. This chapter analyzes the Agreement in Principle reached in 2019 in the context of EU interregionalism, its recent Global Strategy (2016), and its vocation to promote global free trade and to fulfill its role as a regulatory power.

Empirically, the focus is on two policy areas: trade facilitation and intellectual property rights (IPR) in special reference to health. Both policy areas are characterized as behind-the-border or "deep integration" issues that touch upon domestic regulations. Therefore, the negotiation of these complex behind-the-border issues goes beyond the adoption of market-opening policies and increasingly falls within the universe of regulations, reaching deeply into domestic governance. Despite these commonalities, the comparative assessment of trade facilitation and intellectual property, in terms of both their definitional and normative standardization, shows that these policy areas have resulted in different standardization patterns.

Both policy areas are regulated in reference to international rules and standards as set by the World Trade Organization (WTO) agreements. But, with this in the background, I note the articulation of novel definitional and standardization materials in both areas. This is the case for trade facilitation when it comes to transparency, participation, and the involvement of the business community. In intellectual property, those materials include an explicit commitment to advancing economic and social welfare (and thus, the introduction of a public interest dimension, especially around patents and health). These are noteworthy outcomes which, of course, require explanation.

This chapter argues that these varying standardization patterns respond to ideational and institutional elements. While the first refer to how ideas and discourse evolve in trade policy and the negotiation of standards, the second variable talks to the relevance of history and time, thus emphasizing interregionalism as a process, where context and time play a fundamental role.

To develop the argument, the chapter first presents the conceptual and methodological approach. The third section analytically describes the standardization patterns in trade facilitation and IPR as framed in the Agreement in Principle between the EU and MERCOSUR. This is followed by an assessment of whether and how the EU has exercised a regulatory role and how this has played out across different policy areas based on the interplay between the EU's ideas and discourse on trade and regulation, and outreach and MERCOSUR regulatory governance across time. This is shown through the comparative assessment of the agendas under negotiation and the constellations of actors and preferences involved in the process, and where possible changes over time are also assessed. Second, and to the extent that there may be discrepancies between the EU regulatory model and the norms and regulations in force or under discussion in MERCOSUR, the chapter also addresses these differences. The final section discusses the different standardization patterns observed in trade facilitation and intellectual property and calls for a long-term perspective, not only to assess ideas and preferences in trade and regulation across time and policy areas, but also to capture the interaction dynamics across different regulatory arenas.

Conceptual and Methodological Approach

Conceptually, the chapter builds on the categories and dimensions presented in this volume's Introduction (see also Duina 2004). With a focus on the extent to which the EU promotes standardization through interregional free trade agreements, the chapter assesses two dimensions of standardization and regulation.

First, the analysis focuses on "definitional standardization," taken as those passages or sections that identify and explain "the essential characteristics of objects, activities and agents in the world" (Duina 2004, 360). These definitional notions outline "the nature of what is exchanged and of other items and entities associated with an exchange" (Duina 2004, 360) and thus facilitate trade exchanges. Second, "normative standardization" refers to those passages that convey "the desirability of certain situations" in the world.

Normative notions constitute "shared views of how the world should be" (Duina 2004, 360).

The analysis of the definitional and normative dimensions of the standards is then complemented with an assessment of the *source of regulatory authority*. Being the traditional primary source of regulatory authority, states have gradually surrendered particular areas of such authority to transnational organizations and regimes (Lipschutz and Fogel 2002). Thus, "the locus of regulation has shifted from the domestic to the transnational level" (Lall 2015, 125), including the multilateral and the regional arenas.

Given this variation, determining the source of regulatory authority is relevant. This is especially the case when analyzing behind-the-border impediments to trade—as in the case of trade facilitation and intellectual property—which put regulatory issues on the negotiation table. While it might be relatively easy for governments to produce negative measures (i.e., the elimination of national restraints on trade and distortions of competition) to increase market integration, deep or positive policies may require the harmonization and coordination of norms and standards, or mutual recognition of each other's regulatory processes and standards. The negotiation of these agendas reaches deep into domestic governance arrangements. Agreement on regulatory issues which shape the conditions under which markets operate remains extremely difficult to achieve, or, in many cases, almost impossible because of relevant differences among countries in terms of normative or ideological positions, levels of economic development, and institutional arrangements (Scharpf 1999).

The creation of the WTO in the mid-1990s added to this complexity as it gave greater emphasis to the multilateralization of the deep trade agenda. Given the resistance and opposition of developing countries, these controversial issues would then be moved to other negotiation arenas. Furthermore, rather than just proposing WTO rules, trade agreements would include provisions that deepened (WTO-plus) and expanded (WTO-beyond) multilateral commitments, all of which "is politically costlier than border measure trade liberalization" (Theisinger 2021, 19). In all, this chapter provides a comparative assessment of how EU-MERCOSUR negotiations have resulted in different standardization outcomes based on these three various dimensions.

Analyzing the EU and MERCOSUR agreement is relevant. Both blocs have triggered the articulation of complex webs of standards and regulations which contain abundant definitional and normative notions in a wide variety of policy areas. Yet, these differ significantly both in terms of the target and its content, that is, the subject of standardization and what the definitional and normative notions uphold, respectively (Duina 2004, 361).

Empirically, the analysis looks into the EU-MERCOSUR Agreement in Principle, which is a comprehensive deal including trade in goods and rules of origin and regulating technical barriers to trade; customs and trade facilitation; trade remedies; sanitary and phytosanitary (SPS) measures; services; public procurement; competition; subsidies; state-owned enterprises; and IPR, including geographical indications, trade and sustainable development, transparency, small and medium-sized enterprises, and establishing various mechanisms for dialogue and dispute settlement, together with a regional integration clause.

Clearly, this reflects the EU's focus on standard promotion in trade and its intense advocacy of the deep trade agenda (Young and Peterson 2006). The negotiation process with MERCOSUR was intended to follow similar steps to those of the agreement with Chile signed in 2002, which was then portrayed as the most comprehensive example of the EU's trade policy toward the South and as the bloc's "ideal framework" for its bilateral trade relations (Lamy 2002). Still, while both the EU and Chile decided to launch negotiations to modernize the preferential trade agreement part of the Association in 2013,[2] negotiations with MERCOSUR are still based on the EU-MERCOSUR's negotiating mandate approved in 1999. The 1999 mandate "has been broadly interpreted by the European Commission, but it has not been updated by the Council" (Grieger 2019, 5).[3]

Methodologically, the chapter follows a qualitative approach to analyze and comparatively assess the definitional and normative content of standards and regulations around trade facilitation and IPR, especially in relation to health, and the resulting specific standardization patterns and regulatory regimes in the EU-MERCOSUR trade agreement.

The analysis draws on multiple sources, including the Trade Part of the Agreement in Principle announced on June 28, 2019, and the individual chapters of the agreement as published by the European Commission (EC). These documents are available for information and transparency purposes. The final text will be final upon signature. Other documents included in the analysis are reports on negotiation rounds, official statements published by MERCOSUR and various stakeholders, newspaper articles, and press releases together with relevant secondary literature, among others. NVivo qualitative software was used to assist the coding and analysis of the large volume of text data.

The Agreement and the Regulation of Trade Facilitation and Intellectual Property Rights and Health

Trade Facilitation

The EU-MERCOSUR Agreement in Principle already refers to "Customs and Trade Facilitation," which is then further developed in the corresponding individual chapter.

A *definitional* notion seems elusive, yet the passages in the Agreement in Principle refer to trade facilitation as involving the establishment of "enhanced rules of good governance for customs procedures and high level of transparency" and "includes provisions resulting in maximum transparency, consultation of business prior to the adoption of new rules, streamlining of procedures, regular reviews of the rules in force with a view to meeting the needs of business, reducing red tape, and speeding up clearance—all the while ensuring enforcement" (Agreement in Principle 2019, 5).

This definition relies on the acknowledgment of "the importance of customs and trade facilitation in trade relations and in the evolving global trading environment" (Agreement in Principle 2019, 5). Also, specific indications are given both for the EU and MERCOSUR: these "will undertake to apply modern, and whenever possible, automated procedures for the efficient and expedited release of goods" (Agreement in Principle 2019, 5).

This is the departure point of the specific chapter on customs and trade facilitation, which starts by establishing the relevance of customs and trade facilitation "in the evolving global trading environment" and recognizing "international trade and customs instruments and standards are the basis for import, export and transit requirements and procedures" (Agreement in Principle 2019, "Customs and Trade Facilitation," 1).

From a *normative* dimension, this regulatory agreement is intended "to boost EU-MERCOSUR trade by providing enhanced rules of good governance for customs procedures" (Agreement in Principle 2019, 5). Also, normatively, the agreement recognizes the need to apply customs and other trade-related procedures in a "predictable, consistent and transparent" manner (Agreement in Principle 2019, 5). Emphasis is on related legislation, which should be non-discriminatory and based on the "use of modern methods and effective controls to combat fraud, protect consumer health and promote legitimate trade" (Agreement in Principle 2019, "Customs and Trade Facilitation," 1). Again, it concludes by establishing a normative intention as it compels both parties to "apply modern, and whenever possible, automated procedures for the efficient and expedited release of goods, resorting to risk management and prearrival sending of documentation to speed up clearance. Parties will have the possibility to develop joint initiatives including technical assistance, capacity building and measures to provide effective services to the business community" (Agreement in Principle 2019, 5).

Customs and trade facilitation are also defined as a building block toward further regional integration in MERCOSUR and in the EU. Thus, cooperation between the parties is emphasized as they "agree to work together towards supporting the development of regional integration within both parties" (Agreement in Principle 2019, "Customs and Trade Facilitation," 1). Specific areas of customs cooperation are identified in art. 2 and mainly include information exchange, collaborating on "the customs-related aspects of securing and facilitating the international trade supply chain in accordance with the Framework of Standards to Secure and Facilitate Global Trade (SAFE Framework) of the World Customs Organization (WCO)" (Agreement in Principle 2019, "Customs and Trade Facilitation," 2), the implementation of joint initiatives to promote technical assistance and capacity-building, strengthening cooperation in this policy area within the frame of different international organizations,[4] and establishing mutual recognition of various programs and controls, among others.

In terms of *the source of regulatory authority*, both parties will base their customs provisions and procedures upon the following international instruments and standards: the WTO Trade Facilitation Agreement, the International Convention on the Harmonized Commodity Description and Coding System, the WCO SAFE Framework and Data Model, and the revised Kyoto Convention on the Simplification and Harmonization of Customs Procedures. However, the agreement "goes further than the WTO Trade Facilitation Agreement of 2017" (Agreement in Principle 2019, 5). This is specifically reflected in the fact that the agreement "allows for cooperation in establishing mutual recognition of Authorized Economic Operator programmes" (Agreement in Principle 2019, 6). In other words, the agreement envisages the creation of a new figure: the authorized economic operator, which is granted to those trade operators that fulfill certain criteria and can thus enjoy "prerogatives that facilitate their operations under this designation, such as lower requirements for documents and data, a low number of physical inspections and examinations and fast track for merchandise release, among other things" (Ghiotto and Echaide 2019, 51). Parties have also agreed to go beyond the WTO Trade Facilitation Agreement (TFA) by ensuring transparency and allowing "access to relevant information on customs legislation and procedures" to both traders and the public (Agreement in Principle 2019, 5–6).

The text of the Agreement in Principle (2019, 5) also considers further developments in the regulatory process and establishes some normative considerations by indicating that if new rules were to be applied, "[b]usiness will be properly consulted prior to the adoption" of these. It creates a regular review process in order "to meet the needs of business and reduce red tape" (Agreement in Principle 2019, 5). Thus, the area of customs and trade facilitation emphasizes the relevant role of non-state actors in regulatory developments. More specifically, it underscores the "needs" of the business community. While the rules in force should be reviewed to "meet the needs of business" and joint EU-MERCOSUR initiatives should "provide effective services to the business community," these actors should also be consulted "prior to the adoption of new rules" (Agreement in Principle 2019, 5).

The specific chapter on customs and trade facilitation (art. 10) further develops these mandates, based on "transparency" as a normative precept and a principle that should guide "legislative proposals and general procedures related to customs and trade issues" (Agreement in Principle 2019, "Customs and Trade Facilitation," 8). To this end, the agreement establishes the relevance of timely and appropriate consultations "with trade representatives on legislative proposals and general procedures related to customs and trade issues" and "between the administrations and the business community" in the EU and MERCOSUR (Agreement in Principle 2019, "Customs and Trade Facilitation," 8). This is crucial "to meet the needs of the trading community, follow best practices, and remains as little trade-restrictive as possible" (Agreement in Principle 2019, "Customs and Trade Facilitation," 8). In a similar view, the EU and MERCOSUR's new legislation and procedures should be published "promptly, in a non-discriminatory and easily accessible manner" (Agreement in Principle 2019, "Customs and Trade Facilitation," 8). Moreover, the agreement calls for parties to "provide for regular consultations between border agencies and traders or other stakeholders within its territory" (Agreement in Principle 2019, "Customs and Trade Facilitation," 8). In other words, both blocs should carry on consultations with the business sector when attempting to pass new legislative proposals or changes to existing regulations that may affect the sector. In so doing, the EU and MERCOSUR should guarantee "good regulatory practices and transparency" to support "a transparent and predictable regulatory environment and efficient procedures for trade operators" (Agreement in Principle 2019, 15–16).

Finally, the separate chapter on customs and trade facilitation establishes the creation of a Special Committee on Customs, Trade Facilitation, and Rules of Origin. Made up of representatives of the EU and MERCOSUR, the committee is responsible for the "proper functioning of this Chapter, the [*Protocol xx on Rules of Origin*], and the [*Protocol xx on MAA*][5] and any additional customs and trade facilitation] [*sic*]-related provisions agreed between the Parties, and examine all issues arising from their application" (Agreement in Principle 2019, "Customs and Trade Facilitation," 14).

Intellectual Property Rights, Patents, and Health

The Agreement in Principle offers a *definitional* notion of IPR as understood within the interregional trade deal. More specifically, the chapter on IPR is broad and comprises "comprehensive provisions" in "the full spectrum of IPR, including copyright, trademarks, industrial designs and plant varieties" and "comprehensive rules on the protection of trade secrets, provisions on civil and administrative enforcement of IPR, and provisions on border enforcement," together with patents (Agreement in Principle 2019, 12–13).

From a definitional perspective, the specific chapter on intellectual property refers to "all categories of intellectual property that are the subject" of the Agreement on Trade-Related Aspects of Intellectual Property Rights (TRIPS) (Sections 1–7, Part II) and the specific areas detailed in this chapter (Agreement in Principle 2019, "Intellectual Property Rights," 2). This includes patents, together with copyright and related rights, trademarks, geographical indications, industrial designs, layout designs, protection of undisclosed information, and control of anti-competitive practices in contractual licenses (WTO 1994).

The negotiations are portrayed as having "produced a substantive result," which is mainly given by the fact that: "For the first time the EU and MERCOSUR will have a structured bilateral framework with clear legal commitments and opportunities to discuss issues relating to IPR in detail" (Agreement in Principle 2019, 12). So, this talks about setting an interregional space based on already established commitments and standards in IPR.

There is also a *normative* component by indicating that the "provisions on cooperation demonstrate a mutual interest to improve the protection and enforcement of IPR" (Agreement in Principle 2019, 12–13).

Regarding *the source of regulatory authority* in IPR, and specifically around patents, the Agreement in Principle (2019, 13) explains that these are "fully consistent with WTO/TRIPS rules." While the text acknowledges that the EU and MERCOSUR had shown different preferences regarding IPR and patents, the final agreement is depicted as having considered "the concerns of stakeholders on both sides," and thus, it "strikes a good balance between the interests of the EU and MERCOSUR and provides for progress as compared to the status-quo" (Agreement in Principle 2019, 13).

The parties are then to comply with the rights and obligations under the WTO and TRIPS regulations and "any other multilateral agreement related to intellectual property to which it is a Party" (Agreement in Principle 2019, "Intellectual Property Rights," 1). Building on this and based on the normative notion of further progress in this policy area, the agreement encourages those "MERCOSUR countries that are not yet party to the Patent Cooperation Treaty [. . .] to speed up international patent applications and to provide more legal certainty to the process" (Agreement in Principle 2019, 13). This is reiterated in the chapter on IPR in reference to patents: the EU and MERCOSUR should "make best efforts to adhere to the Patent Cooperation Treaty" (23).

With a normative tone, the agreement is framed by a vision of "a more sustainable, equitable and inclusive economy for the Parties" and by a notion of "favouring social and economic welfare and the balance between the rights of the holders and the public interest" and promoting "research and development, and access to knowledge, including to a rich public domain" (Agreement in Principle 2019, "Intellectual Property Rights," 2). Within this normative understanding, the agreement is thus to enable "access, production and commercialization of innovative and creative products and foster trade and investment between the Parties" and to provide for "an adequate and effective level of protection and enforcement" of IPR (Agreement in Principle 2019, "Intellectual Property Rights," 2).

This normative dimension is also evident in the call to support the attaining of various international commitments, as in the case of the United Nations Sustainable Development Goals (SDGs); the World Health Assembly Resolution WHA 60.28; the Pandemic Influenza Preparedness Framework; and the Global Strategy and Plan of Action on Public Health, Innovation and Intellectual Property; and the Development Agenda recommendations by the General Assembly of the World Intellectual Property Organization (WIPO). Moreover, public health is also normatively considered in the chapter on IPR, as the EU and MERCOSUR acknowledge the relevance of the Doha Declaration, specifically in terms of the TRIPS Agreement and Public Health adopted in 2001. The interregional agreement will ensure consistency with this international treaty and thus introduces a novel public interest dimension in the area of intellectual property and patents.

As an aside, it is noted that this policy area also includes the creation of a special Sub-Committee on Intellectual Property, which will be established to "follow up on the implementation of the provisions of this Chapter and any other relevant issue" (Agreement in Principle 2019, "Intellectual Property Rights," 34). Co-chaired by officials of the EU and MERCOSUR, the sub-committee is to meet at least once a year, and decisions will be adopted by consensus. Specific rules of procedure can also be approved by consensus (Agreement in Principle 2019, "Intellectual Property Rights," 34).

The EU-MERCOSUR Agreement: A Deal in the Making for Twenty Years

The final EU-MERCOSUR agreement, reached in June 2019, was the culmination of twenty long years of negotiations, which were part, in fact, of the broader EU-MERCOSUR Interregional Framework Agreement. Signed in 1995, this agreement relied on three pillars: political dialogue, development cooperation, and trade liberalization. After four years of intense and legally driven relations across the Atlantic, trade negotiations were launched in 1999, when the EC adopted the negotiation directives.

After fifteen rounds, negotiations were abandoned in 2004 due to differences over the trade agenda, which covered not only industrial and agricultural goods but also services, government procurement, IPR, customs and trade facilitation, as well as technical barriers to trade, mainly in manufactured goods, services, and agriculture; it would take a hiatus of six years for negotiations to be relaunched.

The suspension of trade negotiations between MERCOSUR and the EU in 2004 did not bring about a break in interregional relations. These continued through ministerial and technical meetings that ratified the mutual interest in the reopening of negotiations while strengthening political dialogue and technical and financial cooperation in diverse policy sectors (i.e., trade, facilitation, SPS measures, and education), for a total amount of €50 million to be executed between 2007 and 2013. Finally, in May 2010, during the presidential meeting scheduled within the Latin American and the Caribbean-EU Summit under Spain's EU presidency, both sides renewed "their commitment to strive for a conclusion of the negotiations without delay" (Council of the European Union 2010). Despite complaints and opposition from various countries given their agricultural concerns (i.e., France, Germany, Ireland, and Italy), negotiations resumed (MercoPress 2010). Yet, they were to follow a two-speed logic: the development of regulatory frameworks, on the one hand, and the preparation of bids, on the other (Makuc et al. 2015). The four negotiation rounds conducted during 2011 and 2012 lacked an exchange of offers, though some advancements were made in the regulatory chapters, including services, public purchases, and customs and trade facilitation.

Negotiations stalled once again in 2012, and no market offers were made in 2014 and 2015, despite both parties' commitments to do so. In May 2016, an exchange of market access offers was finally made. While these still reflected traditional positions, they represented the first significant concession that would unlock the process. Negotiations regained momentum and took on a clear political tone: apart from defending and supporting its own economic interests (Nolte and Ribeiro Neto 2021), the interregional negotiations were meant to convey a political message in support of free trade and multilateralism as a relevant strategical response to the globalization crisis (Sanahuja and Rodríguez 2019). This was also very much in line with the Global Strategy published in June 2016, which established that the EU would "pursue a comprehensive free trade agreement" with MERCOSUR (European Union 2016, 37, 41) as such agreements were perceived "as building blocks of global free trade and a means to "promote international regulatory standards" and relevant norms in various policy areas, including labor, environment, and health and safety norms (European Union 2016, 37, 41).

From that point on, the following rounds of negotiations showed progress in different agendas, though discrepancies remained in each other's sensitive issues: while the EU maintained a strong agricultural protectionism, MERCOSUR countries were still reticent to make concessions in trade liberalization of services, public procurement, and intellectual property rules. Thus, negotiations showed that the trade pattern of EU-MERCOSUR had not changed much and that the parties had not entered into sectors in which their presence was smaller (Cienfuegos 2016, 231). Preferences had not changed either (Botto and Bianculli 2011).

After thirteen rounds held between October 2016 and April 2019, the final round of negotiations led to the trade part of Association Agreement between the EU and MERCOSUR's four founding members—Argentina, Brazil, Paraguay, and Uruguay.

Standardization Patterns in Trade Facilitation and Intellectual Property in the EU-MERCOSUR Agreement in Principle

Trade facilitation and IPR are part of the Agreement in Principle. Their interregional regulatory setting is detailed in the main text and the corresponding separate chapters.

Definitional and normative standardization show some relevant similarities, but also differences across these policy areas, as detailed in Table 7.1.

In the case of trade facilitation, its *definitional* component appears to be rather vague, except for the emphasis on trade facilitation as rules of good governance and transparency. On the contrary, the essential characteristics of what is regulated under intellectual property is clearly identified in both legal texts. A list of what these rights involve and include in the interregional agreement is provided.

This is related to the characteristics of each policy domain and how these are more broadly defined. There is no universal or standard definition of trade facilitation. In fact, trade facilitation has been depicted as having "a variety of context-dependent meanings" (Hoekman and Shepherd 2013, 1) given that various institutions define trade facilitation differently.

Trade facilitation is part of the so-called Singapore issues. This recalls the WTO Singapore Ministerial Conference of 1996, where some developed members proposed that the WTO should admit some new issues, including investment, competition, transparency in government procurement, and trade facilitation. Because of the opposition of developing countries in Seattle, Doha, and Cancun Ministerial Meetings, these issues were ultimately dropped from the Doha Round Agenda, except for trade facilitation.

The EU was then interested in "promoting the regulation of investment, competition, and government procurement practices, but only the Trade

Table 7.1 Variation in Standardization Patterns in Trade Facilitation and Intellectual Property

	Definitional Component	Normative Component	Source of Regulatory Authority
Trade facilitation	Defined as rules of good governance, transparency, participation, and consultation	Relevance as a buildup to trade and the international global trade system	WTO Trade Facilitation Agreement, International Convention on the Harmonized Commodity Description and Coding System, among others, but goes beyond these sources in transparency and consultation
Intellectual property	Defined as including patents, copyright and related rights, trademarks, geographical indications, industrial designs, layout designs, protection of undisclosed information and control of anti-competitive practices in contractual licenses	Relevance of intellectual property and patents toward the attainment of economic, social, and scientific progress	WTO-TRIPS and TRIPS Agreement and Public Health (2001), which adds to support of the WHA 60.28, Global Strategy and Plan of Action on Public Health, Innovation, and Intellectual Property (WHO 2008), Development Agenda-WIPO (2007), and make efforts toward PCT (though not binding)

Source: Author's elaboration.

Facilitation Agreement (TFA) was concluded" (Theisinger 2021, 35). The WTO defines trade facilitation as "the simplification, modernization and harmonization of export and import processes" (WTO, n.d.). The EU holds a similar approach to the WTO, and all MERCOSUR founding member countries have ratified the TFA.[6]

When it comes to intellectual property, the agreement makes a clear reference to international instruments and adopts the definitional approach of the WTO-TRIPS agreement. More specifically, the interregional framework adopted by the EU and MERCOSUR defines intellectual property in a comprehensive manner, including patents, copyright and related rights, trademarks, geographical indications, industrial designs, layout designs, protection of undisclosed information, and control of anti-competitive practices in contractual licenses. These are spelled out in the agreement, which also ratifies all the rights and obligations enshrined in other multilateral treaties, to the extent that they have been signed by the different parties.

Both policy areas also include a *normative* dimension. Interregional commitments in trade facilitation open with a normative tone by asserting the relevance of these rules in trade and in the international global trade system. Similar normative considerations are given to IPR and patents. However, in the latter, rather than just economic or material considerations, regulations consider the extent to which these rules can also support economic and social welfare, an area where public health concerns are also relevant and include the achievement of the objectives subscribed under the framework of the World Health Assembly at the WHO and the SDGs. Thus, intellectual property and patents, more specifically, are given a novel and broader normative foundation based on the notion of health as a public good, including universal access to medicines.

When exploring the *source of regulatory authority* of these standards, both trade facilitation and intellectual property standards and regulations emanate from the international level, mainly from WTO multilateral regulations and standards. However, the agreement acknowledges that commitments in trade facilitation go beyond the WTO-TFA as they endorse transparency, consultation, and public access to business and relevant stakeholders.

Finally, as an aside, the EU-MERCOSUR agreement includes the establishment of specific institutional mechanisms to oversee the functioning and implementation of this accord, and to promote, when necessary, further developments in both policy areas. A special committee is to be created in customs and trade facilitation, while a subcommittee is envisaged to manage intellectual property. However, the agreement only supports active consultation with and participation of the business community in trade facilitation.

Again, international organizations seem of relevance here; more specifically, the role of the Organisation for Economic Co-operation and Development in the promotion of "good regulatory practices" in trade and international regulatory cooperation (Ghiotto and Echaide 2019). These good regulatory practices cover various principles, including transparency and participation in the regulatory process (OECD 2012). These principles refer to the creation of mechanisms to make public all new rules and regulations, and to allow for consultation with and participation of stakeholders. In this respect, art. 10 of the chapter on trade facilitation clearly establishes a novel definitional and normative standardization by requiring of states and regulators transparency and consultation with the business sector, together with the creation of spaces for dialogue with this actor. Also, and as explained below, already in the first decade of the twenty-first century, the business sector was actively involved in the discussions on customs and trade facilitation in the negotiation process between the EU and MERCOSUR (Bianculli 2016).

Explaining Variation in Standardization Patterns in the EU-MERCOSUR Agreement in Principle

Trade facilitation and intellectual property have resulted in different standardization patterns, which can be more readily explained by a combination of ideational and institutional elements. First, in empirical terms, this entails examining the evolution of ideas and discourses in trade policy and, more specifically, regarding those areas where calls for regulatory standardization have increased. Second, the analysis also underscores the significance of history and time. Thus, it highlights the idea of interregionalism and regulatory standardization as a process, where context and time play a fundamental role.

From an ideational perspective, the analytical narrative confirms the extent to which the EU privileges multilateral and international regulations. The interregional trade Agreement in Principle addresses standards in trade facilitation and intellectual property and patents that point to internationally adopted standards. This is in line with the EU's "new generation" preferential trade agreements, where the EU seems to have a preference for international rules and regulations (Theisinger 2021; Young 2015).

In the first decade of the twenty-first century, the EU had agreements with Chile, Mexico, and South Africa; during the second half of that first decade, the EC would strongly promote bilateral trade relations with relevant parties. More specifically, the EC communication "Global Europe: Competing in the World" identified MERCOSUR, along with the Association of Southeast Asian Nations and Korea, "as priorities" of such strategy, as they combined "high levels of protection with large market potential and they are active in concluding FTAs [free trade agreements] with EU competitors" (European

Commission 2006, 9). In 1996, EU trade policy was "to reduce technical barriers in overseas markets and prevent the emergence of new ones" and to encourage their trading partners "to adopt standards and regulatory approaches based on, or compatible with international and European practice" (Commission of the European Communities 1996, 4).

Ten years later, the emphasis was on "regulatory convergence wherever possible and [. . .] strong trade facilitation provisions" (European Commission 2006, 9). Additionally, and in terms of IPR, agreements should include "stronger provisions [. . .] including for example provisions on enforcement of IP rights along the lines of the EC Enforcement Directive" (European Commission 2006, 9). In 2013, the EU leaned toward a more open notion of dealing with "complex regulatory issues," while also supporting the multilateral trading system and "championing international approaches" in bilateral agreements: the EU stated its intention to refer "as much as possible to internationally agreed standards (or at least plurilateral processes) and thereby use bilateral agreements as a lever to pull our partners towards these international set ups" (European Commission 2013, 1, 13).

More recently, the EU has restated its emphasis on international standards and set objectives. The EU Global Strategy emphasized the EU's commitment "to ensure that all its trade agreements are pursued in a manner that supports returning the World Trade Organization (WTO) to the center of global negotiations," while also promoting "international regulatory standards" (European Union 2016, 41).

In all, this shows that since 2006 the EU trade policy has been increasingly attentive to regulatory barriers to trade and has devised different strategies to moderate or narrow these differences in its external trade relations. These range from exporting or assuring compatibility with its own standards to regulatory convergence and cooperation.

The standardization patterns in trade facilitation and intellectual property seem to follow this approach. They do not refer to EU norms and regulations, and MERCOSUR countries are not to adopt EU rules. Rather, standardization pins regulatory convergence to existing international rules and regulations as established by multilateral organizations and bodies (Young 2015, 1268), as in the case of the WTO for trade facilitation and WTO-TRIPS and the Doha Declaration on public health for the area of intellectual property and patents. In this respect, it is worth mentioning that, after years of crisis, the WTO managed to pass the first multilateral agreement in 2014—the Trade Facilitation Agreement, which entered into force in 2017.

In the case of patents, the EU-MERCOSUR agreement also pushes for regulatory coordination as it requires the ratification of existing agreements (Young 2015, 1262), as in the case of the Patent Cooperation Treaty (PCT). However, the agreement does not establish binding obligations and only requires countries to make their "best efforts" to sign the PCT under WIPO. While all EU member states are party to the PCT, only Brazil is a member. The PCT has yet to be signed by Argentina (though a member of WIPO since 1980), Paraguay (not a member of WIPO), and Uruguay (a member since 1979).

These findings are in line with empirical studies showing that, despite the EC's declaratory claims, and even expected outcomes based on the EU-as-a-global-regulator literature (see, inter alia, Damro 2012; Drezner 2007), the EU has not managed to "export" its regulatory standards in the new generation of FTAs (Theisinger 2021; Young 2015). Furthermore, contrary to the agreements with countries that are applying or intend to apply for full membership to the bloc, the EU has not really tried to export its own standards and regulations through these agreements (Young 2015). The EU has more readily attempted regulatory convergence on international standards and regulatory coordination, though to a lesser extent.

Two factors account for this. First, aggressive attempts to export its own rules may give way to opposition to the required regulatory changes in the negotiating partners, and this, in turn, could threaten the establishment of agreements that, in principle, could benefit European businesses (Young 2015). Second, the idea of the EU as global regulator, both coherent and efficient, is mostly based on its market power. However, the extent to which the EU can influence regulatory outcomes in trade agreements is also dependent on the partner's power, and even its preferences. In all, context also matters.

Since the EU-MERCOSUR negotiations have been the longest trade negotiations, these twenty lengthy years of negotiations have provided an institutional setting in which interactions occur, promoting communication, socialization, and persuasion. Participation in trade negotiations has promoted a learning-by-doing process (Bianculli 2017). This process has opened a space in which different state and societal actors, operating at the national and (inter)regional levels, promote, negotiate, and contest not only trade liberalization rules but also regulatory frameworks reaching into economic, social, and political domains.

Trade facilitation was part of the agenda of the EU-MERCOSUR Bi-regional Negotiations Committee (BNC), the main negotiating body between the EU and MERCOSUR.[7] Based on the idea that trade facilitation was one of the most relevant requirements achieved already in 2004, with the relaunch of interregional negotiations in 2010, the issue gained space in the BNC's agenda. That same year, MERCOSUR agreed to their Common Customs Code, leading in turn to further progress in the interregional arena in terms of customs and trade facilitation as the EU and MERCOSUR clarified positions and exchanged proposals in this area in October 2012 (Bianculli 2016). Shortly after negotiations were resumed in 2016, both parties had "practically an agreed text on: customs and trade facilitation" and the "text was closed with the exception for some horizontal issues" (European Commission 2017, 2). The business sector had been actively involved in the discussions on customs and trade facilitation since 2002 (Bianculli 2016).

This has not been the case with intellectual property. During the initial negotiation rounds, MERCOSUR had already systematically rejected opening negotiations on this front as required by the EU and proposed a "bi-regional dialogue" on the matter instead. The Southern bloc assumed that "the EU would aim at imposing TRIPS-plus obligations as a trade-off for agricultural market access" (Blasetti and Correa 2021, 5). This same stance was maintained in 2010: even if a Working Group on Intellectual Property, Geographical Indications and Wines and Spirits was set and met, no proposal was discussed as required by MERCOSUR countries for the relaunch of negotiations.

In 2016, negotiations were reopened again, and the EU presented a proposal for a chapter on intellectual property which included higher standards and regulations than multilateral ones (i.e., TRIPS) (Blasetti 2020). One year later, MERCOSUR finally agreed to negotiate this chapter based on its own proposal, which incorporated the discussion of the WIPO Development Agenda, including, among other issues, access to health (Blasetti 2020). Public health was already part of the MERCOSUR agenda in 2004 (EU-MERCOSUR 2004). In fact, that same year, Argentina and Brazil submitted the first proposal for the establishment of a development agenda for WIPO. Interregional negotiations on intellectual property were then "accomplished in record time, despite the parties' widely different perspectives" (Blasetti and Correa 2021, 5).

The final agreement turned out to be quite balanced for both parties. MERCOSUR accepted the inclusion of a chapter on intellectual property and patents but managed to incorporate the protection of public health in the agreement, along with that of universal access to medicines. This outcome is very much the result of a long-standing consensus within MERCOSUR in relation to the negative impact the interregional agreement could have if it allowed the extension of patents beyond the limits set in the WTO-TRIPS as required by the EU. Thus, MERCOSUR succeeded in keeping this "red line" as a negotiating strategy built upon the concerns of the private sector and civil society—non-governmental organizations and experts (Aoun et al. 2020; Blasetti and Correa 2021; Ghiotto and Echaide 2019).

In all, the resulting agreement is the only non-binding text signed by the EU—it only provides for "best efforts" for the PCT and not its ratification—and one of the least ambitious in terms of TRIPS-plus commitments (Aoun et al. 2020). In exchange, however, the EU achieved the most exceptional protection for geographical indications since regulations in this area imply much higher standards of protection than the TRIPS agreement. Negotiations in this area are not closed and will proceed on a bilateral basis with each of the MERCOSUR countries and remains a challenge for the bloc.

Conclusion

The Agreement in Principle and the different chapters are not the final documents. These texts must go through the legal scrubbing process and translation into the various official languages of the two regional actors. Additionally, it is still to be determined whether the FTA will be split from the other components of the association agreement; this affects the validation procedures to be applied, which remain unclear. Moreover, the ratification process may take several years. In fact, such processes may take up to three years in the EU. In all, it is difficult to foresee when a final agreement will be signed and what this would finally look like. The analysis presented in this chapter is based on the currently available documents as published by the EC.

The analytical narrative shows that interregional negotiations on trade facilitation and intellectual property, especially in terms of patents and health, have resulted in different standardization patterns. Both areas are structured around multilateral agreements and regulations, while also including novel standardization material, as shown by the request for transparency and consultation in trade facilitation. Intellectual property even goes further by explicitly committing to economic and social welfare and introducing a public interest dimension.

To fully understand these noteworthy outcomes, this chapter proposes a long-term perspective assessing ideas and preferences in trade and regulatory standards across time and policy areas. Thus, it emphasizes the relevance of comparative and international political economy to also capture the interaction dynamics across different levels of regulation: regional, interregional, and multilateral/global.

Notes

1. This chapter is part of the "Rethinking the Fundamentals of Regions and Interregionalism: The European Union and Latin America Through the Lenses of Regional Regulatory Governance" project (Reg-EULAC), which is funded by the Spanish Ministry of Science and Innovation (PID2019-105997GB-I00).
2. Similarly, in 2016, the EU launched negotiations with Mexico to modernize the free trade agreement, and two years later, they reached an Agreement in Principle.
3. Therefore, "the EU-MERCOSUR FTA [free trade agreement] does not have a separate chapter on investment including investment protection standards or an investor state dispute settlement mechanism but covers some market access provisions in the services and establishment chapter. General rules on e-commerce can also be found there. There is a chapter on trade and sustainable development (TSD) but none on anti-corruption or trade and gender equality" (Grieger 2019, 5).
4. These include the WTO, the WCO, and the United Nations Conference on Trade and Development.
5. In the Trade part of the EU-MERCOSUR Association Agreement—Protocol on Mutual Administrative Assistance in Customs Matters, it is agreed that: "In respect to the applicability and implementation of this Protocol, the Parties shall consult each other to resolve the matter in the framework of the [Committee on Customs, Rules of Origin and Trade Facilitation, set up under Article XXX of this Agreement] (Art. 17, 8)." Similarly, the Trade part of the EU-MERCOSUR Association Agreement— Protocol on Rules of Origin, refers to this committee as a relevant actor and mechanism in relation to consultations (art. 26, 16).
6. The MERCOSUR Trade Facilitation Agreement was approved in December 2019; its provisions are more ambitious than those agreed multilaterally in the WTO Trade Facilitation Agreement (Herreros 2020).
7. The BNC is made up of Council members, members of the EC's General Directorates for Trade and Foreign Affairs, and the foreign ministers of MERCOSUR countries.

References

Aggarwal, V., and E. Fogarty. 2005. "The Limits of Interregionalism: The EU and North America." *Journal of European Integration* 27 (3): pp. 327–346.

Aoun, A., A. Barrenechea, R. Blasetti, M. Cortese, G. Gette, N. Hermida, J. A. Kors, V. Lowenstein, and G. E. Vidaurreta. 2020. *Estudio Preliminar del Capítulo Sobre Propiedad Intelectual del Acuerdo MERCOSUR—UE*. Research Paper No. 110. Geneva: South Centre.

Bianculli, A.C. 2016. "Regulatory Governance Regimes and Interregionalism: Exploring the Dynamics of EU-Mercosur Negotiations." *Canadian Journal of Latin American and Caribbean Studies* 41 (2): pp. 173–196.

Bianculli, A. C. 2017. *Negotiating Trade Liberalization in Argentina and Chile: When Policy Creates Politics*. New York: Routledge.

Bianculli, A. C. 2021. "Regulatory Cooperation and International Relations." *Oxford Research Encyclopedia of International Studies*. https://oxfordre.com/internationalstud ies/view/10.1093/acrefore/9780190846626.001.0001/acrefore-9780190846626-e-658.

Blasetti, R. 2020. "Geographical Indications: A Major Challenge for MERCOSUR." *GRUR International* 69 (11): pp. 1113–1122.

Blasetti, R., and J. I. Correa. 2021. *Intellectual Property in the EU–MERCOSUR FTA: A Brief Review of the Negotiating Outcomes of a Long-Awaited Agreement*. Research Paper No. 128. Geneva: South Centre.

Börzel, T. A., and T. Risse. 2012. "When Europeanisation Meets Diffusion: Exploring New Territory." *West European Politics* 35 (1): pp. 192–207.

Botto, M., and A. C. Bianculli. 2011. "Comparative Asymmetric Trade Negotiations in the Southern Cone: FTAA and EU-MERCOSUR. In *Asymmetric Trade Negotiations*, edited by S. Bilal, P. De Lombaerde, and D. Tussie, pp. 83–120. Aldershot, UK: Ashgate.

Cienfuegos, M. 2016. "La anhelada asociación euromercosureña tras quince años de negociaciones." *Revista CIDOB d'Afers Internacionals* no. 112: pp. 225–253.

Commission of the European Communities. 1996. *Community External Trade Policy in the Field of Standards and Conformity Assessment*. Brussels.

Council of the European Union. 2010. *IV EU-Mercosur Summit Joint Communiqué*. Madrid, May 17. Brussels. https://www.consilium.europa.eu/uedocs/cms_data/docs/ pressdata/en/er/114486.pdf.

Damro, C. 2012. "Market Power Europe." *Journal of European Public Policy* 19 (5): pp. 682–699.

De Lombaerde, P., and M. Schulz. 2009. *The EU and World Regionalism: The Makability of Regions in the 21st Century*. Aldershot, UK: Ashgate.

Drezner, D. W. 2007. *All Politics Is Global: Explaining International Regulatory Regimes*. Princeton, NJ: Princeton University Press.

Duina, F. 2004. "Regional Market Building as a Social Process: An Analysis of Cognitive Strategies in NAFTA, the European Union and Mercosur." *Economy and Society* 33 (3): pp. 359–389.

European Commission. 2006. *Global Europe: Competing in the World. A Contribution to the EU's Growth and Jobs Strategy*. Brussels: European Commission External Trade.

European Commission. 2013. *Trade: A Key Source of Growth and Jobs for the EU. Commission Contribution to the European Council of 7–8 February 2013*. Brussels: European Commission.

European Commission. 2017. *Report from the XXVIIIth Round of Negotiations of the Trade Part of the Association Agreement between the European Union and Mercosur*. Brussels: European Commission.

EU-MERCOSUR. 2004. *Twelfth Meeting of the Bi-regional Negotiations Committee—Final Conclusions*. Buenos Aires.

European Union. 2016. *Shared Vision, Common Action: A Stronger Europe: A Global Strategy for the European Union's Foreign and Security Policy*. Brussels: European External Action Service.

Farrell, M. 2009. "EU Policy Towards Other Regions: Policy Learning in the External Promotion of Regional Integration." *Journal of European Public Policy* 16 (8): pp. 1165–1184.

Ghiotto, L., and J. Echaide. 2019. *Analysis of the Agreement between the European Union and the Mercosur*. Berlin: PowerShift e.V. and Anna Cavazzini.

Grieger, G. 2019. *The Trade Pillar of the EU-Mercosur Association Agreement*. Briefing: International Agreements in Progress. Brussels: European Parliamentary Research Service. https://www.europarl.europa.eu/RegData/etudes/BRIE/2019/640 138/EPRS_BRI(2019)640138_EN.pdf.

Herreros, S. 2020. *América Latina y el Caribe y la Asociación de Naciones de Asia Sudoriental: experiencias comparadas en el ámbito de la facilitación del comercio*. Santiago: Economic Commission for Latin America.

Hoekman, B., and B. Shepherd. 2013. "Who Profits from Trade Facilitation Initiatives?" Asia-Pacific Research and Training Network on Trade Working Paper No. 129. Bangkok: United Nations Economic and Social Commission for Asia and the Pacific.

Lall, R. 2015. "Timing as a Source of Regulatory Influence: A Technical Elite Network Analysis of Global Finance." *Regulation & Governance* 9 (2): pp. 125–143.

Lamy, P. 2002. Statement of Commissioner Lamy announcing successful end to negotiations on EU-Chile Association Agreement. IP/02/630. Brussels, April 26.

Lipschutz, R.D., and C. Fogel. 2002. "'Regulation for the Rest of Us?' Global Civil Society and the Privatization of Transnational Regulation." In *The Emergence of Private Authority in Global Governance*, edited by R. B. Hall and T. J. Biersteker, pp. 115–140. Cambridge: Cambridge University Press.

Majone, G. 1994. "The Rise of the Regulatory State in Europe." *West European Politics* 17 (3): pp. 77–101.

Makuc, A., G. Duhalde, and R. Rozemberg. 2015. *La Negociación MERCOSUR-Unión Europea a Veinte Años del Acuerdo Marco de Cooperación: Quo Vadis?* Buenos Aires: Banco Interamericano de Desarrollo.

MercoPress. 2010. "EU Countries Divided over Extent of Agriculture Talks with Mercosur." May 18. https://en.mercopress.com/2010/05/18/eu-countries-divided-over-extent-of-agriculture-talks-with-mercosur.

Nolte, D., and C. C. Ribeiro Neto. 2021. "MERCOSUR and the EU: The False Mirror." *Lua Nova: Revista de Cultura e Política* no. 112: pp. 87–122.

Organisation for Economic Co-operation and Development (OECD). 2012. *Recommendation of the Council on Regulatory Policy and Governance*.

Sanahuja, J. A., and J. D. Rodríguez. 2019. "Veinte años de negociaciones Unión Europea—Mercosur: Del interregionalismo a la crisis de la globalización." *Documentos de Trabajo* No. 13. Fundación Carolina.

Scharpf, F. W. 1999. "Negative and Positive Integration in the Political Economy of European Welfare States." In *Governance in the European Union*, edited by G. Marks, F. W. Scharpf, P. C. Schmitter, and W. Streeck, pp. 15–39. London: SAGE.

Söderbaum, F., and L.Van Langenhove. 2005. "Introduction: The EU as a Global Actor and the Role of Interregionalism." *Journal of European Integration* 27: pp. 249–262.

Theisinger, M. 2021. "New Approaches in the Promotion of EU Standards." In *The Evolving Nature of EU External Relations Law*, edited by W. Th. Douma, C. Eckes, P. Van Elsuwege, E. Kassoti, A. Ott, and R. A. Wessel, pp. 19–40. The Hague: T. M. C. Asser Press.

World Trade Organization (WTO). 1994. Agreement on Trade-Related Aspects of Intellectual Property Rights (unamended). https://www.wto.org/english/docs_e/lega l_e/27-trips_01_e.htm.

World Trade Organization (WTO). n.d. "Trade Facilitation." https://www.wto.org/engl ish/tratop_e/tradfa_e/tradfa_e.htm#II.

Young, A. R. 2015. "Liberalizing Trade, Not Exporting Rules: The Limits to Regulatory Co-ordination in the EU's 'New Generation' Preferential Trade Agreements." *Journal of European Public Policy* 22 (9): pp. 1253–1275.

Young, A. R., and J. Peterson. 2006. "The EU and the New Trade Politics." *Journal of European Public Policy* 13 (6): pp. 795–814.

8

Conflicting Standards of Sustainable Biofuel in the EU-ASEAN Trade Negotiations

Daniela Sicurelli

Introduction

The European Union (EU) has historically used its trade power as a foreign policy tool, but its ambition to emerge as a "power through trade" has clearly emerged especially since the first decade of the twenty-first century, when the EU started negotiating comprehensive trade agreements. According to Meunier and Nicolaïdis (2006), the EU has increasingly used access to its large market as a bargaining chip to promote principles and standards in the negotiations with its trading partners. As Postnikov (Chapter 5 of this volume) has demonstrated, the chapters on sustainable development included in all the new-generation trade agreements of the EU show the commitment of the Union to building its own international identity as a green power and to gain external legitimacy. Several studies have investigated the attempt of the EU to promote environmental standards through trade agreements and, more precisely, in the field of climate change (Bastiaens and Postnikov 2017; Carrapatoso 2011; Silander 2022). While the self-representation of the EU as an environmental leader and normative power is indeed an aspect of the EU's identity-building process (von Lucke et al. 2021; Wunderlich 2020), the strategy of the EU can also be read under rationalist lenses. Literature on the EU's attempt to use trade agreements to export its stringent environmental standards has emphasized the influence of protectionist interests. Examples of these standards include those applied to

Daniela Sicurelli, *Conflicting Standards of Sustainable Biofuel in the EU-ASEAN Trade Negotiations* In: *Standardizing the World*. Edited by: Francesco Duina and Crina Viju-Miljusevic, Oxford University Press. © Oxford University Press 2023. DOI: 10.1093/oso/9780197681886.003.0009 pesticides (LaForce 2014), genetically modified organisms (GMOs) (Schulze and Tosun 2016), and fisheries (Mcneill 2021).

This chapter focuses on a case of a failed attempt by the EU to play the role of environmental standard-setter, regarding the promotion of standards of sustainable biofuel in its trade negotiations. The attempt of the EU to lead by example in promoting its own standards of biofuels sustainability in the trade negotiations has raised the attention of international political economy scholars (Afionis and Stringer 2012; Fischer and Meyer 2020; Poletti and Sicurelli 2016; Renckens et al. 2017). In 2009, with the Renewable Energy Directive (RED), the EU adopted the strictest standards of sustainability and applied those standards to imported biofuels as well. In so doing, the EU aspired to set the incentives for foreign firms to adjust to EU sustainability criteria and push their governments to adopt the EU-sponsored standards. Under this point of view, one should expect that the perspective of having access to a large market such as that of the EU would persuade its trading partners of the necessity to endorse those sustainability standards. So far, though, the EU has failed in its attempt to export those standards in its relations with the US and Brazil, the world's largest producers of ethanol and biodiesel (Renckens et al. 2017). Moreover, it was not able to reach an agreement on biofuel sustainability standards in the trade negotiations with palm oil–producing countries. By focusing on negotiations with the largest producers of palm oil, Indonesia and Malaysia, this chapter aims to investigate the reasons for such resistance to EU standards.

According to Renckens et al. (2017) and Kupzok (2020), one of the reasons for the weakness of EU leadership in this field is the fragile legitimacy of European sustainability criteria in a field which is subject to epistemic contestation. As these authors emphasize, EU targets and criteria are based on weak scientific evidence and, therefore, are largely questionable. Furthermore, accusations against the attempt of the EU to use sustainability standards as an instrument to restrict biofuel imports have led to a widespread perception of the lack of credibility of the EU as a promoter of development cooperation through trade.

This chapter provides a complementary explanation of the failure of the EU attempt to promote its sustainability criteria. It argues that a political economy perspective accounts for the failure of the European strategy to promote sustainability standards as part of comprehensive trade agreements with Malaysia and Indonesia. The protectionist implications of EU standards on Asian palm oil, the centrality of palm oil as an export good for Indonesia and Malaysia economies, and the low dependency of those partners on the EU as a trade partner have reduced the bargaining power of the latter in the negotiations. The open dispute over the World Trade Organization (WTO) compatibility of European sustainability criteria has further challenged the self-attributed image of the EU as a global leader in the promotion of sustainable development.

This chapter is structured as follows. The next section specifies the method used for the empirical analysis, followed by a section that compares the conflicting sustainability standards adopted in the EU and in the two palm oil–producing countries. The subsequent section traces the attempt of the EU to include biofuel sustainability standards in the trade negotiations with the two countries. The final section provides a political economy explanation for the reasons why the strategy of the EU did not succeed.

Method

As the introduction of this volume has clarified, in its trade relations, the EU engages in the international promotion of standards that can have either a definitional or a normative dimension (or both). This chapter considers both dimensions. Throughout the trade negotiations with Malaysia and Indonesia, the EU has promoted both a definition of green energy and of risks associated to specific sources of energy for the environment, on the one hand, and binding prescriptions to produce sustainable energy, on the other.

The selection of cases (trade agreements with Malaysia and Indonesia launched in 2010 and 2016, respectively) is based on the relevance of those countries for biofuel production since they produce 80 percent of the world's palm oil. Since the late 1990s, palm oil has been increasingly used as a source for biodiesel, a form of renewable energy intended to tackle global warming. Given the centrality of climate change governance as a venue for the identity-building process of the EU as a normative leader and, at the same time, the interests of European biofuel producers in protecting their industry, trade agreements with the two Asian countries represent crucial cases for the emergence of the Union as a standard-setter. The trade agreement that the EU concluded in 2015 with another ASEAN country, Vietnam, is considered both as confirmation of the ambition of the EU to emerge as a standard-setter in the field of sustainable biofuel and as a reference for identifying the negotiating options with Malaysia and Indonesia. The reason beyond the selection of Vietnam as a reference case is that, according to the European Commission, the trade agreement the EU has concluded with the country is meant to be a template for future trade agreements with ASEAN members. Trade commissioner Cecilia Malmström explained that the EU-Vietnam trade agreement represents a "stepping stone" for Europe's trade agreements in Southeast Asia, "paving the way" for a future interregional trade agreement (Valero 2018).

The chapter discusses data from secondary and primary sources. The time frame under consideration is 2009–2022, which coincides with the adoption of stringent sustainability standards in the EU and the subsequent promotion of those standards in the trade negotiations with Malaysia and Indonesia. The chapter compares the standards of biofuel sustainability adopted by the EU, Malaysia, and Indonesia, analyzing the EU environmental directives and delegated acts, on the one hand, and the sustainability criteria of the Roundtable on Sustainable Palm Oil (RSPO) and the Indonesian Sustainable Palm Oil (ISPO) certification schemes, respectively recognized by the two Asian countries, on the other hand.

In order to trace the effort of the EU to promote sustainability standards, this chapter analyzes the content of sustainability impact assessments carried out by the Directorate-General for Trade (DG Trade) for supporting trade negotiations with the two countries, the text of the partnership and cooperation agreements (PCAs) concluded with the same countries, press releases, and newspaper articles.

Moreover, the chapter captures the motivations for opposition to EU standards by carrying out an analysis of the discourse of Indonesian and Malaysian governments, based on press releases, newspaper articles, and WTO documents. Finally, in order to explain the lack of success of the EU in exporting its green energy standards, the chapter complements the analysis of the position of Asian leaders with an analysis of data concerning trade flows and trade dependency from EU and World Bank documents.

European and Asian Standards of Sustainable Biofuel

Since 2009, after a decade of global consensus on the representation of biofuels as a relevant instrument to tackle global warming, the EU has emerged as a staunch defender of the idea that even renewable energy can be unsustainable and that not all biofuels contribute to the fight against climate change. Based on this assumption, the EU has adopted the most stringent standards worldwide on sustainable biodiesel. What is more relevant for the purposes of this chapter is that those standards are not compatible with standards recognized in Asian countries. This section compares the standards of sustainable biofuel the EU aims to promote in the trade deals with the standards upheld by Indonesia and Malaysia.

EU Standards of Sustainable Biofuel

By the end of the 1990s, international organizations, and the EU itself, considered biofuels a solution to the problem of climate change. Based on new scientific evidence, EU biofuel policy went through a "full normative turn" (Kupzok 2020) in 2009, when the EU stated that biofuels that do not fulfill given sustainability criteria may represent a potential threat for the environment.

Since the end of the 1990s, biofuels entered the agenda of EU environmental policy as a promising alternative energy to oil and fossil fuel. This source of energy found large support since it is renewable and competitive due to its low production costs. Based on these considerations, in the first decade of the twenty-first century, the EU heavily invested in cereals and sugar beet for the production of biofuels and in research for improving production of more efficient and convenient biofuels. Such an investment in domestic sources of biofuel was also consistent with the aim of EU farmers to protect European rapeseed and biodiesel producers from cheaper imported ethanol. As a matter of fact, by 2010, the EU imposed high EU tariffs on Brazilian ethanol imports (Afionis et al. 2016; Renckens et al. 2017). In 2003, the Council of the EU and the European Parliament approved the so-called biofuels directive, namely Directive 2003/30, on the promotion of the use of biofuels or other renewable fuels for transport. The directive aimed at promoting the production of biofuels and set the target of 2 percent for the market share of biofuels by December 2005 and 5.75 percent by December 2010. Furthermore, in 2006, the European Commission's (2006, 5) strategy for biofuels further clarified the opportunity of a transition to biofuel, stating, "Replacing a percentage of diesel or petrol with biofuels is [. . .] the simplest way for the transport sector to make an immediate contribution to the Kyoto targets, particularly given that the benefits would apply to the entire vehicle fleet."

This policy, though, raised the opposition of environmental non-governmental organizations (NGOs) (EEB 2005; WWF 2006) and scientists concerned about the potential consequences of massive biofuel production for deforestation. A report of the Joint Research Centre of the European Commission (Edwards et al. 2008) questioned the contribution of biofuels to emissions reduction and warned against its potential impact on one of the main causes of climate change, namely deforestation. In this respect, it claimed that uncertainty on the risks of deforestation associated with biofuel production question the effectiveness of the targets established by the biofuel directive as instruments to tackle global warming. These critical positions also raised support among business groups representing European biofuel producers. The latter had competing interests with biofuel imported by countries where biofuel production, especially in the sector of palm oil, is considered responsible for high deforestation rates (Fischer and Meyer 2020).

The RED (2009) addressed those concerns and established a distinction between sustainable and unsustainable biofuels and set the criteria to define acceptable biofuels. On the one hand, according to the directive, the use of biofuels has to produce at least 35 percent emission savings compared to fossil fuels (50 percent from 2007 onward and 60 percent from 2008 onward). On the other hand, biofuels should not be produced from raw materials grown on land with high biodiversity value with a high carbon stock (such as forests) and peatland. Thus, the directive introduced a new definition of green and sustainable energy. It prescribed that, besides being extracted through renewable sources, green energy should be produced through processes that do not contribute to deforestation and that do not harm biodiversity.

Finally, the directive stated that these criteria apply both to biofuels produced in the EU and to imported ones. Such a clarification set the legal groundwork for the EU's effort to emerge as a promoter of standards beyond its borders. By anticipating the potential criticism for the protectionist undertones of those standards, and, therefore, the likely dispute against those norms in the framework of the WTO, the EU proactively engaged in promoting the distinction between sustainable and non-sustainable biofuels in the context of the multilateral negotiations of the Doha Round and of the preferential trade negotiations with single trade partners.

In the revised Renewable Energy Directive 2018/2001/EU (the so-called RED II), it further distinguishes between low- and high-risk biofuels. It started addressing the indirect land-use change (ILUC) effects of an increasing use of biofuel, namely the effects of conversion of forest land for palm oil plantations. ILUC would ultimately determine whether biofuels can be considered more sustainable than fossil fuels. Besides defining the conditions for biofuel to be considered sustainable, the sustainability standards included in the directive also had a normative dimension. The EU introduced a cap for conventional biofuels, namely biofuel produced on agricultural land, and adopted a risk-based approach, where the definition of risk is broad enough to account for the uncertainty in calculations of ILUC effects. The directive prescribed that biofuels produced from feedstocks with high ILUC risks must be phased out by 2030. Finally, the EU member states and the European Parliament issued a delegated act of the revised RED in 2019 (European Commission 2019a) which set out the criteria for determining high-ILUC-risk feedstock for biofuels and for certifying low-ILUC-risk biofuels, bioliquids, and biomass fuels.

Asian Standards of Sustainable Biofuel

Southeast Asia is the region where most of the global production of palm oil originates. Indonesia is the first producer worldwide of crude palm oil, followed by Malaysia and Thailand, respectively, the second and third producers (Statista 2022) (see Figure 8.1). As a matter of fact, palm oil is one

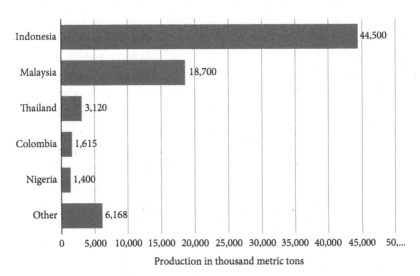

Figure 8.1 Leading producers of palm oil worldwide, 2021–2022 (in 1,000 metric tons).
Source: Statista (2022).

Table 8.1 Criteria for Environmental Sustainability of Biofuel

	European Union	RSPO	ISPO
Status	Binding targets	Voluntary standards	Legally mandatory certification
Scope	Regulation of indirect land-use change (ILUC) risk	No regulation of ILUC	No regulation of ILUC
Obligation/Incentive	Biofuels produced from feedstocks with high ILUC risks will be phased out by 2030	Market price premium for sustainable biofuel	License to operate for sustainable biofuel

of the biggest industries in the region. The governments of Southeast Asian countries do recognize the need to comply with sustainability standards and to produce green energy, but they rely on different sustainability criteria and certification schemes (see Table 8.1).

The RSPO is the first and most influential international multi-stakeholder organization that originated in 2004 following demands of international environmental NGOs, such as the World Wide Fund for Nature (WWF), with the purpose of tackling the negative consequences for the environment of the growing global demand for palm oil. The origins of the RSPO were also explicitly linked with the emerging global consensus on the United Nations Millennium Development Goals, which set the global goal of pursuing environmental sustainability. The RSPO is a "voluntary business initiative whose members agree to a process of certification [. . .] with the aim of producing and using sustainable palm oil. Plantation practices must adhere to these principles of following applicable laws and regulations that focus on environmental sustainability, planning, and implementation for the long-term socio-economic wellbeing and continuous improvement of the sector" (Suharto et al. 2015). The membership of RSPO includes business groups (oil palm producers, processors and traders, consumer goods manufacturers, retailers, banks, and investors) and NGOs. The secretariat of the RSPO is in Kuala Lumpur. The Malaysian Palm Association is a member of the RSPO; nevertheless, the RSPO membership is de facto dominated by European companies and NGOs (Choiruzzad et al. 2021).

In March 2011, the government of Indonesia also established its own national certification scheme, ISPO. The new regime originated as a critical reaction to the predominance of European companies and organizations in the RSPO (Choiruzzad et al. 2021). Unlike the RSPO, which is a voluntary scheme, ISPO is a government regulation and imposes binding norms. Adhering to ISPO standards is mandatory for all Indonesian palm oil plantations and mills, while it is voluntary for smallholders. The ISPO regulation was updated in the 2015 reform, which led to what is now called the Indonesian Sustainable Palm Oil Certification System.

In contrast to EU sustainability standards, RSPO and ISPO do not regulate the effects of ILUC.

The Controversy on Sustainable Biofuel in the EU-ASEAN Trade Negotiations

The EU has tackled the implications of trade agreements for sustainable development since 1999, when the European Commission started carrying out sustainability impact assessment exercises on the potential economic, social, and environmental implications of trade negotiations (Kirkpatrick and George 2006). It was in the following decade, though, that the EU adopted a more assertive position on the trade and environment nexus. All the trade agreements concluded by the EU since 2009 have a chapter devoted to sustainable development, which calls on the parties to adhere to environmental and labor norms.

Moreover, given the comprehensive nature of the trade agreements negotiated by the EU since 2009, trade deals are commonly framed into more explicitly political agreements that are usually titled PCAs or Framework agreements. These political agreements contain provisions on sustainable development and may include reference to cooperation in specific sectors, such as green energy. Even though trade agreements tend to integrate broader political agreements, the legal relationship between the two types of agreements varies according to the partner (see Table 8.2). The PCAs with Singapore, Vietnam, and Malaysia, for instance, contain a clause that establishes that the PCA will be an integral part of the overall bilateral relations, while the PCA with Indonesia lacks such a clear linkage with the trade agreement.

Following two years of interregional negotiations, the EU launched trade negotiations with single Association of Southeast Asian Nations (ASEAN) member states in 2009. By coincidence, negotiations with Indonesia and Malaysia started just after the reform of EU biofuel policy that led to stringent

Table 8.2 Sustainable Biofuels in the PCAs among the EU, Vietnam, Malaysia, and Indonesia

	EU-Indonesia PCA (2014)	EU-Malaysia PCA (2015)	EU-Vietnam PCA
Institutional linkage with the trade agreement	No: Art. 43: "neither this Agreement nor action taken hereunder shall in any way affect the powers of the Member States to undertake bilateral cooperation activities with Indonesia."	Yes: Art. 52: "The present Agreement shall be an *integral part of the* [...] *overall bilateral relations* as governed by the Framework Agreement."	Yes: Art. 55: "Existing agreements relating to specific areas of cooperation falling within the scope of this Agreement shall be considered *part of the overall bilateral relations* as governed by this Agreement and as forming part of a *common institutional framework*."
Distinction between sustainable and unsustainable biofuels	No: No mention of biofuels.	No: Art. 36: Parties should cooperate to develop "new, sustainable, innovative and renewable forms of energy, including biofuels."	Yes: Art. 42: Parties should cooperate to "develop new innovative and renewable forms of energy, including *sustainable biofuels*."

sustainability standards. While promoting sustainability standards through trade negotiations, the EU has tried to reach an agreement on the same topic with the same members in the framework of the talks for PCAs.

When negotiations with Malaysia started (2010), the European Commission stressed the need to improve cooperation with the country on the definition of sustainable biofuel. Its mandate for negotiating the trade agreement made explicit reference to tariff barriers on biofuels. The draft chapter on sustainable development proposed by the EU referred to the implications of trade of biofuels. Similarly, the annex on Malaysia in the sustainability assessment of the trade agreement with ASEAN (European Commission 2011) highlighted the lack of compliance with sustainability criteria by Malaysian biofuel companies. On September 11, 2013, the European Parliament resolution containing recommendations for a PCA with Malaysia included a call for sustainable biofuel avoiding deforestation.

The EU, however, was not able to promote a commitment to developing sustainable biofuel in the PCAs with Indonesia (2014) and Malaysia (2015), while it succeeded to include a reference to sustainable biofuel in the PCA with Vietnam (2016). The PCA with Indonesia calls on the two parties to cooperate on sustainable forest management but does not refer to biofuel. According to the agreement, "The Parties agree on the need to protect, conserve, and manage in a sustainable manner forest resources and their biological diversity for the benefit of current and future generations. The Parties endeavor to continue their cooperation to improve forest and land fire management, combating illegal logging and its associated trade, forest governance, and the promotion of sustainable forest management" (EU 2015, art. 28).

The Council Decision of the EU on the signing of a PCA with Malaysia concluded in 2018 explicitly requires "cooperation for developing sustainable forms of energy, including biofuels," but does not distinguish between sustainable and unsustainable biofuels (EU 2018, art. 36).

The EU-Vietnam PCA, instead, distinguishes sustainable biofuels from unsustainable ones and states that "Parties agree to enhance cooperation in the energy sector with a view to diversifying energy supplies in order to improve energy security, and develop new innovative and renewable forms of energy, including sustainable biofuels" (EU 2016, art. 42).

The EU, though, reiterated its call on Indonesia to agree on criteria of sustainable palm oil in the second Joint Committee which took place in Brussels in 2017. In regard to the environment and climate change, as a result of the Joint Committee, the two parties "see the pursuit of the Sustainable Development Goals and actions to mitigate climate change as important objectives" and "are exploring concrete cooperation on the implementation of Nationally Determined Contribution (NDC), forestry and environment, including sustainable palm oil and social forestry" (European Union External Action 2017). At the same time, though, DG Trade expressed its concern for the implications for climate change of palm oil production in the sustainable impact assessment (SIA) with the two countries. It issued the "Sustainability Impact Assessments in support of Free Trade Agreement negotiations between the European Union and Malaysia Draft Inception Report" in 2018, where it criticized Malaysian biofuel policy, reporting that Friends of the Earth Malaysia (Sahabat Alam Malaysia) has collaborated with Friends of the Earth from other countries to "reject the state's claims on palm oil's carbon footprint and the impact of deforestation on minority communities" (DG Trade 2018). In the same report, it stated: "Between 1990 and 2014, the expansion of palm oil cultivation has increased to nearly five million hectares, significantly reducing peat land and rainforests in Malaysia" (DG Trade 2018, 108). Finally, in 2019, the EU published the SIA in support of the trade agreement with Indonesia, where it expressed concern "with regard to working conditions, and environmental issues including deforestation" (European Commission 2019b, 12).

Trade negotiations with Indonesia and Malaysia are still ongoing. Divergences with the EU concerning the criteria of sustainability and what the governments of the two countries have called "crop apartheid" (Reuters 2018) in reference to the EU's de facto ban against palm oil represent one of the major obstacles to concluding the deals.

While trade negotiations with the two Asian partners are still ongoing, one may safely conclude that the EU did not succeed in its attempt to export its biofuel sustainability norms. The EU has indeed contributed to put the issue of sustainable biofuel on the agenda of Asian governments, but did not prove effective in its attempt to include its prescriptions for sustainable sourcing of palm oil in trade agreements. In fact, the Indonesian government established ISPO primarily as a reaction to the European attempt to promote sustainability standards throughout the trade negotiations. Nevertheless, the EU was ultimately unable to promote its criteria of sustainable biofuels in the trade negotiations with Indonesia and Malaysia. Alternative models to that of the EU found greater support among international partners. Most notably, the Chinese government, with WWF China, the Carbon Disclosure Project, and the RSPO, launched the China Sustainable Palm Oil Alliance, which supports Indonesian and Malaysia interpretations of sustainable biofuel and remarks once again that the EU is not taking the lead in shaping international sustainability norms in the palm oil sector (Business and Human Rights Resource Centre 2019). According to Hai (2013), it was the RSPO, instead, that seemed to emerge as a benchmark for international standards of sustainable palm oil. Most notably, the Chinese government is currently discussing the possibility of localizing the RSPO's sustainability standards (Yifan 2021).

Explaining Resistance to EU Standards

Ideational explanations of the resistance of trade partners to EU standards have pointed to the lack of legitimacy of EU standards, due to the ambiguous concept of ILUC and the difficulty of measuring the risks associated with it (Kupzok 2020; Renckens et al. 2017). Another possible ideational explanation is based on the inner lack of coherence between EU biofuel sustainability norms with the development cooperation aims of EU trade policy. Finally, opposition to the EU sustainability standards may also have identity and nationalist connotations and reflect the anti-colonial sentiment of Southeast Asian countries (Nessel 2021).

Analysis of the discourse of leaders of the Indonesian and Malaysian governments confirms these hypotheses. The ideational explanation alone does account for the lack of authoritativeness of EU standards and the lack of credibility of the latter as a norm promoter, but it does not explain why, by opposing sustainability norms, trade negotiators have accepted the risk of undermining the conclusion of the comprehensive agreement with the EU.

A political economy explanation complements the ideational reading and helps explain the refusal of the Malaysian and Indonesian governments to endorse the EU-sponsored standards. This explanation sheds light on the conflicting interests of European and Asian biofuel producers and on the way the low dependency of those countries on trading with the EU has further reduced the bargaining power of the latter in negotiating the comprehensive trade agreements with those countries. The lack of a clear legal framework in the international trade law setting the conditions when environmental concerns should take precedence over free trade provides an opportunity for ASEAN countries to challenge European sustainability criteria under the dispute settlement mechanism of the WTO.

The biofuel sustainability standards adopted by the EU since 2009 hit powerful interest groups in Malaysia and Indonesia. As a matter of fact, while the EU is one of the top biodiesel producers of the world, crude palm oil is listed among the top commodities exported by Indonesia, together with oil and gas, minerals, electrical appliances, and rubber products, and by Malaysia, beside electrical and electronics products, chemicals, petroleum products, and liquefied natural gas.

Indonesian and Malaysian palm oil producers mobilized in order to shape the sustainable development chapter of the trade agreements. As far as Indonesia is concerned, the Vision Group to Enhance Trade and Investment between Indonesia and the EU (Delegation of the European Union and the Government of Indonesia Ministry of Trade 2011, 43), comprising Indonesian and European government, private interests, and academics, expressed the concerns of Indonesian business over "assuring fair access to the trade preferences under the EU's Renewable Energy Directive." Instead of including the EU sustainability standards in the trade agreement, the Indonesian entrepreneur association APINDO (2014) proposed that the EU consider the trade deal as a channel to institutionalize a bilateral dialogue on sustainability. According to the business group, Indonesia should have the opportunity to socialize its palm oil sustainability standards to EU consumers, NGOs, and private sectors. Palm oil producers especially observed that Indonesian standards are less demanding than EU standards and, therefore, argued against the trade barriers imposed by the EU (Damuri et al. 2016). Palm oil also emerged as the key offensive interest for Malaysia since the early stage of the negotiations. For this reason, and due to the heavy involvement of the state in the palm oil industry, Malaysian palm oil exporter interests lobbied the national negotiators and voiced criticism against the sustainability requirements the EU aims at including in the trade agreement (Tham 2012).

In 2017, palm oil imports from Indonesia, Malaysia, and Thailand amounted to three-quarters of EU imports of this type of oil (Copenhagen Economics 2018). Thus, European import competing interests joined a coalition with NGOs to pressure for the inclusion of stringent sustainable development criteria in the trade relations with Asian countries (Fischer and Meyer 2020; Poletti and Sicurelli 2016). When the European Parliament called on the EU to ban imports of biofuel produced by palm oil because of its implications for deforestation in 2018, Indonesia and Malaysia warned that they would retaliate against what amounted, in their view, to protectionist measures. In December 2019, Indonesia requested WTO dispute consultations with the EU concerning the amended RED. Malaysia participated in the dispute against the EU as a third party.

The Indonesian government claimed that EU sustainability measures are not consistent with the WTO's Agreement on Technical Barriers to Trade, the General Agreement on Tariffs and Trade 1994, and the Agreement on Subsidies and Countervailing Measures (WTO 2019b). It further complained that the EU accepted the inclusion of ILUC in assessing the implications of biofuel production for deforestation even recognizing that "ILUC cannot be observed or measured." Furthermore, the delegation of Indonesia to the delegation of the EU pointed out that "[t]he European Union has also acknowledged that 'ILUC emissions cannot be measured with the level of precision required to be included in the EU GHG [greenhouse gas] emission calculation methodology'" (WTO 2019a). According to Indonesian foreign affairs deputy minister Mahendra Siregar, proof of the protectionist undertones of EU green energy policy is that the European criteria of sustainability seem to discriminate against palm oil but do not target other sources of biofuels. The diplomat observed, instead, that "[s]tudy showed rapeseed and soya plantations produce massive pollution on soils, rivers, and seas in their respective regions with the use of pesticides and inorganic fertilizers. They are also destroying biodiversity" (Nada Shofa 2021).

The Malaysian delegation warned that, by discriminating against palm oil producers, EU sustainability criteria "will have significant detrimental effects on palm oil producing countries who depend on this industry to raise the socio-economic wellbeing of their people and to help these nations achieve the United Nation Sustainable Development Goals" (Sapp 2019). The governments of Indonesia and Malaysia further warned that the de facto ban of palm oil in the EU risks undermining the potential for economic development in the two countries, having implications for small landholders who have found in palm oil production a way to fight poverty (Jong 2019). As a compensatory measure, the two governments financially supported smallholders, which further reduced the attractiveness of adhering to the sustainability criteria proposed by the EU for this category of producers (Leng 2022).

The ability of the EU to strategically use access to its attractive market as a bargaining chip to promote sustainability standards in Malaysia and Indonesia is strongly conditioned by the low dependency of those economies on the EU. According to World Bank data referring to 2020, Indonesian trade in goods and services only amounted to 17.5 percent of its gross domestic product (GDP) (World Bank 2022). Furthermore, despite growing attention on the European market and the willingness of the government to negotiate a trade deal with the EU, Indonesia mainly looks to eastern markets. Its strongest trade ties are currently oriented toward Asian countries, namely Japan, China, Singapore, and South Korea. Malaysia is more dependent upon international trade than Indonesia, as its exports in goods and services amount to 61 percent of its GDP. Even in this case, though, the EU is Malaysia's fifth largest trading partner, after China, Singapore, South Korea, and the United States.

Palm oil export to the EU increased exponentially from 2001 to 2012 (see Figure 8.1), which made the EU the second largest palm oil export destination after India for Malaysia and Indonesia (*Euractiv* 2017). At the same time, China started to emerge as an attractive export destination. In 2013, the Indonesian employer association registered an escalation of China's demand for crude palm oil, which counts as one of the two favorite import commodities for Indonesia (APINDO 2013). Two years later, the Malaysian Palm Oil Council and China Chamber of Commerce of Import and Export of Foodstuffs, Native Produce and Animal By-Products signed the first Memorandum of Understanding on China's import of palm oil from Malaysia. It was only after the European palm oil ban, though, that China replaced it in this prominent role as the second largest destination for Southeast Asian palm oil (Statista 2021). On April 25, 2019, the Malaysian Palm Oil Council and the Chinese Chamber of Commerce signed a second memorandum of understanding, in which China agreed to increase the import of Malaysian palm oil (Bernama 2019).

As the Malaysian plantation industries and commodities minister, Datuk Zuraida Kamaruddin, commented, the EU's refusal to recognize Malaysian and Indonesian standards of sustainable palm oil "is ironic, considering Europe only represents 6.4% of the global palm oil market" (Hazim 2022). Similarly, the European NGO Fern (Speechly and Ozinga 2019) noticed that the EU accounts for an export destination for Indonesian palm oil that is declining in importance, while other major importers, especially China and India, are emerging.

At the time of writing, the dispute in the WTO is still ongoing. According to international lawyers, the decision of the EU to target palm oil seems deliberate and raises doubts concerning the legitimacy of those measures on the basis of environmental considerations (Mayr et al. 2021). The WTO has ruled against the EU in previous environmental and food safety disputes, most notably in the beef hormone (1998) and GMO cases (2006). A ruling of the WTO Dispute Settlement Body against the EU environmental standards in the biofuels case would further undermine the ability of the Union to emerge as a global standard-setter through trade.

Conclusion

The attempt of the EU to export its rules and emerge as a standard-setter in the field of sustainable biofuel in its relations with palm oil–producing countries has failed so far. The EU did contribute to the growing international attention on the risks of deforestation associated with this source of biofuel, but was not able to export its sustainability norms even though it used the access to its market as a carrot. The reasons for such a failure can be mainly found in the diverging interests of biofuel producers in Europe and in the Asian countries and in the low trade dependency of Malaysia and Indonesia on the EU.

These countries have found an institutional channel to pursue their opposition to the protectionist undertones of EU standards in the WTO, which agreed to Indonesia's request to establish a panel examining EU law on the import of palm oil–based biofuels. The recent conciliatory approach adopted by the EU in promoting an EU and ASEAN Joint Working Group on palm oil, which met for the first time in January 2021, seems to suggest that the Union has recently opted to engage in a dialogue with palm oil–producing countries and to support, with capacity-building, sustainability efforts and practices of local palm oil producers. Even though it does not represent a second U-turn in the EU biofuel policy, this new cooperative approach seems based on the recognition that, in light of WTO norms on non-discrimination, the EU should accept to support the implementation of Malaysian and Indonesian standards rather than imposing regulatory barriers to importation.

Negotiations on sustainable biofuel allow for generalizations concerning the ability of the EU to promote stringent sustainability standards in trade agreements. The cases considered in this chapter suggest that low trade dependency on the EU empowers offensive interest groups in its trade partners and ultimately represents a powerful obstacle for the attempt of the Union to promote sustainability standards in the framework of trade negotiations. The growing attractiveness of China as a trade partner in the region and its emergence as ASEAN's largest two-way trading partner in 2020 is expected to further constrain the ability of the EU to promote regulatory standards in the region. The ruling of the WTO Dispute Settlement Body will clarify whether EU rules are compatible with global international trade law and will affect the legitimacy of the standards the EU promotes in the trade negotiations and, therefore, its ability to act as a standardizer in the broader field of trade and environment.

References

Afionis, S., and L. C. Stringer. 2012. "European Union Leadership in Biofuels Regulation: Europe as a Normative Power?" *Journal of Cleaner Production* 32: pp. 114–123.

Afionis, S., L. C. Stringer, N. Favretto, J. Tomei, and M. S. Buckeridge. 2016. "Unpacking Brazil's Leadership in the Global Biofuels Arena: Brazilian Ethanol Diplomacy in Africa." *Global Environmental Politics* 16 (3): pp. 127–150.

Asosiasi Pengusaha Indonesia (APINDO). 2013. "Indonesia-China Trade in ACFTA: Mapping of Competitiveness and Specialization." Active Working Paper No. 1.

Asosiasi Pengusaha Indonesia (APINDO). 2014. APINDO Position Paper on Indonesia-European Union (EU) Comprehensive Economic Partnership Agreement (CEPA).

Bastiaens, I., and E. Postnikov. 2017. "Greening Up: The Effects of Environmental Standards in EU and US Trade Agreements." *Environmental Politics* 26 (5): pp. 847–869.

Bernama (Malaysian National News Agency). 2019. "New Palm Oil MOU with China Not Extension of Old Agreement under BN." *New Straits Times*, April 30. https://www.nst.com.my/business/2019/04/484283/new-palm-oil-mou-china-not-extension-old-agreement-under-bn.

Business and Human Rights Resource Centre. 2019. "Six Major Brands Join China Sustainable Palm Oil Alliance, Taking Lead in Making Sustainable Palm Oil the Norm." Press Release. October 31. https://www.business-humanrights.org/en/latest-news/six-major-brands-join-china-sustainable-palm-oil-alliance-taking-lead-in-making-sustainable-palm-oil-the-norm/#:~:text=Six%20major%20brands%20are%20now,CDP%20China's%20Forests%20Program%20Manager.

Carrapatoso, A. 2011. "Climate Policy Diffusion: Interregional Dialogue in China–EU relations." *Global Change, Peace & Security* 23 (2): pp. 177–194.

Choiruzzad, S. A. B., A. Tyson, and H. Varkkey. 2021. "The Ambiguities of Indonesian Sustainable Palm Oil Certification: Internal Incoherence, Governance Rescaling and State Transformation." *Asia Europe Journal* 19 (2): pp. 189–208.

Copenhagen Economics. 2018. *EU Imports of Palm Oil from Indonesia, Malaysia and Thailand*. May. https://copenhageneconomics.com/publication/eu-imports-of-palm-oil-from-indonesia-malaysia-and-thailand/.

Damuri, Y. R., R. Atje, and A. Soedjito. 2016. *Study on the Impact of an EU-Indonesia CEPA*. Centre for Strategic and International Studies. http://eeas.europa.eu/archives/delegations/indonesia/documents/more_info/pub_2015csiscepa_en.pdf.

Delegation of the European Union and the Government of Indonesia Ministry of Trade. 2011. *Invigorating the Indonesia-EU Partnership: Towards a Comprehensive Economic Partnership Agreement*. http://eeas.europa.eu/archives/delegations/indonesia/documents/press_corner/20110615_01_en.pdf.

Directorate-General for Trade (DG Trade). 2018. Sustainability Impact Assessments (SIAs) in support of Free Trade Agreement (FTA) negotiations between the European Union and Malaysia. Draft Inception Report. May 25. Brussels. https://circabc.europa.eu/ui/group/09242a36-a438-40fd-a7af-fe32e36cbd0e/library/ea0ad72d-61a3-4324-b9a7-ad6965f66c67/details?download=true.

Edwards, R., S. Szekeres, F. Neuwahl, and V. Mahieu. 2008. *Biofuels in the European Context: Facts and Uncertainties*. European Commission Joint Research Centre. https://www.etipbioenergy.eu/images/jrc_biofuels_report_march_2008.pdf.

Euractiv. 2017. "Palm Oil for Fighter Jets: Under EU Attack, Producers Seek Alternatives." September 13. https://www.euractiv.com/section/biofuels/news/palm-oil-for-fighter-jets-under-eu-attack-producers-seek-alternatives/.

European Union. 2015. Framework Agreement on Compehensive Partnership and Cooperation between the European Community and its Member States, on the one part, and the Republic of Indonesia, of the other Part, 22014A0426(02).

European Union. 2016. Framework Agreement on Comprehensive Partnership and Cooperation between the European Union and its Member States, of the one part, and the Socialist Republic of Viet Nam, of the other part, 22016A1203(02).

European Union. 2018. Council Decision on the signing, on behalf of the European Union, and provisional application of the Framework Agreement on Partnership and Cooperation between the European Union and its Member States, of the one part, and Malaysia, of the other part, 18 September, 10798/18.

European Commission. 2006. Communication from the Commission—an EU Strategy for Biofuels {SEC(2006) 142}. February 8. Brussels. https://op.europa.eu/en/publicat ion-detail/-/publication/be8e2853-075b-4ed3-a0ca-ef3991690714/language-en.

European Commission. 2011. "Commission's Services' Annex on Malaysia to the Position Paper on the Trade Sustainable Impact Assessment of the Free Trade Agreement between the EU and ASEAN." http://trade.ec.europa.eu/doclib/docs/2011/january/tradoc_147337.pdf.

European Commission. 2019a. Commission Delegated Regulation Supplementing Directive (EU) 2018/2001 as regards the determination of high indirect land-use change-risk feedstock for which a significant expansion of the production area into land with high carbon stock is observed and the certification of low indirect land-use change-risk biofuels, bioliquids and biomass fuels. Non legislative act, March 13. Brussels. https://eur-lex.europa.eu/legal-content/EN/TXT/PDF/?uri=CELEX:320 19R0807.

European Commission. 2019b. Sustainability Impact Assessment (SIA) in support of Free Trade Agreement (FTA) negotiations between the European Union and Republic of Indonesia Draft Final Report. April 4. Brussels. https://trade.ec.europa.eu/doclib/docs/2019/april/tradoc_157836.docx.pdf.

European Environmental Bureau (EEB). 2005. EEB Position on Biomass and Biofuels: The Need for Well-Defined Sustainability Criteria. December. http://np-net.pbworks.com/f/EEB+(2005)+Position+on+bioenergy+-+need+for+well+defined+sustainability+criteria.pdf.

European Union External Action. 2017. The EU and Indonesia hold second Joint Committee. Press Release. December 6. https://www.eeas.europa.eu/node/36911_en.

Fischer, C., and T. Meyer. 2020. "Baptists and Bootleggers in the Biodiesel Trade: EU–Biodiesel (Indonesia)." *World Trade Review* 19 (2): pp. 297–315.

Hai, T. C. 2013. "Malaysian Corporations as Strategic Players in Southeast Asia's Palm Oil Industry." In *The Palm Oil Controversy in Southeast Asia: A Transnational Perspective*, edited by O. Pye and J. Bhattacharya, pp. 19–47. Singapore: ISEAS.

Hazim, A. 2022. "Malaysia Not a Nation to Be Fooled Around With—Zuraida Tells EU on Palm Oil." *Malaysian Reserve*, April 26. https://themalaysianreserve.com/2022/04/26/malaysia-not-a-nation-to-be-fooled-around-with-zuraida-tells-eu-on-palm-oil/.

Jong, H. N. 2019. "Europe, in Bid to Phase Out Palm Biofuel, Leaves Fans and Foes Dismayed." *Mongabay*, March 15. https://news.mongabay.com/2019/03/europe-in-bid-to-phase-out-palm-biofuel-leaves-fans-and-foes-dismayed/.

Kirkpatrick, C., and C. George. 2006. "Methodological Issues in the Impact Assessment of Trade Policy: Experience from the European Commission's Sustainability Impact Assessment (SIA) Programme." *Impact Assessment and Project Appraisal* 24 (4): pp. 325–334.

Kupzok, N. 2020. "Fragile Legitimacy: The Rise and Crisis of the EU's 'Sustainable Biofuels' Policy." *Socio-Economic Review* 18 (1): pp. 235–256.

LaForce, V. C. 2014. "The EU–Caribbean Trade Relationship Post-Lisbon: The Case of Bananas." *Journal of Contemporary European Research* 10 (2): pp. 266–279.

Leng, K. Y. 2022. "As War Drives Up the Price of Palm Oil, Is Sustainable Production at Risk?" *China Dialogue*, April 28. https://chinadialogue.net/en/food/as-war-drives-up-the-price-of-palm-oil-is-sustainable-production-at-risk-2/.

Mayr, S., B. Hollaus, and V. Madner. 2021. "Palm Oil, the RED II and WTO Law: EU Sustainable Biofuel Policy Tangled Up in Green?" *Review of European, Comparative & International Environmental Law* 30 (2): pp. 233–248.

Mcneill, J. 2021. "Exporting Environmental Objectives or Erecting Trade Barriers in Recent EU Free Trade Agreements." *Australian and New Zealand Journal of European Studies* 12 (1): pp. 40–53.

Meunier, S., and K. Nicolaïdis. 2006. "The European Union as a Conflicted Trade Power." *Journal of European Public Policy* 13 (6): pp. 906–925.

Nada Shofa, J. 2021. "Asean Leads by Example in Sustainable Vegetable Oil: Indonesia." *Jakarta Globe*, April 1. https://jakartaglobe.id/business/asean-leads-by-example-in-sustainable-vegetable-oil-indonesia/.

Nessel, C. 2021. "Colonialism in Its Modern Dress: Post-colonial Narratives in EUrope-Indonesia Relations." *Asia Europe Journal* 19 (1): pp. 59–74.

Poletti, A., and D. Sicurelli. 2016. "The European Union, Preferential Trade Agreements, and the International Regulation of Sustainable Biofuels." *JCMS: Journal of Common Market Studies* 54 (2): pp. 249–266.

Renckens, S., G. Skogstad, and M. Mondou, M. 2017. "When Normative and Market Power Interact: The European Union and Global Biofuels Governance." *JCMS: Journal of Common Market Studies* 55 (6): pp. 1432–1448.

Reuters. 2018. "European Move to Ban Palm Oil from Biofuels Is 'Crop Apartheid'—Malaysia." January 17, https://www.reuters.com/article/malaysia-palmoil-eu-idUSL3 N1PD1NJ.

Sapp, M. 2019. "Malaysia Tells Brussels Palm Oil Unfairly Labeled as High ILUC Risk." *Biofuel Digest*, March 6. https://www.biofuelsdigest.com/bdigest/2019/03/06/malay sia-tells-brussels-palm-oil-unfairly-labeled-as-high-iluc-risk/.

Schulze, K., and J. Tosun. 2016. "Rival Regulatory Regimes in International Environmental Politics: The Case of Biosafety." *Public Administration* 94 (1): pp. 57–72.

Silander, D. 2022. "The European Commission on Sustainable Development: A New Normative Power in Its Making?" *Forum for Social Economics*. Published online, early view. doi: https://doi.org/10.1080/07360932.2022.2032255.

Speechly, H., and S. Ozinga. 2019. *Indonesian–EU Palm Oil Trade and Consumption: Improving Coherence of EU Actions to Avoid Deforestation and Human Rights Abuses*. Fern. October. https://www.fern.org/fileadmin/uploads/fern/Docume nts/2020/EU-Indonesia_palm_oil_trade_and_consumption.pdf.

Statista. 2021. "Import Volume of Palm Oil in China from Marketing Year 2015/16 to 2020/21 with a forecast for 2021/22." https://www.statista.com/statistics/1063102/ china-palm-oil-import-volume/.

Statista. 2022. "Leading Producers of Palm Oil Worldwide from 2021/2022." https://www. statista.com/statistics/856231/palm-oil-top-global-producers/.

Suharto, R., K. Husein, Sartono, D. Kusumadewi, A. Darussamin, D. Nedyasari, D. Riksanto, Hariyadi, A. Rahman, T. Uno, P. Gillespie, C. Arianto, and R. Prasodjo. 2015. Joint study on the similarities and differences of the ISPO and the RSPO certification systems. Jakarta: Ministry of Agriculture of the Republic of Indonesia, Secretariat of ISPO Commission. https://www.undp.org/sites/g/files/zskgke326/files/migration/gcp/ISPO-RSPO-Joint-Study_English_N-8-for-screen.pdf.

Tham, S. Y. 2012. *Negotiating for a Malaysia-EU FTA: Contesting Interests from Malaysia's Perspective*. Asie.Visions 57. Ifri Center for Asian Studies. November. https://www.ifri.org/sites/default/files/atoms/files/asievisions57thammalaysiaeufta.pdf.

Valero, J. 2018. "EU-Vietnam Deal Seen as 'Stepping Stone' for Agreement with ASEAN, Says Commission." *Euractiv*, October 17. https://www.euractiv.com/section/asean/news/eu-vietnam-deal-seen-as-stepping-stone-for-agreement-with-asean-says-com mission/.

von Lucke, F., T. Diez, S. Aamodt, and B. Ahrens. 2021. *The EU and Global Climate Justice: Normative Power Caught in Normative Battles*. London: Routledge.

World Bank. 2022. "Exports in Goods and Services (% of GDP)." https://data.worldbank.org/indicator/NE.EXP.GNFS.ZS.

World Trade Organization (WTO). 2019a. European Union—Certain Measures concerning palm oil and palm oil crop-based biofuels. Dispute Settlement, DS593. https://www.wto.org/english/tratop_e/dispu_e/cases_e/ds593_e.htm.

World Trade Organization (WTO). 2019b. "Indonesia Initiates WTO Dispute Complaint against EU Biofuels Measures." December 16. https://www.wto.org/english/news_e/news19_e/ds593rfc_16dec19_e.htm#:~:text=DISPUTE%20SETTLEMENT-,Indonesia%20initiates%20WTO%20dispute%20complaint%20against%20EU%20biofuels%20measures,WTO%20members%20on%2016%20December.

World Wide Fund for Nature (WWF). 2006. WWF & the EU Biofuels Communication. Press Release. February. http://awsassets.panda.org/downloads/wwf_on_biofuels_c omm_q_a_2006___final_080206.pdf.

Wunderlich, J. U. 2020. "Positioning as Normative Actors: China and the EU in Climate Change Negotiations." *JCMS: Journal of Common Market Studies* 58 (5): pp. 1107–1123.

Yifan, J. 2021. "Stalemate: Sustainable Palm Oil Struggles to Take Off in China." *China Dialogue*, April 27. https://chinadialogue.net/en/food/stalemate-sustainable-palm-oil-struggles-to-take-off-in-china/.

9

Standardization among the Like-Minded

The EU-Asia Case

Julia Grübler

Introduction: Push from the West toward the East

The European Union (EU) has only four trade agreements with East Asian economies in place.[1] All of them entered into force during the past decade, are deep in nature, and are in the center of recently emerging mega-regional trading blocs.

While long regarded as stumbling blocks for a multilateral outcome, bilateral, plurilateral, and mega-regional trade agreements have become established features of the global trade landscape (Dür et al. 2014; WTO 2011). Taking a closer look at the evolution of the latter seems particularly worthwhile, in terms of the future of global trade policy practices, as well as the EU's trade integration and standardization efforts with East Asian economies.

The year 2013 marked the start of the EU's Transatlantic Trade and Investment Partnership (TTIP) negotiations with the United States (US). Back then, trade flows of the EU and the US accounted for almost 40 percent of global merchandise exports and half of worldwide exports of commercial services.[2] The economic magnitude and timing of these negotiations have to be kept in mind when considering the EU's recent regulatory standardization efforts with other economies, as they absorbed the political, industrial, media, and civil society attention in Europe. It is one reason why EU negotiations for a deep trade agreement with Japan kicked off almost unnoticed the same year (Young 2017).

This context changed significantly in early 2017. In the US, the Trump administration decided to withdraw from the Trans-Pacific Partnership (TPP) and to stop TTIP negotiations. These decisions marked the start of trade policy tensions among multiple trading partners, with import tariffs experiencing a dramatic comeback.[3] In particular, economies like the EU

Julia Grübler, *Standardization among the Like-Minded* In: *Standardizing the World*. Edited by: Francesco Duina and Crina Viju-Miljusevic, Oxford University Press. © Oxford University Press 2023. DOI: 10.1093/oso/9780197681886.003.0010 and Japan faced increased tariffs (e.g., on steel and aluminum) or the risk of tariff hikes on other export products of great economic and political importance, such as motor vehicles and parts. In addition, the US decided to block appointments of new members to the World Trade Organization's (WTO) Appellate Body, which weakened the multilateral trading system.[4]

For the EU, a functioning multilateral trade order is particularly relevant with respect to its trading partners in Asia. Until recently, the Republic of Korea (henceforth Korea) has been the only economy in East Asia with which the EU had a bilateral free trade agreement (FTA). Trade relations with other Asian economies were built upon the principles of the WTO.[5]

In this fragile trade environment, characterized by increased unpredictability and rivalry, it appears intuitive that efforts to conclude bilateral EU trade agreements with East Asian trading partners were given renewed impetus (see, e.g., Frenkel and Walter 2017). Also, it seemed fit that they would be incorporating strong normative affirmations of the rules-based multilateral trade order and the WTO. In this vein, the years 2019 and 2020 were particularly eventful. On February 1, 2019, the EU-Japan Economic Partnership Agreement entered into force, followed by the EU-Singapore FTA on November 21, 2019, and the EU-Vietnam FTA on August 1, 2020. Together with the EU-Korea FTA, which has been applied since July 2011 and entered fully into force in December 2015, the EU currently has only four FTAs in place in this region.

The significance of these economies for the EU stretches beyond their bilateral relationship as they form an integral part of an increasingly overlapping, cross-regional network of trade agreements and are actively engaging in multilateral negotiations.

This chapter focuses on the standardization characteristics of the EU trade agreements with Korea and Japan. Korea is a particularly interesting case, as it was the EU's very first established deep trade agreement, labeled by the European Commission as a "second generation" trade agreement, and simultaneously the first EU trade agreement with an East Asian economy. In 2019, the EU-Japan agreement was the second EU agreement with a trading partner in East Asia and was declared by the European Commission as the new "gold standard" of EU trade relationships (European Commission 2019a).

Korea and Japan are also well suited for comparison in terms of their geographical proximity, economic development, and structure of trade relations with the EU. Some comparisons are drawn with the two other remaining EU trade agreements in the region, those with Vietnam and Singapore, and at times with the mega-regionals to which the East Asian trading partners are parties to. However, as will be shown, the characteristics of these economies (e.g., level of development) and their trade relations with the EU (e.g., traded products) substantially differ from those with Japan and Korea, such that patterns in the agreements and also the drivers behind their design (e.g., political economy considerations) are expected to be different.

For the purpose of this analysis, standardization refers to the agreement on definitions and normative principles, with special attention devoted to the parties' approach toward international standards, standard-setting bodies and organizations, and the multilateral trade order under the WTO. Zooming in, the chapter will have a closer look at two sectors: First, the automotive sector was chosen due to its economic significance for Korea, Japan, and the EU, as well as challenges that this sector has recently been facing, including a surge in trade policy uncertainty. Second, the digital sector was considered for multiple reasons: It is (1) dynamically evolving; (2) so far little regulated but subject to various bilateral, plurilateral, and multilateral negotiations; (3) of geopolitical importance; and (4) an economic field and trade policy area where Asia is expected to take a leading role. The sector could almost be considered the diametrical opposite of the automotive sector in terms of established standardization practices and economically powerful players in the EU.

The analysis shows that the EU focuses on strengthening existing international standards with East Asian trading partners. This is in line with a historical institutionalist framework. The EU and East Asian economies, whose trade relationships were governed by the multilateral rulebook for decades, continue to do so by underlining their commitment to WTO rules and procedures and other international standards; all the more so, as these negotiations coincided with the US turning its back on mega-regional agreements and partly on the WTO. Limited impact of interest groups and civil society actors can be attributed to both the focus on established institutions and convergence toward existing standards, as well as the timing of negotiations—with the bulk of attention by public and private sectors devoted to transatlantic trade talks.

In addition to strengthening established international standards, the EU and East Asian FTA partners agree to actively engage in developing new *international* standards, especially in areas for which no such standards exist, for example, in the digital sphere, or where the existing ones are considered to be no longer appropriate by at least one party. The automotive sector is traditionally featured prominently in EU trade agreements, and provisions—especially for competitive exporters like Korea and Japan—are shaped by the national and supranational lobbies in the EU. For the digital sector, however, cultural accounts with shared values among the *like-minded* are emphasized. It is here where normative text passages (e.g., on the access to source code, electronic contracts, e-signatures, or unsolicited commercial electronic messages) can be found that left a footprint in international negotiations.

Finally, the "gold standard" agreement with Japan is indeed more comprehensive and specific in terms of definitions and normative standards than the eight years older Korea FTA. Nevertheless, in view of the texts of the agreements with Singapore and Vietnam, whose market sizes and economic structures differ substantially from Japan's, the shallower agreement with Korea still seems to remain the blueprint for standardization efforts in EU agreements with Asian partners.

Like-Minded Partners: Economic Integration from Various Angles

Most of the EU's agreements can be ascribed to the group of first-generation agreements, which were negotiated prior to the announcement of the Global Europe Strategy and mostly were focused on tariff reductions (European Commission 2006). The FTA between the EU and Korea—provisionally applied since 2011 and in force since 2015—marked the starting point for so-called second-generation agreements.[6] These stretch far beyond the traditional means of reducing bilateral tariffs. "The EU-South Korea FTA is the first of a new generation of comprehensive trade agreements which, apart from market opening commitments also offers a basis for regulatory co-operation in key sectors as well as a substantial chapter on sustainable development with binding provisions upholding and promoting social and environmental standards" (European Commission 2021a, 15).

To date, the number of countries with applied second-generation EU agreements has grown to fourteen. Almost a decade had passed between the application of the first new generation FTA with Korea and the second modern FTA in Asia, namely with Japan, which entered into force in early 2019. Shortly thereafter, the agreements with Singapore and Vietnam entered into force in 2019 and 2020, respectively. The agreements with Japan,

Singapore, and Vietnam are the latest three agreements of the EU that were successfully concluded and entered into force. In addition, negotiations on an investment protection agreement are ongoing with Japan, while investment protection agreements have been concluded with Singapore and Vietnam but need to be ratified by EU members before they can enter into force.[7]

These economies also stand out with respect to the EU's ambitions related to the digital transformation of the EU economy. The EU's trade policy review, published in February 2021, highlights the support for Europe's digital agenda as a key priority for EU trade policy. Listed actions to be undertaken by the European Commission include exploring the possibility of closer regulatory cooperation with like-minded partners on digital trade issues and seeking the fast conclusion of a WTO agreement on digital trade that covered rules on data flows while ensuring a high level of consumer protection (European Commission 2021c).

Importantly, the EU makes clear in the Strategy for Cooperation in the Indo-Pacific, which was announced in September 2021, that Korea, Japan, and Singapore are regarded as like-minded partners as they are the first three countries with which the EU aimed to establish non-binding digital partnerships: "They will allow the EU and like-minded partners to ensure the development of standards for emerging technologies, including in areas like artificial intelligence, in line with democratic principles and fundamental rights. They will be underpinned by a toolbox, drawing on regulatory cooperation, capacity building and skills, and investment in international cooperation and research partnerships" (European Commission and HR/VP 2021, 10).

The designation as "like-minded" is not trivial in the context of trade policy standardization. It assigns these countries to share the same or similar values in the contentious domain of the digital economy, with the main normative values repeatedly underlined by the EU being consumer protection and the safe and ethical use of emerging technologies. It is with these economies that we can expect the emergence of increased definitional standardization (e.g., on digital identities and digital services) and normative standardization (e.g., on trusted data flows and artificial intelligence) at bilateral, plurilateral, and multilateral levels.

The choice of three out of four Eastern Asian economies with which the EU has concluded deep trade agreements as like-minded countries for cooperation in the development of standards in the evolving field of the digital economy indicates the gravitational force of the recently established regional trade networks centered around the Association of Southeast Asian Nations (ASEAN) and the two remaining new mega-regionals:[8] the Comprehensive and Progressive Agreement for Trans-Pacific Partnership (CPTPP), which evolved from the TPP after the US withdrawal and entered into force in December 2018; and the Regional Comprehensive Economic Partnership (RCEP), which includes China and entered into force in January 2022 (Figure 9.1).

Given that the EU cultivates the largest network of trade agreements globally, it is a central hub.[9] However, in the context of Asian trade networks, and with a focus on mega-regionals, the EU is in the periphery, while countries at the heart of ASEAN + 3, CPTPP, and RCEP form the hubs. In its trade policy review, the European Commission (2021c, 16) states that "[t]he ability to influence the development of regulations and standards of global significance is an important competitive advantage." However, it also acknowledges that its "relative weight is shrinking given the emergence of new regulatory powers and rapid technological development, which is often driven from outside the EU."

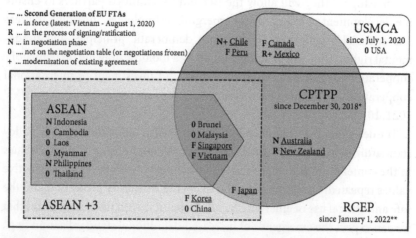

Figure 9.1 EU trade agreements with members of mega-regional trade agreements in Asia.

Notes: * Comprehensive and Progressive Agreement for Trans-Pacific Partnership (CPTPP): in force since December 30, 2018, for the first six countries that have ratified it (AUS, CAN, JPN, MEX, NZL, SGP); January 14, 2019, for Vietnam; September 19, 2021, for Peru; November 29, 2022 for Malaysia.

** Regional Comprehensive Economic Partnership (RCEP): in force since January 1, 2022, for the first ten countries (AUS, BRN, KHM, CHN, JPN, LAO, NZL, SGP, THA, VNM); February 1, 2022, for Korea; March 18, 2022, for Malaysia; January 2, 2023 for Indonesia.

Source: Updated from Grübler and Stöllinger (2020). Author's illustration.

The discussion of this chapter on EU FTAs with East Asian trading partners should therefore be seen in the broader context of these gravitational forces, not least due to the fact that mega-regional agreements are seen as potential hubs for future standardization.[10]

Korea and Japan: Characterizing Gold Standard Holders

Korea, Japan, and China belong to the ASEAN + 3, an economic cooperation with the ten ASEAN states that started in 1997. Both Korea and Japan are also part of the RCEP agreement that entered into force on January 1, 2022, for Japan, and a month thereafter for Korea. Japan, in addition, is also part of the CPTPP agreement, that entered into force on December 30, 2018. Singapore and Vietnam are both parties of RCEP and CPTPP, as well as ASEAN. Overall, nine of eleven CPTPP economies,[11] and six of fifteen RCEP economies either have a second-generation trade agreement with the EU in place or are in the process of modernizing their existing agreements.

These mega-regionals are characterized by a great diversity among members (Figure 9.2) in several basic dimensions that are potential candidates for determinants of the level of ambition for cooperation and

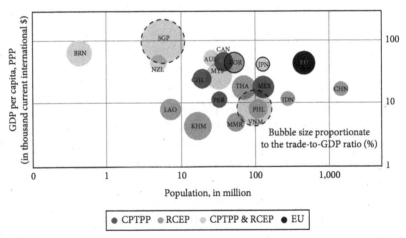

Figure 9.2 Economic size and openness of members of mega-regional trade agreements in Asia.

Notes: Axis in log scales. Trade-to-GDP ratio for Lao PDR for the year 2016.

Data source: World Bank (2022). Author's illustration.

standardization efforts in FTAs, including market size, purchasing power, level of development, significance of international trade, relative importance of trading partners, and the type of trade flows occurring. In other words, reviewing these characteristics gives a flavor of how important explanatory frameworks—regarding political economy considerations, involvement of interest groups, and power asymmetries—for observed patterns could be.

In terms of gross domestic product (GDP) and population size, all countries except China are much smaller than the EU. However, income levels for Korea and Japan were closest to the EU. The GDP per capita at purchasing power parities in 2020, at current international dollars, was around $45,000 for Korea and approximately $42,000 for Japan, compared to about $45,000 for the EU (World Bank 2022). Both countries can be found among the top twenty-five countries in the world with respect to their level of development. The Human Development Index of the United Nations (UN) ranked Japan 19th and Korea 23rd (compared to 11th for Singapore and 117th for Vietnam; all twenty-seven EU member states feature in the top sixty countries) (UNDP 2020).

A proxy for the relative importance of international trade across countries is the trade-to-GDP ratio (corresponding to the bubble sizes in Figure 9.2). It is worth noting that among all CPTPP and RCEP economies, Japan has the lowest trade-to-GDP ratio (31 percent), while at the other end, Singapore has the highest ratio (321 percent), followed by Vietnam (208 percent). Korea (69 percent) features right in the middle. In essence, the four Asian economies with which the EU has established deep trade agreements cover the entire spectrum of trade-openness levels among the nineteen CPTPP and RCEP countries.

For the EU, Korea and Japan represent top-ten trading partners and the two biggest trading partners in Asia after China (Table 9.1). For both countries, the value of trade in goods is multiple times bigger than the value of trade in services. For the year 2020, both are characterized by relatively balanced trade flows in goods, whereas the EU exports about twice as many services to Korea and Japan than it imports. Changing perspective, the EU constitutes the third biggest trading partner for Korea and Japan after China and the US, with a share of roughly 10 percent.[12] Singapore and Vietnam exhibit distinctly different trade relationships with the EU.

Table 9.1 EU Trade Ranking in 2021

Goods	Total			Exports			Imports			Balance
	Rank	Mio EUR*	Share	Rank	Mio EUR	Share	Rank	Mio EUR	Share	Mio EUR
KOR	9	107,297	2.5	9	51,857	2.4	9	55,440	2.6	−3,584
JPN	8	124,621	2.9	7	62,351	2.9	8	62,269	2.9	82
SGP	20	42,880	1.0	18	27,276	1.3	28	15,604	0.7	11,672
VNM	16	49,136	1.1	33	10,628	0.5	11	38,507	1.8	−27,879

Services	Total			Exports			Imports			Balance
	Rank	Mio EUR	Share	Rank	Mio EUR	Share	Rank	Mio EUR	Share	Mio EUR
KOR	17	18,631	1.0	14	12,346	1.4	17	6,284	0.7	6,062
JPN	7	40,400	2.3	5	27,672	3.0	9	12,729	1.5	14,943
SGP	5	50,284	2.8	6	21,565	2.4	7	28,719	3.3	−7,155
VNM	32	5,622	0.3	27	4,158	0.5	38	1,464	0.2	2,694

* – Trade/export/import/trade balance values in million euros

Source: DG Trade (2022a), based on Eurostat (Comext). May 2022.

Industrial products drive trade between the EU and its East Asian partners. Notably, exports as well as imports between the EU and Korea and Japan are strongly concentrated in the EU's three main exporting sectors (Harmonized System [HS] sections): machinery and appliances (XVI); products of the chemical or allied industries, including pharmaceutical products (VI); and transport equipment (XVII).[13] Across all extra-EU trading partners, these three sectors accounted for 43 percent of EU imports and 57 percent of EU exports in 2021. However, they represented more than 70 percent of imports from Korea and Japan and more than 55 percent of EU exports to these trading partners (Table 9.2).

Already this rough overview suggests that from the abovementioned frameworks, primarily political economy aspects could have influenced the standardization ambitions: EU trade with Korea and Japan is centered around its own main goods export sectors and thus in its internationally most competitive industries, backed by strong lobbies. These sectors are furthermore facing a high number of technical barriers to trade (TBT), many in the form of technical standards and regulations (Grübler and Reiter 2021) whose implicit trade costs could be reduced through efforts of harmonization or mutual recognition. They are, however, typically less sensitive politically than regulations affecting agricultural and food products, which received considerably more attention by media and civil society actors in TTIP trade talks. With similar levels of development, trade structures, and importance for each other's trade flows, it can be argued that, by and large, power asymmetries frameworks can be neglected for the analysis of FTAs with Korea and Japan (but might well be considered when turning to other partners in the region, such as Vietnam).

Table 9.2 EU Sectoral Trade Composition 2021 (%)

EU	Machinery (XVI)		Transport (XVII)		Chemicals (VI)		Sum	
	Imports	Exports	Imports	Exports	Imports	Exports	Imports	Exports
KOR	36.7	31.0	20.4	17.2	14.2	16.1	71.3	64.3
JPN	40.8	14.9	20.7	16.4	12.8	26.5	74.3	57.8
SGP	27.8	31.3	2.0	8.8	38.3	19.3	68.1	59.4
VNM	50.7	27.2	1.7	10.1	0.6	22.8	53.0	60.1
Extra-EU	24.8	24.3	6.8	13.8	11.2	18.6	42.8	56.7

Source: DG Trade (2022b), based on Eurostat (Comext). May 2022.

Cooperation Design: The Structure of EU FTAs with Asian Partners

The structure of chapters in FTAs gives a first indication of the standardization of formalized EU trade ties with East Asian economies in the broadest sense (i.e., in terms of topics successfully covered in negotiations). These are summarized in Table 9.3, with a comparison drawn with the CPTPP and RCEP agreements.

The EU agreements with Korea, Singapore, and Vietnam are organized in fifteen, sixteen, and seventeen chapters, respectively, while the agreement with Japan has twenty-three. At first glance, the rough structure of the EU agreements and CPTPP looks rather homogeneous. However, not least the considerable differences in the number of pages of the agreements (Table 9.4)—and in particular, the distinction between the annex covering tariff elimination/reduction schedules and the remainder of the trade agreements that provides the room for definitional and normative standardization—suggest that a second look is worthwhile.

The agreement with Korea is 1,338 pages long; the legal text comprises 80 pages, while the annex on the elimination or reduction of customs duties constitutes the bulk of the agreement with a length of 1,050 pages. This composition has changed for the more recent EU agreements in Asia, which is partly due to the continued reduction of tariffs (Figure 9.3) at most-favored nation (MFN) basis (i.e., for all WTO members). In particular, tariffs imposed by Japan on EU products *prior* to the establishment of the FTA were already in the range of Korean tariffs *after* the implementation of the FTA (Grübler et al. 2021). Nonetheless, the schedule for further tariff reductions is comprehensive. The FTA with Japan is 897 pages long, with the main text capturing 172 pages, and the annex on tariffs being regulated across 442 pages. And, indeed, as will be shown in more detail below, the "gold standard" agreement with Japan is more comprehensive and specific in terms of definitions and normative standards than the eight years older Korea Agreement.

The agreement with Vietnam is the longest among the four, incorporating a large section devoted to tariff elimination schedules. Singapore, by contrast, is very different, given that it provides duty-free market access to almost all goods at the MFN basis and has a strong focus on services trade, such that the elimination of duties corresponds to only 15 percent of the agreement (compared to 49 percent, 59 percent, and 78 percent for Japan, Vietnam, and Korea, respectively).

Table 9.3 Chapters of Deep EU Trade Agreements in Asia and Mega-Regionals

Chapters	KOR	JPN	SGP	VNM	CPTPP	RCEP
Objectives and general definitions / General provisions	1	1	1	1	1	1
Trade in goods (national treatment and market access)	2	2	2	2	2	2
Rules of origin and origin procedures		3			3	3
Textile and apparel goods					4	
Customs matters and trade facilitation	6	4	6	4	5	4
Trade remedies	3	5	3	3	6	7
Sanitary and phytosanitary measures	5	6	5	6	7	5
Technical barriers to trade / Standards, technical regulation, and conformity assessment procedures	4	7	4	5	8	6
Non-tariff barriers to trade and investment in renewable energy generation			7	7		
Trade in services	7	8	8	8	10	8
Financial services					11	
Telecommunications					13	
investment liberalization / establishment / investment	7	8	8	8	9	10
Temporary entry of business persons / Temporary movement of natural persons	(7)	(8)	(8)	(8)	12	9
e-commerce	7	8	8	8	14	12
Capital movements, payments and transfers, and temporary safeguard measures	8	9		17 (8)		
Government procurement	9	10	9	9	15	16
Competition policy	11	11	11	10	16	13

Subsidies	(11)	12	(11)	(10)		
State-owned enterprises, enterprises granted special rights or privileges and designated monopolies	11	13		11	17	
Intellectual property	10	14	10	12	18	11
Corporate governance		15				
Trade and sustainable development / Labor / Environment / Development	13	16	12	13	19, 20, 23	
Competitiveness and business facilitation					22	
Transparency / Transparency and anti-corruption	12	17	13	14	26	
Good regulatory practices and regulatory cooperation / Regulatory coherence		18			25	
Cooperation and capacity-building / Economic and technical cooperation				15	21	15
Cooperation in the field of agriculture		19				
Small and medium-sized enterprises		20			24	
Dispute settlement / Mediation mechanism	14	21	14, 15	17	28	
General provisions (and exceptions)	15		16	16	29	
(Administrative and) institutional provisions	15	22	16	16	27	
Final provisions	15	23	16	16	30	
Number of pages (in the case of EU agreements: in the *Official Journal of the European Union*)	80 + annexes = 1,338	172 + annexes = 897	126 + annexes = 751	163 + annexes = 1,396	~580 incl. annexes; excl. schedules	510

Notes: Information collected based on texts of the agreements.

Sources: For Korea (European Union 2011); for Japan (European Union 2018); for Singapore (European Union 2019); for Vietnam (European Union 2020); for RCEP (ASEAN Secretariat n.d.); for CPTPP (New Zealand MFAT n.d.).

Table 9.4 Space Devoted to Tariff Elimination and Reduction in EU FTAs

Pages	KOR	JPN	SGP	VNM
Total	1,338	897	751	1,396
Main legal text	80	172	126	163
	6%	19%	17%	12%
Annex	1,258	725	625	1,233
Thereof annex on the elimination and reduction of customs duties	1,050	442	111	828
% of total annex	83%	61%	18%	67%

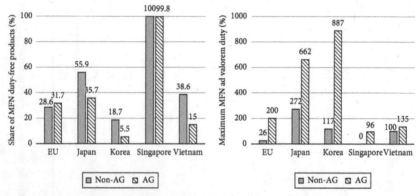

Figure 9.3 Relevance of MFN tariffs of Asian FTA partners in 2020.
Data source: WTO Stats (https://stats.wto.org/). Author's illustration.

Using the legal texts of fifty-six FTAs signed since 2010 as data, a recent quantitative analysis suggests that around 30 percent of the legal text of RCEP was duplicated from CPTPP/TPP.[14] The most influential EU agreements were those deep agreements which have been established since 2017 and are at the core of this chapter: Japan (15 percent overlap of text), Vietnam (10 percent), Singapore (10 percent), Canada (10 percent), and Korea (8 percent) (Francois and Elsig 2021).

Following a chapter on the objectives of the agreements and general definitions, all agreements start with provisions on trade in goods, focusing on market access and national treatment, and subsequently lay down the trade rules in four areas: (1) customs matters and trade facilitation; (2) trade remedies; as well as two chapters on standard-like non-tariff measures, that is, (3) sanitary and phytosanitary measures, related to human, animal, and plant health; and (4) technical barriers to trade. The subsequent chapter on services, investment, and e-commerce is particularly interesting from an economic perspective and considering FTAs' potential for standardization, as these areas are less regulated internationally. They are also less streamlined in EU agreements and across mega-regionals.

Keeping the context of mega-regionals in mind, the following analysis focuses on the agreements with Korea and Japan, with comparisons drawn with Singapore and Vietnam, summarizing definitional and normative passages embedded in the preamble, first chapter, articles on international standards and links to international organizations, and provisions agreed upon for the automotive industry and digital trade.

The Preamble: A Note on Values

The preamble of FTAs is setting the stage for the economic partnership. All four EU FTAs in East Asia start off by highlighting the strong partnership based on "common principles and values." With respect to these values, they have in common that they recognize the importance of transparency and emphasize that the strengthened relationship arising from the FTA should be "in accordance with the objective of sustainable development, in its economic, social and environmental dimensions" (European Union 2011, 7). They commit to the UN Charter (1945), the Universal Declaration of Human Rights (1948), and state that the bilateral relationship is building on the rights and obligations under the Marrakesh Agreement Establishing the World Trade Organization (WTO Agreement, 1994), and other multilateral, regional, and bilateral agreements to which they are party.

Overall, the preambles of the agreement with Singapore and Vietnam are closer to the one with Korea. However, the three newer agreements—Japan, Singapore, and Vietnam—contain a normative passage on parties' determination to "promote trade and development in a manner mindful of high levels of environmental and labour protection and relevant internationally recognized standards and agreements," whereas international standards are not referred to in the case of the Korea FTA, where parties aim to "strengthen the development and enforcement of labour and environmental laws and policies" (European Union 2011, 7).[15]

In the context of the mega-regionals introduced above, it is noteworthy that in the agreement of Vietnam and Singapore, who are members of

ASEAN, but not for Japan or Korea, parties recognize that the bilateral FTA with the EU would "complement and promote regional economic integration efforts" (European Union 2019, 3).

Global Trade Order: Linkages to the WTO, International Organizations, and Standards

The EU agreements with Korea, Singapore, and Vietnam start chapter one with almost identical wording on the establishment of a free trade area between the parties in conformity with art. XXIV of the General Agreement on Tariffs and Trade 1994 and art. V of the General Agreement on Trade in Services (i.e., in line with multilateral trade rules of the WTO).

An exception is the EU agreement with Japan, where the article on the establishment of an FTA is completely absent. In general, the notions of free trade and free trade areas were completely avoided in the main EU-Japan agreement text.[16] It directly starts with the objective, formulated in one sentence to "liberalise and facilitate trade and investment, as well as to promote a closer economic relationship between the Parties." The second part of the objective formulation on a closer economic relationship does not occur in other EU-Asia FTAs.[17]

The first chapter is also used to specify the parties of the agreement, provide definitions of specific terms (such as person, goods, measure, or customs authority), and clarify abbreviations of agreements between the parties on which they build, as well as WTO agreements to which they refer.[18]

Furthermore, each of the four agreements contains an article explaining the relation with other agreements. Notably, the parties agree that nothing in the FTA shall require action in a manner inconsistent with obligations under the WTO Agreement. In addition to the Marrakesh Agreement, at least fourteen WTO agreements are referred to. Parties are affirmative of their existing rights and obligations under the WTO Agreement and its annexes for trade in goods (except trade-related investment measures), trade in services, trade-related aspects of intellectual property rights, dispute settlement, and also the plurilateral agreement on government procurement.

With WTO agreements being incorporated into FTAs, *mutatis mutandis*, they set the level playing field for definitional standardization, especially for goods trade. What can be observed, however, is that the scope of WTO agreements is partially extended to a greater number of goods or institutions among FTA parties. For example, in the EU agreement with Japan, art. 10.3 specifies additional rules for government procurement extending the coverage from the annexes of the WTO government procurement agreement to the procurement of central and subcentral government authorities, bodies governed by public law (e.g., hospitals or universities) specified for Japan and each EU member state, as well as to services not covered by the WTO agreement and procurement in the transport sector.

An exception to this rule of building upon WTO definitions is the EU-Japan chapter on rules of origin, which makes no referral to the WTO agreement on rules of origin and is packed with definitions for terms as basic as exporter, importer, material, product, or production, to elaborate articles on requirements for originating products and their sophisticated technical specifications (e.g., for wholly obtained products, insufficient processing of goods, or the treatment of packaging materials).

Overall, however, they continue the trend observed by Allee et al. (2017) for FTAs signed between 1994 and 2014. They found that the average FTA made about twenty-five WTO-related references. Furthermore, they suggest that larger countries and those most active in establishing FTAs most likely included strong WTO presence in their FTAs. Without double counting of referenced agreements annexed to the WTO agreement, this figure is greater than fifty for the four EU-Asia FTAs.

The WTO agreements provide a multilateral framework. Within this room to maneuver, the parties agree either on standards or standard-setting *bodies*. This is mainly the case for customs and trade facilitation (World Customs Organization), sanitary and phytosanitary measures (Codex Alimentarius, World Organisation for Animal Health, International Plant Protection Convention), and TBTs.

The universe of TBT-related standards is particularly diverse. Though all four agreements mention relevant standards for specific industries, only the EU-Japan agreement lists a series of international *organizations* (in art. 7.6), whose standards shall be considered as *relevant* international standards.[19]

In addition, the FTA with Japan encourages regional and national standardizing bodies to engage in the preparation of international standards, and to use international standards as the basis for their standards development with "a view to harmonising standards on as wide a basis as possible" (European Union 2018, 51). The endeavor toward harmonization makes the EU-Japan agreement stand out from the others. The Committee on Regulatory Cooperation established under the FTA shall support this process.[20]

In line with findings based on a text analysis for the EU FTAs with Canada, Central America, Singapore, and Korea by Young (2015), the EU agreements with Asia show a strong focus on international organizations and standards. Hence, most standards and regulations they refer to might not be new by themselves; but FTA parties' agreement to align their standards to these international standards makes them new to their companies engaging in trade, as prominently highlighted in the cases of motor vehicles and medical devices.

Beyond that, this focus is a normative statement in itself, fitting with what the EU often states how it wants the global trade landscape to be: transparent, open, and anchored in a rules-based multilateral system.

Driving Standardization of Technical Barriers: The Automotive Industry

As mentioned earlier, the transport sector represents a significant portion of EU trade with Korea and Japan (see Table 9.2).[21] Hence, vehicles and parts received considerable attention in these FTA negotiations. All four agreements with East Asian partners contain a separate annex for this sector, stating under their objectives to secure the protection of human health, safety, and environment, and to promote the compatibility of regulations based on international standards. These annexes are most elaborate for Korea and Japan, which emphasize that the parties recognize the importance of motor vehicles and parts for trade, employment, and growth.[22]

While there was still a stronger focus on the elimination of tariffs in the case of the agreement with Korea,[23] the other three agreements solely focus on non-tariff provisions, in particular the acceptance of international standards and standard-setting bodies.

At the core, parties of all agreements recognize that the World Forum for Harmonization of Vehicle Regulations (WP.29) within the framework of the UN Economic Commission for Europe (UNECE) is the relevant international standard-setting body and that UNECE regulations or Global Technical Regulations (GTR) are the relevant international standards for the products covered. In essence, the annexes address international standards in four ways: They (a) take stock of differences between domestic and international regulations (in a very detailed way for Korea); (b) set time frames for the harmonization between these; (c) lay out aspirations to develop international standards, especially in underregulated areas; and (d) commit parties to refrain from introducing domestic technical regulations diverging from UNECE regulations.

References are also made to the TBT Agreement with respect to notifications (Korea) and definitions for conformity assessment procedures and technical regulations (Japan). The product coverage itself is defined through the internationally applied HS product classification (chs. 40, 84, 85, 87, and 94, though with exceptions varying by FTA partner).[24]

In the case of the Korea agreement, the parties worked out correspondence tables between their national regulations and UNECE regulations. Whenever a product complies with the requirement listed, parties accept these for type approval as complying with their national technical regulations. More than seventy EU regulations and fifty Korean regulations were matched. For those where no matching with respective UNECE regulations was achieved, the parties shall harmonize their regulations with UNECE regulations or GTR within five years from the entry into force of the agreement—which was only one in the case of the EU but were twenty-one in the case of Korea. The EU Agreement with Japan lists only four UN regulations, which are applied by one party but not by the other and should be applied no later than seven years after the FTA's entry into force. Overall, this indicates that the EU had relatively more to gain from standardization efforts in this sector and even more so in the case of Korea, as more domestic regulations were not in line with international standards that the EU already had applied. The scope for future standardization is also greater with Korea, which was more restrictive in its vehicle-types coverage in the FTA.

No equivalence tables are included in the annexes for Japan, Vietnam, or Singapore. Here, at the core of the vehicle type approval is the UN Regulation No. 0 of the "1958 Agreement" (i.e., the "Agreement concerning the Adoption of Uniform Technical Prescriptions for Wheeled Vehicles, Equipment and Parts Which can be Fitted and/or be Used on Wheeled Vehicles and the Conditions for Reciprocal Recognition of Approvals Granted on the Basis of these Prescriptions"), administered by the WP. 29. The parties agreed to accept products for which, in accordance with the 1958 Agreement, an International Whole Vehicle Type Approval certificate has been issued without requiring any further testing, documentation, certification, or marking. This is true even for Singapore and Vietnam, which have not been but are encouraged in the annex to become signatories of the 1958 Agreement.

A special feature in the motor vehicles annex of the Korea agreement is art. 5 on MFN treatment, the core principle of non-discrimination among WTO members. It is explicitly applied to internal taxes and emission regulations and is deeper than the general MFN principle in that no less favorable treatment should be accorded than that to the like products originating in third countries, including as provided in any FTA with third countries.

For the agreement with Japan, a distinct feature is a safeguard mechanism laid out in art. 18, specifying that during the first ten years of the agreement, each party reserves the right to suspend equivalent concessions or obligations if the partner country does not apply UN regulations. Given the economic importance of this export sector, parties clearly opted for a carrot and stick approach, making sure that enforcement of regulatory convergence is not restricted only to soft power.

Specialized working groups have been established with Korea, Japan, and Vietnam for the effective implementation of the annex and to address market access problems "before they arise." A special feature of the Vietnam agreement regarding standardization beyond technicalities is the focus on capacity-building (testing competence, procedures for type approvals), including internships and exchanges of experiences for officials of Vietnamese type-approval authorities in the EU.

Both agreements with Korea and Japan aspire to shape the international standards in this sector in areas where no UNECE regulations or GTR exist. For example, at the second meeting of the Working Group in March 2021, the EU and Japan confirmed their cooperation in establishing a new harmonized UN Regulation that should provide the framework for the "close-proximity field of vision requirements" with a view to improving the safety of pedestrians.

Furthermore, if one party introduces or maintains a technical regulation, the parties consult on the possibility for developing international standards, or where this is not an option, to approximate their regulations. The agreement with Japan goes further in that parties agree to cooperate to facilitate the *worldwide* use of UN regulation No. 0 of the 1958 Agreement and in enlarging its coverage to additional vehicle categories.

Another forward-looking feature with multiple normative components that all four agreements have in common is an article on the non-discrimination of products with new technologies or features. Their market access should not be delayed unless "scientific or technical information" demonstrates that the new technology or feature creates a risk for human health, safety, or the environment.

Emerging Trade Topics: Rules for the Digital Economy

FTA chapters on cross-border investments, international trade in services,[25] and e-commerce address internationally scarcely regulated but in economic terms dynamically evolving areas, where multi- and plurilateral negotiations at the level of the WTO are ongoing. The EU FTAs with East Asian partners are similarly organized in six sections, on (1) general provisions; (2) either investment liberalization (Japan, Vietnam) or establishment (Korea, Singapore); (3) cross-border trade in services; (4) the entry and temporary stay of natural persons for business purposes; (5) the regulatory framework; and (6) electronic commerce.

All four agreements cover subsections on services particularly relevant for the digital economy: postal services, telecommunication services, financial services, and international maritime transport services. All except the one with Japan cover computer services in a separate subsection.

In the case of Korea, Japan, and Vietnam,[26] these chapters should be effectively implemented by specialized committees.

The general provisions—reaffirming parties' rights and obligations under the WTO Agreement—however, make clear that the emphasis is on services and investments, which are aimed to be reciprocally liberalized, while the provisions on e-commerce aim "only" for cooperation. These cooperation efforts are in line with what is sought at the international level.

The only multilateral agreement that exists for e-commerce specifies that members of the WTO follow the practice of not imposing customs duties on electronic transmissions. However, they do so based on regular decisions to extend this agreement until the following ministerial conference,[27] whereas the EU and its Asian FTA partners established a permanent solution.

In addition to the multilateral approach, e-commerce has been subject to plurilateral (the so-called Joint Statement Initiative [JSI]) negotiations among more than seventy WTO members since early 2019. It is worth noting in this context that the three co-convenors of the WTO e-commerce negotiations are Australia, Japan, and Singapore. Topics listed in EU-Asia FTA articles on cooperation on regulatory issues overlap with discussion in the JSI talks.

For all four agreements, these include the recognition of certificates of electronic signatures, the facilitation of cross-border certification services, the treatment of unsolicited e-commerce communication, and the protection of consumers.

The agreements with Korea, Singapore, and Vietnam furthermore list the liability of intermediary service providers with respect to the transmission or storage of information as an area for dialogue. Korea also mentions the development of paperless trading, whereas the list is longer for Japan, covering cybersecurity, challenges for small and medium-sized enterprises, intellectual property, and electronic government.

As observed earlier, the agreements with Singapore and Vietnam more closely resemble the FTA with Korea than the agreement with Japan. The former list a shorter number of areas for cooperation, defining that cooperation may take the form of exchange of information on legislation and its implementation, and—in the case of Korea and Singapore—underline in their objectives that the development of e-commerce must be fully compatible with the international standards of data protection, to ensure the confidence of users, however, without further specifications regarding relevant standards.

The agreement with Japan differs in the scope and depth of its articles on e-commerce. For example, it sets out in the objectives that parties recognize the importance of the principle of technological neutrality in e-commerce. It also provides definitions and articles on topics for cooperation and active participation in *multilateral* fora. For example, art. 8.73 specifies that parties may not require the access to source code of software owned by a person of the FTA partner. This corresponds to the small portion of cleared JSI text on business trust. Likewise, art. 8.76 lays out that parties shall not treat electronically concluded contracts differently from others with respect to their legal effect, validity, or enforceability. Almost in the same wording, an article in the JSI negotiations has been cleared for electronic contracts. The same holds true for the article on electronic authentication and e-signatures (art. 8.77) and detailed text on measures to limit unsolicited commercial electronic messages (art. 8.79). So, again, the reader finds international texts in the EU FTAs—however, even before they were agreed as such.

By contrast, for the topic of free flow of data, for which no clean plurilateral text has emerged so far with proposals for paragraphs by more than ten countries on the table, the EU and Japan agreed in art. 8.81 to reassess within three years the need for the inclusion of provisions on this issue.

Conclusion

Until recently, the EU has built its trade relations with Asian economies solely upon multilateral rules. With the global trade order having been threatened and mega-regionals emerging around the ASEAN economies, new deep FTAs with major trading partners in East Asia were concluded, which place a strong emphasis on the WTO and international standards in line with a historical institutionalist view. These economies are also considered like-minded partners with whom the EU aims to explore closer regulatory co-operation, especially in quickly evolving areas, such as new technologies and the digital economy. These highlight cultural accounts, emphasizing shared values, for example, regarding high standards for consumer protection.

The FTAs with Korea and Japan have been used to agree on international standards and standard-setting bodies, to take stock of differences between domestic and international regulations, and to set a time horizon for the harmonization between the two. For the economically important vehicle sector, this mainly implies Asian economies' regulations converging toward international standards that the EU has already in place. At the same time, however, they affirm their aspirations to co-design international standards, particularly in areas for which internationally recognized standards do not yet exist or are deemed no longer fit for purpose. The example of e-commerce, where Asian economies show a strong engagement on the multilateral level, illustrates how texts of FTAs may shape global rules.

The dynamic reciprocal approach of agreeing on international standards, standard-setting bodies, and reinforcing multilateral agreements in FTAs while aiming for cooperation in the development of new international standards brings together the EU's motivations to promote its values and support its economy, while defending a predictable, rules-based trading system. This forward-looking feature is more pronounced in the "gold standard" agreement with Japan; nevertheless, the agreement with Korea appears to continue to be the blueprint for EU agreements in Asia.

Notes

1. The opinions expressed in this chapter are those of the author. The chapter builds on her research as an economist at the Vienna Institute for International Economic Studies. It stands in no relation with the author's work at the United Nations Conference on Trade and Development or the WTO.

2. See, for example, data extractable from the WTO's stats portal (https://stats.wto.org/).

3. See Bown (2020) for extensive updates on US tariff hikes on imports from China and vice versa.

4. After the terms of two judges expired in 2019, the Appellate Body became dysfunctional. On March 27, 2020, the EU and fifteen WTO members, including China, decided on a contingency appeal arrangement for the period of paralysis of the WTO appeal function (European Commission 2020a).

5. In East Asia, all countries but three are members of the WTO. These three are Bhutan and Timor-Leste, which hold an observer status and are in the accession process, and North Korea.

6. See, for example, the EU's reports on the implementation of trade agreements until 2019. Starting in 2020, the reports were structured geographically; first- and second-generation agreements were still mentioned. In the 2021 report on the implementation and enforcement of trade agreements, these distinctions are no longer featured (European Commission 2019b, 2020b, 2021b).

7. Originally, the agreements were envisaged as trade and investment agreements. However, based on a ruling by the Court of Justice of the European Union, they have been split into a trade agreement under the competence of the EU and an investment protection agreement that requires the ratification by EU member states. As of May 2022, the investment protection agreements with Singapore and Vietnam had not been ratified by fifteen and sixteen members, respectively. The last round of discussions on an investment protection agreement with Japan took place in March 2019.

8. If the EU agreement with the Common Market of the South economies (Argentina, Brazil, Paraguay, and Uruguay) were ratified (see Chapter 7 in this volume), it would constitute another intercontinental mega-regional agreement. However, its potential impact for cooperation efforts on the regulations of future technologies is more limited compared to those in Asia, given the different economic structure.

9. A hub economy in international trade would be one that has many bilateral links with partners, which do not necessarily have direct links among them.

10. Employing deep multi-country agreements decreases the complexity and trade costs arising from applying a "spaghetti bowl" of heterogeneous standards and trade rules (Baldwin 2006; Dür et al. 2014), potentially reducing regulatory distance for standard-like non-tariff barriers between trading partners by more than 40 percent (Cadot and Ing 2015). In that vein, it is worth noting that some empirical literature suggests that FTA components in accordance with the multilateral trade rules of the WTO show particularly high economic impacts (Kohl et al. 2016). Furthermore, intercontinental and overlapping agreements seem to contribute more to the dissemination of standards than other constellations of FTAs (Brandi et al. 2019; Morin et al. 2019), with so-called hubs appearing to be in the most beneficial situation (Hur et al. 2010; Reiter and Grübler 2020; Sopranzetti 2018).

11. On February 1, 2021, the United Kingdom submitted a formal accession request.

12. Source: Directorate-General for Trade, based on the International Monetary Fund (May 2022).

13. These feature also among the overall top five importing sectors, together with mineral products (V) and base metals and articles thereof (XV).

14. The CPTPP agreement is almost identical to the initial TPP agreement. Only twenty specific elements were changed, and US-specific commitments were suspended (Elms 2018). Still, its trade rules are laid out in about 580 pages (dropping from 620), which is more than the four EU-Asia agreements taken together. This legal text is accompanied by hundreds of pages of member-specific schedules. The RCEP agreement stretches over 510 pages, again coming with a huge number of pages related to market access schedules.

15. Where Singapore's preamble deviates significantly from the other three agreements is its demand for flexibility. While the latter express their belief that the agreement would create a stable and predictable commercial environment for trade and investment expansion, the agreement with Singapore points toward necessary flexibilities "reaffirming each Party's right to adopt and enforce measures necessary to pursue legitimate policy objectives such as social, environmental, security, public health and safety, promotion and protection of cultural diversity."

16. It appears in the appendix on the relation with third countries with respect to originating materials for the production of certain vehicles and parts thereof (p. 677) and the joint declaration regarding the need for the establishment of an FTA between Japan and countries with which the EU forms a customs union on the last text page of the agreement (p. 899).

17. The EU-Japan FTA is called an economic partnership agreement (EPA), which can result in confusion, given that EU EPAs have been established with African, Caribbean, and Pacific economies to address special development needs.

18. For South Korea, the Framework Agreement for Trade and Cooperation (signed in October 1996) and the Agreement on Cooperation and Mutual Administrative Assistance in Customs Matters (signed in April 1997); for Vietnam, the Framework Agreement on Comprehensive Partnership and Cooperation (signed in June 2012); and for Singapore, the Partnership and Cooperation Agreement (signed in October 2018).

19. International organizations such as the International Organization for Standardization, the International Electrotechnical Commission, the International Telecommunication Union, the Codex Alimentarius Commission, the International Civil Aviation Organization, the WP. 29 within the framework of UNECE, the UN Sub-Committee of Experts on the Globally Harmonized System of Classification and Labelling of Chemicals, and the International Council for Harmonisation of Technical Requirements for Pharmaceuticals for Human Use.

20. For example, during the third meeting, in December 2021, Japan's plans to revise its technological standards for offshore wind power facilities, as well as related questions to the conformity assessment, tendering process, and licensing were discussed.

21. The Vietnamese automotive and vehicle parts industry has been growing fast, and it has been gaining significance in international trade. For the EU, so far, its economic importance has been more limited, in particular, in terms of EU imports. Singapore did not have an automotive industry; however, Korea's Hyundai started the

construction of a research and development center with an electric vehicle production facility in 2020.

22. The weight of this sector is further underlined by an article on compliance, which states that disputes shall be considered a matter of urgency, reducing time frames for consultations and reports compared to those listed in the general dispute settlement chapter by half or more.

23. Upon entry into force, tariffs were eliminated by both parties for vehicle parts; after three years for medium-sized and large cars; and after five years for small cars.

24. Korea: excluded products are listed in a separate sub-appendix, covering tractors, snow mobiles, golf carts, and construction machinery. Japan: excludes motor vehicles and parts that are used exclusively for agriculture and forestry. Singapore: no exceptions. Vietnam: covering only particular categories of motor vehicles (M1) and parts (M2, N3) as defined in UNECE regulations, with the option to discuss the coverage extension to categories L, M, and N, but not before ten years from the date of entry into force of the agreement.

25. For a detailed account on chapters on trade in services and investment (liberalization), see Chapters 2 and 4 in this volume.

26. For Vietnam, this committee also covers government procurement.

27. For example, at the 12th Ministerial Conference in Geneva in June 2022, this moratorium was extended until the next conference or March 31, 2024, the latest (WT/MIN(22)/32; WT/L/1143).

References

Allee, T., M. Elsig, and A. Lugg. 2017. "The Ties between the World Trade Organization and Preferential Trade Agreements: A Textual Analysis." *Journal of International Economic Law* 20 (2): pp. 333–363.

ASEAN Secretariat. n.d. Legal Text of the RCEP Agreement. https://rcepsec.org/legal-text/.

Baldwin, R. 2006. "Multilateralising Regionalism: Spaghetti Bowls as Building Blocs on the Path to Global Free Trade. *World Economy* 29 (11): pp. 1451–1518.

Bown, C. 2020. "US-China Trade War Tariffs: An Up-to-Date Chart." Peterson Institute for International Economics (PIIE). February 14 [as of]. https://www.piie.com/research/piie-charts/us-china-trade-war-tariffs-date-chart.

Brandi C., D. Blümer, and J. F. Morin. 2019. "When Do International Treaties Matter for Domestic Environmental Legislation?" *Global Environmental Politics* 19 (4): pp. 14–44.

Cadot, O., and L. Y. Ing. 2015. "Non-tariff Measures and Harmonisation: Issues for the RCEP." Working Papers DP-2015-61. Economic Research Institute for ASEAN and East Asia. September.

Directorate-General for Trade (DG Trade). 2022a. *EU27 Trade in Goods by Partner*. https://trade.ec.europa.eu/doclib/docs/2006/september/tradoc_122530.pdf.

Directorate-General for Trade (DG Trade). 2022b. Factsheets. https://webgate.ec.europa.eu/isdb_results/factsheets/.

Dür, A., L. Baccini, and M. Elsig. 2014. "The Design of International Trade Agreements: Introducing a New Dataset." *Review of International Organizations* 9 (3): pp. 353–375.

Elms, D. 2018. "The Comprehensive and Progressive Trans-Pacific Partnership: Policy Innovations and Impacts." Global Economic Dynamics Focus Paper. Gütersloh: Bertelsmann Stiftung.

European Commission. 2006. Global Europe—Competing in the World. A Contribution to the EU's Growth and Jobs Strategy. Communication by the Commission, COM(2006)0567 final. https://eur-lex.europa.eu/LexUriServ/LexUriServ.do?uri=COM:2006:0567:FIN:en:PDF.

European Commission. 2019a. EU-Japan Trade Agreement Enters into Force. Press Release. January 31. https://ec.europa.eu/commission/presscorner/detail/en/IP_19_785.

European Commission. 2019b. Report on Implementation of EU Free Trade Agreements. 1 January 2018–31 December 2018. Report from the Commission to the European Parliament, the Council, the European Economic and Social Committee and the Committee of the Regions, COM(2019) 455 final. https://eur-lex.europa.eu/legal-content/EN/TXT/PDF/?uri=CELEX:52019DC0455&from=FR.

European Commission. 2020a. EU and 15 World Trade Organization Members Establish Contingency Appeal Arrangement for Trade Disputes. Press Release. March 27. https://ec.europa.eu/commission/presscorner/detail/en/IP_20_538.

European Commission. 2020b. Report on the Implementation of EU Free Trade Agreements. 1 January 2019–31 December 2019. Report from the Commission to the European Parliament, the Council, the European Economic and Social Committee and the Committee of the Regions, COM(2020) 705 final. https://eur-lex.europa.eu/legal-content/EN/TXT/PDF/?uri=CELEX:52020DC0705&from=DE.

European Commission. 2021a. Individual information sheets on implementation of EU Trade Agreements, Commission Staff Working Document accompanying the Report from the Commission to the European Parliament, the Council, the European Economic and Social Committee and the Committee of the Regions on Implementation and Enforcement of EU Trade Agreements, SWD(2021) 297 final. https://ec.europa.eu/transparency/documents-register/detail?ref=SWD(2021)297&lang=en.

European Commission. 2021b. Report on Implementation and Enforcement of EU Free Trade Agreements. Report from the Commission to the European Parliament, the Council, the European Economic and Social Committee and the Committee of the Regions, COM(2021) 654 final. https://eur-lex.europa.eu/legal-content/EN/TXT/PDF/?uri=CELEX:52021DC0654&from=EN.

European Commission. 2021c. Trade Policy Review—An Open, Sustainable and Assertive Trade Policy. Communication from the Commission to the European Parliament, the Council, the European Economic and Social Committee and the Committee of the Regions, COM(2021) 66 final. https://eur-lex.europa.eu/resource.html?uri=cellar:5bf4e9d0-71d2-11eb-9ac9-01aa75ed71a1.0001.02/DOC_1&format=PDF.

European Commission and High Representative of the Union for Foreign Affairs and Security Policy (HR/VP). 2021. The EU Strategy for Cooperation in the Indo-Pacific. Joint communication to the European Parliament and the Council, JOIN(2021) 24 final. https://eur-lex.europa.eu/legal-content/EN/TXT/PDF/?uri=CELEX:52021JC0024&from=EN.

European Union. 2011. Free Trade Agreement between the European Union and its Member States, of the one part, and the Republic of Korea, of the other part. *Official Journal of the European Union* 54, L 127, May 14: pp. 6–1343.

European Union. 2018. Agreement between the European Union and Japan for an Economic Partnership. *Official Journal of the European Union* 61, L 330, December 27: pp. 3–899.

European Union. 2019. Free Trade Agreement between the European Union and the Republic of Singapore. *Official Journal of the European Union* 62, L 294, November 14: pp. 3–755.

European Union. 2020. Free Trade Agreement between the European Union and the Socialist Republic of Viet Nam. *Official Journal of the European Union* 63, L 186. June 12: pp. 3–1400.

Francois, J., and M. Elsig. 2021. Short Overview of the Regional Comprehensive Economic Partnership (RCEP), European Parliament, Briefing requested by the INTA committee, PE 653.625, February. https://www.europarl.europa.eu/RegData/etudes/BRIE/2021/653625/EXPO_BRI(2021)653625_EN.pdf.

Frenkel, M., and B. Walter. 2017. "The EU-Japan Economic Partnership Agreement: Relevance, Content and Policy Implications." *Intereconomics* 52 (6): pp. 358–363.

Grübler, J., and O. Reiter. 2021. "Characterising Non-Tariff Trade Policy." *Economic Analysis and Policy* 71: pp. 138–163.

Grübler, J., and R. Stöllinger. 2020. "EU-Freihandelsabkommen: Was liegt auf dem Tisch? " *FIW Policy Brief* 47. September: pp. 1–16.

Grübler, J., O. Reiter, and R. Stehrer. 2021. "On the New Gold Standard in EU Trade Integration: Reviewing the EU-Japan EPA." *Empirica* 48 (3): pp. 611–644.

Hur, J., J. D. Alba, and D. Park. 2010. "Effects of Hub-and-Spoke Free Trade Agreements on Trade: A Panel Data Analysis." *World Development* 38 (8): pp. 1105–1113.

Kohl, T., S. Brakman, and H. Garretsen. 2016. "Do Trade Agreements Stimulate International Trade Differently? Evidence from 296 Trade Agreements." *The World Economy* 39 (1): pp. 97–131.

Morin, J.-F., D. Blümer, C. Brandi, and A. Berger. 2019. "Kick-starting Diffusion: Explaining the Varying Frequency of Preferential Trade Agreements' Environmental Provisions by Their Initial Conditions." *The World Economy* 42 (9): pp. 2602–2628.

New Zealand Ministry of Foreign Affairs and Trade (MFAT). n.d. Comprehensive and Progressive Agreement for Trans-Pacific Partnership Text and Resources. https://www.mfat.govt.nz/en/trade/free-trade-agreements/free-trade-agreements-in-force/cptpp/comprehensive-and-progressive-agreement-for-trans-pacific-partnership-text-and-resources/.

Reiter, O., and J. Grübler. 2020. "Greater than the Sum of Its Parts? How Does Austria Profit from a Widening Network of EU Free Trade Agreements?" The Vienna Institute for International Economic Studies Working Paper No. 186, September.

Sopranzetti, S. 2018. "Overlapping Free Trade Agreements and International Trade: A Network Approach." *World Economy* 41 (6): pp. 1549–1566.

United Nations Development Programme (UNDP). 2020. Human Development Report 2020. The Next Frontier: Human Development and the Anthropocene. New York. https://hdr.undp.org/en/content/human-development-report-2020.

World Bank. 2022. "Databank: World Development Indicators." https://databank.worldbank.org/source/world-development-indicators.

World Trade Organization (WTO). 2011. *The WTO and Preferential Trade Agreements: From Co-existence to Coherence.* World Trade Report 2011. Geneva: WTO.

Young, A. R. 2015. "Liberalizing Trade, Not Exporting Rules: The Limits to Regulatory Co-ordination in the EU's 'New Generation' Preferential Trade Agreements." *Journal of European Public Policy* 22 (9): pp. 1253–1275.

Young, A. R. 2017. "European Trade Policy in Interesting Times." *Journal of European Integration* 39 (7): pp. 909–923.

10

The Indian Response to the EU's Regulatory Standardization

The Case of Public Procurement and Social Standards under the EU-India Free Trade Agreement

Sangeeta Khorana

Introduction

European Union (EU) trade policy has been focused on negotiating free trade agreements (FTAs), and deals have been concluded with seventy-six partner countries (European Union 2021). Over the past several years, the FTAs not only have increased in number but also have become "deeper." The agreements include provisions on regulatory cooperation that address unnecessary non-tariff barriers and even go beyond the realm of World Trade Organization (WTO) mandates by pursuing commitments in areas such as investment, movement of capital, and competition policy. Studies highlight the rationale for using the EU's FTAs with third countries as a successful mechanism to promote values that the EU finds important across diverse regions (see, e.g., Meissner and McKenzie 2019; Poletti et al. 2021; van 't Wout 2022). Studies find that trade talks between the EU and its partners were ascribed to the EU's normative aspirations to export a preferred model of liberalization, governance, and multilateral regulation to partner countries (Khorana and Garcia 2014, 481). Not only do these FTAs cover conventional trade liberalization, but recent EU trade agreements also focus on the pursuit of non-trade objectives (Falkenberg 2020). Most recent FTAs

Sangeeta Khorana, *The Indian Response to the EU's Regulatory Standardization* In: *Standardizing the World*.
Edited by: Francesco Duina and Crina Viju-Miljusevic, Oxford University Press. © Oxford University Press 2023.
DOI: 10.1093/oso/9780197681886.003.0011

are, in fact, guided by the EU's desire to implement the "spirit" of the relevant texts and its aspiration to be a geopolitical actor. The geopolitical aspiration, which continues to be imbedded in EU policymaking, has been reviewed, and the latest narrative within EU trade policy focuses on the "open strategic autonomy" discourse. This aims at shaping the new system of global governance and developing mutually beneficial bilateral relations, while protecting businesses and firms from unfair and abusive practices.

The open strategic autonomy concept is broad and still evolving, and a number of conceptualizations have been offered in policy and academic literature. For example, the Commission (European Union 2020) emphasizes that the EU will be open to trade and will promote stable rules in order to be strong economically and have geopolitical influence. Anghel et al. (2020) defines this as the ability to act autonomously and cooperate with partners in strategic areas when required. In essence, the open strategic autonomy is a strategy that goes beyond the traditional role of addressing market access barriers to a more holistic approach that focuses on environment and sustainable development.

This chapter argues that while the overarching aim of EU trade policy continues to be guided by its aspiration to export a preferred model of liberalization and governance in partner countries, it is not always the case that the partner country shares the same viewpoint. FTA negotiations for the EU-India deal, which commenced in 2007, were mainly driven by the EU's interest-led motivation to open markets and further business opportunities for its firms, but, to an extent, they were also propelled by the need to consolidate its geostrategic influence in the region (European Commission 2006, 2010). The EU and India talks, which stalled in 2013 over differences on tariff reductions, patent protection, human rights, procurement liberalization, and data security, were relaunched in May 2021.

This chapter examines two interrelated issues. First, and briefly, how has EU trade policy evolved in light of the open strategic autonomy approach? Second, using the EU-India FTA as a case study, I discuss how the EU's efforts to advance certain normative standards in the public procurement and sustainable development chapters stalled the talks. Both these areas were major elements of the EU policy discourse but were "red lines" for India. I thus argue that the willingness to adopt EU's regulatory standardization may vary between countries and that the "one-size-fits-all" approach may not always apply.

Evolving EU Trade Policy in Light of "Open Strategic Autonomy"

The EU has developed a complex architecture of interregional agreements, varying from framework agreements at an intercontinental level to those with restricted scope. Often these relationships result in "complex inter-regionalism" (Hardacre and Smith 2009, 2014), in which multiple actors at a variety of levels and scales of operation in different regions come into collision or collaboration with each other. Trade policy plays a significant role given that this allows the EU's firms the opportunity to gain market access on favorable terms to groups of countries, and, in this manner, it is a significant incentive to the building of interregional ties (Smith 2018). The strategic relations with India are no exception.

As this volume makes clear, EU trade policy focuses on regulatory standardization through trade agreements with third countries (see also Khorana and Garcia 2014, 481), but this approach has varied over time in terms of the broader context in which trade policy itself is set—from developing strategic partnerships to the EU being an exporter of broad-level principles and values, and more recently to the open strategic autonomy framework. Even so, EU trade policy has consistently sought to foster market access for EU firms by addressing barriers and generating momentum for regulatory cooperation and, in many cases, convergence. There is, indeed, an extensive literature on the role of the EU as an actor that aims to export its principles and values through FTAs (see Woolcock 2010). The rationale for this approach is explained not only by the economic benefits it brings, but also by the fact that EU norms or approaches to regulation are distinctive and reflective of how it perceives its identity.

Here it can be noted that the strategic partnership approach was formulated in 2008, and it became an important foreign policy instrument thereafter. The European Council observed that the partnership approach provided "a useful instrument for pursuing European objectives and interests" (European Council 2010, 3) and served as a means to find "a balance of mutual advantages and commitments" (Van Rompuy 2010). As part of this, trade was seen as an increasingly important element (Jain and Sachdeva 2019, 1).

The recent open strategic autonomy approach has, however, taken on increased importance. It is broad, and its interpretation is rapidly evolving

(European Union 2021). The EU specifically alludes to the trade policy dimension of this policy and states that its "openness shows that the EU will be open to trade and will promote stable rules in order to be strong economically and have geopolitical influence." Grevi (2019, 3) views the open strategic autonomy approach as being able to set objectives, make decisions, and "mobilize the necessary resources in ways that do not primarily depend on the decisions and assets of others." Anghel et al. (2020, 1) define open strategic autonomy as "the ability to act autonomously, to rely on one's own resources in key strategic areas and to cooperate with partners whenever needed." Akgüç (2021), however, argues that the open strategic autonomy of the EU should be understood in broader terms, beyond the geopolitical, technological, and economic domains to one that incorporates socioeconomic and environmental considerations to better reflect societal challenges and global realities. The EU (2020, 7) accepts that the discourse is shifting, and it is "shaping the system of global economic governance and developing mutually beneficial bilateral relations, while protecting ourselves [the EU] from unfair and abusive practices."

Importantly for this volume, the strategic autonomy framework specifically focuses on increasing the resilience of EU supply chains through common regulation in certain expanding sectors (e.g., e-commerce, investment, and climate change) and accessing critical raw materials through new trade partnerships. This reflects the subtle change in EU trade policy (i.e., use FTAs as a means to rebalance EU firms' interdependence in certain geographical areas and sectors, as well as to diversify supply sources).

The strategic open economy approach should be seen as the context for the EU-India FTA talks. India is an attractive partner: the growth rate of consumption of the Indian middle class has been on an increasing trend, unlike in developed countries where growth is broadly flat, at between 0.5 and 1 percent per year. The growing Indian middle class is expected to spend more on services (such as healthcare and education), seek premium offerings and new product categories (such as organic food), and have consumption preferences significantly driven by digital connectedness—trends that are likely to benefit EU firms. Thus, an FTA with India would allow the EU to pursue business interests (i.e., enhance market access for EU firms in India, while at the same time supporting its post-pandemic recovery and promoting values through FTAs). Yet, the EU-India FTA talks came to a grinding halt due to differences in negotiating "asks": in the language of this volume, the standards pushed by the EU proved unacceptable to India. The next section delves into the specifics of this outcome.

The EU-India FTA Case Study

The Landscape for Public Procurement in India

Government procurement comprises nearly 20–25 percent of India's gross domestic product (GDP). The EU-India FTA negotiations aimed to liberalize market access and to open the public procurement market, among others, because European companies do not enjoy similar access to India, where they face both de jure (e.g., "buy national" provisions) and de facto (e.g., lack of transparency, corruption) market access barriers. What makes India particularly attractive to the EU is not only the size of India's public procurement market and the untapped potential, but also its rapidly growing economy and growing demand for infrastructure, an area that is covered under public procurement.

Public procurement was a roadblock and a bone of contention in the EU-India talks (Khorana and Asthana 2014; Khorana and Garcia 2013; Khorana et al. 2011). At the onset of the 2007 talks, India, in no unclear terms, indicated that it did not wish to open its government procurement market. The EU indicated that "*it cannot envisage a deal that does not include market commitments on procurement* [emphasis added]" (CEC 2007). But India's then Commerce Minister Kamal Nath categorically stated that "we will not include points like public procurement in the talks of India-EU FTA" (*OneIndia News* 2007). The main issue that derailed the EU-India FTA talks was the EU's demand to increase the level of transparency in procurements. The EU insisted as well that India should liberalize the government procurement of goods and services, including public utilities, at the state, provincial, and local government levels (Witchterich and Menon-Sen 2009). These were normative positions reflective of a broader drive, by the EU, to pursue its vision of the world—a mindset that India was not willing to adopt (Khorana and Asthana 2014). Specifically, the push by the EU to enhance transparency was comprehensible in light of its aim to establish a procurement framework which overlaps with the WTO Government Procurement Agreement (GPA) (i.e., its desire to employ WTO-GPA style commitments, which make it imperative to have full transparency in FTAs).

The EU's demands became a negotiating hurdle for India, which is an observer to the WTO-GPA and, as such, does not have the obligation to have GPA-style commitments in areas such as tendering and transparency. The ground realities of different systems contributed to divergence in negotiating perspectives, which led to government procurement being a non-mover in the FTA talks.

It seems important to understand the reasons behind India's resistance. From India's perspective, its reservations stemmed from a lack of consolidated data on government procurement, including the breakdown of the value of contracts by procurement methods. At the international level, as a WTO-GPA observer, India is not required to report procurement data. Moreover, government procurement is decentralized and procurement activity is conducted by public entities, including public enterprises, at the central and state levels. The central government is also empowered to designate procuring entities at the central level. We may call these differences in regulatory and institutional approaches between India and the EU.

Further, and again on the institutional front, India does not have any procuring agencies at the central level. Until 2017, the Directorate General of Supply and Disposals was the procuring entity at the central level for commonly used goods and services; it was dissolved in 2017 when the government e-marketplace (e-GeM) was introduced. Government procurement is regulated by several pieces of legislation, in particular the General Financial Rules (GFRs). The GFRs are issued by the Ministry of Finance. The GFRs contain general provisions, such as the methods and thresholds of procurement that apply to all sectors. Generic guidelines to implement the GFRs are provided in procurement manuals, also issued by the Ministry of Finance; these were last revised in 2017 (goods and services) and 2019 (works) (Government of India 2017). Indian procuring entities, such as the Ministries of Defence and Railways, are empowered to issue their own internal procurement manuals as long as these are consistent with the GFRs. States have their own procurement provisions, which should follow the GFRs; however, some states have enacted their own procurement acts. States such as Tamil Nadu and Karnataka have enacted specific laws on public procurement, while others are in the process of drafting relevant legislation.

It is important to note that in recent years, India introduced changes to the procurement framework and amended the GFRs in 2017, 2019, and 2020. When the EU-India FTA talks commenced in 2007, India's procurement framework did not have any provisions on the use of the e-GeM for goods and services. But this became mandatory following recent changes. Other changes made include the introduction of new methods, namely e-reverse auction and two-stage bidding. In addition, e-procurement was made mandatory for all tenders, and other changes were made in the evaluation criteria for the procurement of consultancy services and removal of fees to obtain tender documents. Further, the participation of start-ups in procurement has been facilitated, and requirements for previous turnover and experience were removed. Finally, the procurement system has been refined to include environmental considerations in the procurement process, and the Code of Integrity was adopted. The demand for higher transparency may, in the present circumstances, no longer be a stumbling block given that India has implemented reforms since 2017.

It should be noted as well that recent government polices to open up India have resulted in foreign investors being granted greater access to India's procurement market. Parliament approving further liberalization in investment, complemented by the easing of investment caps, and the opening up of previously restricted sectors to overseas investors are also steps that are making the procurement market ready for competition. This was not the case in 2007 when the EU commenced trade talks with India.

Yet, despite these recent reforms, hurdles to public procurement liberalization remain for EU firms. The Public Procurement (Preference to Make in India) Order, 2017, revised in 2018 and 2019, was issued to promote the manufacturing and production of goods and services in India, with a view to enhancing income and employment. Under the Order, only local suppliers are eligible to bid for contracts (goods, services, and works) that are less than INR 5 million or a higher threshold, if allowed by the contracting entity. In the event of sufficient local supply and competition in the domestic market, irrespective of the value of the contract, non-local suppliers are not eligible to bid. For contracts above INR 5 million, a 20 percent preference margin is granted to local suppliers. The Order allows entities to award local suppliers that are part of the contract or to allow them to match the offer of the foreign supplier. In addition, a local content requirement of at least 50 percent applies. However, procuring entities may notify a lower/different local content requirement; for instance, the minimum local content notified by the Ministry of Heavy Industry ranges from 40 percent to 95 percent. Procurement of less than INR 500,000 is not subject to the provisions contained in the Order. Finally, under the Make in India initiative, the procurement of local goods and services containing domestically owned intellectual property rights (IPR) is preferred under the 2018 National Digital Communications Policy.

Sustainability: Human Rights and Labor Standards

Modern trade agreements contain rules on trade and sustainable development. There is an increasing recognition in the EU that the effects of trade and trade policy are far too great to be treated separately from other development goals such as human rights. Over 80 percent of all EU trade agreements signed since 2013 include labor provisions, and more than 40 percent of agreements since 2000 include anti-corruption and anti-bribery clauses that go beyond the WTO rules. This evidences that the trade agreements of the EU are increasingly including clauses that require the partners to meet certain conditions on human rights, which may include labor conditions, political participation, environmental issues, and standards in relation to specific goods. Studies find that non-trade issues, especially binding labor provisions (Raess and Sari 2018), are particularly prevalent in EU FTAs.

The Lisbon Treaty is at the center of the EU's external relations, and there is an underlying aim to have global influence on human rights enforcement (Woolcock 2010). The EU is committed to incorporating human rights standards into its trade policies. The human rights clauses built into EU FTAs are termed "democracy clauses," and they are phrased as an essential clause, which allow parties to partially or fully suspend an agreement unilaterally in case of violation. These are included in the sustainable development chapter that covered fundamental human rights and the eight core International Labour Organization (ILO) conventions. Human rights are mostly included in EU political framework agreements under "essential elements" clauses, which are complemented by provisions on cooperation and dialogue between trading partners on human rights. In nearly all cases, reference to human rights norms and the commitments of partners feature in FTA preambles. Core labor rights that form part of human rights in a broader sense are specifically covered in the more recent trade and sustainable development chapters of EU FTAs.

The major route for trade and human rights in trade agreements is the EU's insistence on placing non-trade issues, such as human rights, as part of trade policy, usually done through two modalities. The first is that the often-preferential market access is conditional on compliance with such human rights objectives. The second is the EU's Generalized System of Preferences (GSP), where its unilateral scheme also makes eligibility conditional on ratification of twenty-seven international conventions and to cooperate with the EU to monitor the implementation of these conventions related to environment, climate change, and good governance. FTA partners have been required by the EU to make commitments similar to GSP+, though there is no formal obligation to ratify the ILO Conventions.

With this said, for trade policy, as part of trade agreements, there is limited scope to enforce conditionalities, given the reciprocal nature necessary for these. For instance, both the EU and US preferential frameworks effectively promote values in beneficiary countries, but the standards reinforced through the schemes and implementation differ. While both have a labor rights standard, the US scheme includes a direct reference to IPRs as a necessary standard, unlike the EU. The GSP preferences have a review and enforcement mechanism, and preferences can in fact be suspended based on conditionality. Yet, there have been few cases where this has happened (as with Myanmar and Belarus, where EU preferences were withdrawn). Unlike the US, the EU has preferred a constructive engagement to more restrictive measures and has not activated the human rights clause to suspend trade preferences under any of its trade agreements. Civil society and the European Parliament have, however, encouraged the European Commission to use the clause in a more robust way to respond to breaches of human rights and democratic principles.

This has certainly taken place in the case of the EU-India talks. The European Parliament pressed for a "progressive" trade policy, linking trade with environment, labor, and human rights (ETUC 2017; Jean et al. 2018). Within the context of the EU-India FTA, the European Parliament underlined the need for sustainable development chapter (European Parliament 2009, 2011). The Parliament highlighted concerns on the persecution of religious minorities and human rights activists in India by underlining that "*human rights and democracy clauses constitute an essential element of the FTA* [emphasis added]" (EP 2009, 2). It stressed that the environmental and human rights objectives are "*a minimum, compliance with the ILO's eight core conventions and four priority conventions* [emphasis added]" (European Parliament 2011, para. 30).

This stance by the Parliament led to inclusion of human rights in the FTA negotiations (Frennhoff Larsén 2017; Leeg 2014). But it proved to be a major obstacle, given India's historic antipathy toward international agreements on labor standards (Rodgers 2011). In particular, India did not agree with the EU approaching trade policy and human rights issues as intertwined (as the EU has done in many FTAs). For example, the core labor rights that form part of human rights in a broader sense are specifically covered in the Trade and

Sustainable Development Chapters of the EU's FTAs. According to EU practice, human rights are included in EU political framework agreements under "essential elements" clauses. The human rights clause states that if no political framework agreement exists, then essential elements clauses are to be included in FTAs, and serious breaches of the essential elements clauses may trigger the suspension in whole or part of the overall framework agreement and all the linked agreements, including the trade agreement (non-execution clause). In the framework agreements, the clause is usually complemented by provisions on cooperation and dialogue between the parties on human rights. The "essential elements" human rights clause enables one party to take appropriate measures in case of serious breaches by the other party, highlighting the EU approach which considers human rights and trade as being intrinsically linked.

India's position was that its own constitutional mandate governs the understanding and interpretation of human rights. Therefore, there is no need to link those rights to any trade initiatives. And while the current scenario needs to be acknowledged, with the voice of civil society and domestic groups undoubtedly diluted, India has had a historically important role in the framing of the Universal Declaration of Human Rights. It is worth mentioning that the EU and India refer to the *shared* values of human rights, but the perspectives and legal implementation of human rights in the partners vary. There may be agreement over the definition of human rights, but not over how they should be protected. Thus, Gupwell and Gupta (2009, 91) write that India's insistence was motivated by the "*sensitivity and prestige in not wanting to be subjected to any pressure on these issues where trade relations are involved* [emphasis added]." In addition, Indian businesses feared that the EU's "social clause" agenda was inspired by protectionist motives and that the sanctions-based approach in the FTA would augur negative trade implications, mainly for the labor-intensive industries in which India specializes, such as clothing and carpets (Jha and D'Souza 2012).

There is thus obviously a need for a continued dialogue on human rights because a bilateral agreement cannot be skewed toward any one party, and mutual understanding of each other's sensitivities will be a key issue, along with respect for sovereignty in dealing with contentious issues. Both India and the EU handle human rights with different conceptions and approaches. These differences are normal and natural given the different histories, cultures, traditions, political systems, worldviews, and geographical and geopolitical realities, and because the two are at different levels of socioeconomic development. And this is where the EU-India Human Rights Dialogue, which was initiated in 2004, can provide the direction to achieving a balanced approach. An immediate way forward for the partners may be a joint memorandum of an understanding on human rights.

Conclusion

The bilateral agreements of the EU are structured partnerships that facilitate mutual understanding and rapprochement, boost multilateral efforts, and allow partners to address shared concerns on global challenges (Grevi 2012). There is evidence that FTAs concluded by the EU with third countries are a step forward in the direction of overcoming the shortcomings of the WTO, in that the FTAs include commitments from partner countries to provide market access and remove barriers to trade at a bilateral level, and the commitments, in most cases, go beyond the level of WTO provisions. Further, the FTAs require partners to make specific commitments which allow the EU to employ FTAs as a means to "promote consensus among like-minded partners and to develop a network of relations that can promote not only economic but also political goals, including in the social and environmental areas" (Business Europe 2019, 24). In many cases, the EU thus appears to have been able to advance its standards in those areas by securing critical passages in the resulting FTAs.

As evidenced by the EU-India trade deal talks, however, this may not always be the case. The requirement to have transparency in procurement—and an adaptation of the Indian system to international norms—led to strong opposition. India's regulatory and administrative realities could not be easily reconciled with EU demands. Similarly, different understandings around human rights (themselves reflective of different histories, cultures, traditions, political systems, worldviews, and geographical and geopolitical realities, and different levels of socioeconomic development) also proved to be major hurdles.

We can conclude with reflections for possible ways forward. The case of failed negotiations in the sectors examined (i.e., public procurement and human rights) highlight the importance of not having an off-the-shelf trade deal and of understanding country-specific issues. In addition, to ensure that the EU can carry forward its standardization of FTAs with its trade partners, it should, first, support capacity-building through technical assistance programs in less developed countries and, second, follow international recognized standards that allow all partners to reform policies in line with international norms.

References

Akgüç, M. 2021. "Europe's Open Strategic Autonomy: Striking a Balance between Geopolitical, Socioeconomic and Environmental Dimensions." ETUI Research Paper—Policy Brief. doi: http://dx.doi.org/10.2139/ssrn.3873804.

Anghel S., B. Immenkamp, E. Lazarou, J. L. Saulnier, and A. B. Wilson. 2020. *On the Path to "Strategic Autonomy": The EU in an Evolving Geopolitical Environment.* Brussels: European Parliament.

Business Europe. 2019. *A Trade Strategy for the 21st Century.* April. https://www.busines seurope.eu/sites/buseur/files/media/reports_and_studies/april_2019_-_a_trade_ strategy_fit_for_the_21st_century_light_0.pdf.

Commission of the European Communities (CEC). 2007. EU and India Hold Bilateral Discussions on New Trade and Investment Agreement. Press Release. June 28. Brussels: Commission of the European Communities.

European Commission. 2006. A Contribution to the EU's Growth and Jobs Strategy. COM(2006) 567 final. Brussels: European Commission.

European Commission. 2010. Report on Progress Achieved on the Global Europe Strategy, 2006–2010. Commission Staff Working Document, SEC(2010) 1268/2. Brussels: European Commission.

European Council. 2010. General Secretariat. Conclusions—16 September 2010. EUCO 21/1/10, CO EUR 16, CONCL 3. https://www.consilium.europa.eu/uedocs/cms_data/ docs/pressdata/en/ec/116547.pdf.

European Parliament. 2009. *European Parliament Resolution of 26 March 2009 on an EU-India Free Trade Agreement.* P6_TA (2009) 0189. Brussels: European Parliament.

European Parliament. 2011. *European Parliament Resolution of 11 May 2011 on the state of play in the EU-India Free Trade Agreement negotiations,* P7_TA (2011) 0024. Brussels: European Parliament.

European Trade Union Confederation (ETUC). 2017. *Reflection Paper on Harnessing Globalisation—ETUC Assessment.* Brussels: European Trade Union Confederation.

European Union. 2020. Strategic Plan 2020–2024: Directorate-General Trade. https:// trade.ec.europa.eu/doclib/docs/2020/november/tradoc_159104.pdf.

European Union. 2021. "An Open, Sustainable and Assertive Trade Policy: Open Strategic Autonomy." https://trade.ec.europa.eu/doclib/docs/2021/february/tradoc_ 159434.pdf.

Falkenberg, R. 2019. "Trade Policy: Is There a Way Back to Global Governance? A European View." In *Perspectives on the Soft Power of EU Trade Policy,* edited by S. Bilal and B. Hoekman, pp. 31–37. London: VoxEU/Centre for Economic Policy Research.

Frennhoff Larsén, M. 2017. "The Increasing Power of the European Parliament: Negotiating the EU-India Free Trade Agreement." *International Negotiation* 22 (3): pp. 473–498.

Government of India. 2017. *Manual for Procurement of Goods, 2017; Manual for Procurement of Consultancy and Other Services, 2017; and Manual for the Procurement of Works, 2019.* Department of Expenditure. https://doe.gov.in/procurement-policy-divisions.

Grevi, G. 2012. "Why EU Strategic Partnerships Matter." European Strategic Partnership Observatory, Working Paper 1, June. FRIDE-Egmont.

Grevi G. 2019. "Strategic Autonomy for European Choices: The Key to Europe's Shaping Power." Discussion Paper. July. Brussels: European Policy Centre.

Gupwell, D., and N. Gupta. 2009. "EU FTA Negotiations with India, ASEAN and Korea: The Question of Fair Labour Standards." *Asia Europe Journal* 7 (1): pp. 79–95.

Hardacre, A., and M. Smith. 2009. "The EU and the Diplomacy of Complex Interregionalism." *The Hague Journal of Diplomacy* 4 (2): pp. 167–188.

Hardacre, A., and M. Smith. 2014. "The European Union and the Contradictions of Complex Interregionalism." In *Intersecting Interregionalism: Regions, Global Governance and the EU*, edited by F. Baert, T. Scaramagli, and F. Söderbaum, pp. 91–106. Dordrecht: Springer.

Jain, R. K., and G. Sachdeva. 2019. "India-EU Strategic Partnership: A New Roadmap." *Asia Europe Journal* 17 (3): pp. 309–325.

Jean, S., P. Martin, and A. Sapir. 2018. "International Trade under Attack: What Strategy for Europe?" *Policy Contribution* No. 12. August. Brussels: Bruegel.

Jha, D. Kumar, and S. D'Souza. 2012. "FTA with EU to Benefit Textile Exports." *Business Standard*, July 11. http://www.business-standard.com/india/news/ftaeu-soon-to-bene fit-textile-exports/480043/.

Khorana S., and A. Asthana. 2014. "EU FTA Negotiations with India: The Question of Liberalization of Public Procurement." *Asia Europe Journal* 12 (3): pp. 251–263.

Khorana S., and M. Garcia. 2013. "European Union-India FTA: One Step Forward, One Back?" *Journal of Common Market Studies* 51 (4): pp. 684–700.

Khorana, S., and M. Garcia. 2014. "Procurement Liberalization Diffusion in EU Agreements: Signalling Stewardship?" *Journal of World Trade* 48 (3): pp. 481–500.

Khorana S., N. Perdikis, W. A. Kerr, and M. Yeung. 2011. *Bilateral Trade Agreements in the Era of Globalization: The EU and India in Search of a Partnership*. Aldershot, UK: Edward Elgar.

Leeg, T. 2014 "Normative Power Europe? The European Union in the Negotiations on a Free Trade Agreement with India." *European Foreign Affairs Review* 19 (3): pp. 335–355.

Meissner, K. L., and L. McKenzie. 2019. "The Paradox of Human Rights Conditionality in EU Trade Policy: When Strategic Interests Drive Policy Outcomes." *Journal of European Public Policy* 26 (9): pp. 1273–1291.

OneIndia News. 2007. "India, EU Row over FTA." November 30. https://www.oneindia.com/2007/11/29/india-eu-row-over-fta-1196361259.html.

Poletti, A., D. Sicurelli, and A. Yildirim. 2021. "Promoting Sustainable Development through Trade? EU Trade Agreements and Global Value Chains." *Italian Political Science Review/Rivista Italiana Di Scienza Politica* 51 (3): pp. 339–354. doi: 10.1017/ipo.2020.33.

Raess, D., and D. Sari. 2018. "Labour Provisions in Trade Agreements (LABPTA): Introducing a New Dataset." *Global Policy* 9: pp. 451–466.

Rodgers, G. 2011. "India, the ILO and the Quest for Social Justice since 1919." *Economic and Political Weekly* 46 (10): pp. 45–52.

Smith, M. 2018. "Trade Policy and Foreign Policy in the European Union." In *Handbook on the EU and International Trade*, edited by S. Khorana and M. Garcia, pp. 171–187. Cheltenham, UK: Edward Elgar.

van 't Wout, D. 2022. "The Enforceability of the Trade and Sustainable Development Chapters of the European Union's Free Trade Agreements." *Asia Europe Journal* 20: pp. 81–98.

Van Rompuy, H. 2010. Remarks by President of the European Council at the Press Conference before the G8 Meeting. June 24. Toronto. https://www.consilium.europa.eu/uedocs/cms_data/docs/pressdata/en/ec/116880.pdf.

Witchterich, C., and K. Menon-Sen. 2009. "Trade Liberalisation, Gender Equality, Policy Space: The Case of the Contested EU-India FTA. WIDE Paper Heinrich Böll Stiftung. Brussels.

Woolcock, S. 2010. "The Treaty of Lisbon and the European Union as an Actor in International Trade." ECIPE Working Paper No. 01/2010. Brussels: European Centre for International Political Economy.

11

Conclusion

The Reach and Limits of the EU

Francesco Duina and Crina Viju-Miljusevic

Trade liberalization is no longer focused on tariffs on goods that were easily handled by previous rounds of the General Agreement on Trade and Tariffs. It now includes non-tariff barriers and extends to services, investment, the environment, labor issues, and beyond. In line with the expectations of economic sociology, a truly integrated marketplace requires the articulation of perspectives and values—or, in the language we have used throughout the volume, definitional and normative principles—in all those areas. In domestic markets, agreements on these matters emerge over decades and as organic elements of shared daily life. Negotiating them at the multilateral level is much more difficult. The result of that process, if achieved, is the standardization of worldviews.

The European Union (EU) has been one of the most important advocates for such standardization in multilateral and preferential trade negotiations. It, of course, has followed this approach internally with its Single Market Initiative since the late 1980s. Recently, it has been keen to export its templates to third parties through multilateral and/or bilateral/regional negotiations (Young and Peterson 2006) or through unilateral mechanisms (Bradford 2020; Hadjiyianni 2021) (discussed below).

Given this, we have seen that the current EU trade agreements with partners across the world include World Trade Organization (WTO)-plus provisions, where commitments are made to build and deepen the multilateral trade relationship. Such provisions extend to, but are not limited to, obligations on sanitary and phytosanitary rules, technical barriers to trade, countervailing and anti-dumping duties, services, government procurement, and intellectual property rights (IPR). Importantly, though, the agreements also include WTO-extra provisions, where parties agree on definitional and

Francesco Duina and Crina Viju-Miljusevic, *Conclusion* In: *Standardizing the World*. Edited by: Francesco Duina and Crina Viju-Miljusevic, Oxford University Press. © Oxford University Press 2023. DOI: 10.1093/oso/9780197681886.003.0012 normative principles in areas not covered by the WTO, such as competition policy, data protection, environmental laws, investment, labor market conditions, and human rights. Similar observations apply to the principles advanced by other international organizations, such as the International Labour Organization. At times, the agreements simply refer to those principles. At other times, however, they go well beyond them.

This volume has sought to understand the process and success of the EU in exporting its own preferences to third parties through its various trade agreements. More specifically, the volume had two main objectives. We aimed to paint a picture of the standardizing content in EU trade agreements in various policy areas and with diverse trading partners. We then offered explanations for the emerging patterns. We summarized the main findings of this volume in some detail in the Introduction. It seems, nonetheless, useful to briefly outline them here as well.

First, the EU has been successful at furthering standardization through its trade agreements across policy areas and with diverse trading partners. In certain cases, international standards are indeed widely used as reference (labor, trade facilitation, certain aspects of IPR), while in others the process goes considerably beyond those standards, either by building on them or outright producing original material (e.g., services, geographical indications [GIs], the environment, investments, food safety, rule of law [RoL] and anti-corruption, and certain aspects of IPR). Interestingly, the successful standardization in EU trade agreements has had two important indirect effects. On the one hand, it has allowed the EU to introduce additional measures within its own internal market (e.g., in services and investments). On the other hand, it has influenced non-EU trade agreements in Asia and the Global South (around, for instance, labor, the environment, and investments). All this points to an impressive ability of the EU to shape standards (and thus worldviews) across the globe both directly (through its trade agreements) and as effects of those direct efforts.

Second, the definitional and normative standardization achieved in EU's trade agreements is often highly granular and specific. At the same time, it exhibits a broader characteristic: it aims to liberalize markets in a measured and socially minded manner—around labor and the environment, for instance. This contrasts with what many would consider a more neoliberal approach. Thus, the EU has advanced particular—and rather rich—worldviews as it pursues market building and all that goes with it.

Third, despite these important achievements, the EU has failed to advance its standardizing preferences in certain policy areas and with different trading partners. Some of those partners include the US, Canada, India, Malaysia, and Indonesia, across policy areas such as government procurement, human rights, GIs, food safety, and sustainable biofuels. We observe that some of these partners are not major economic or geopolitical actors. EU power has noteworthy limits.

Fourth, the evidence points to a lack of consistency in terms of negotiated outcomes in certain areas. The result is at times more of a "tapestry" of different standardizing principles than an assertion of homogenous viewpoints as we move across trade agreements. Thus, while in services, for instance, the outcomes are similar across agreements, the same cannot be said for investor protection, for example, or the automotive industry.

Taken together, the findings make clear that the EU has indeed been rather successful at projecting its worldviews across the globe. At the same time, the process has been uneven and inconsistent. We are, of course, in the relatively early phases of the EU's efforts. The future will provide us with further opportunities for assessments and observations.

In terms of our second aim—establishing causality—the preceding chapters emphasize that no single factor can explain the observable outcomes. Various institutional variables (from path-dependency to the constitutional and regulatory tendencies of the partners) are quite important. But political economy considerations (such as the interests of business actors), asymmetries of power, cultural elements and questions of identity, and interest groups and civil society actors have also influenced the direction of standardization. Just as the overall picture around outcomes points to complexity, so does that of the forces driving those outcomes.

These findings encourage us to reflect on several related matters. First, we can begin by recalling how some of our contributors reported that the EU has been more successful at influencing aid-dependent countries, countries that hope to eventually join the EU, and economically weaker partners. Less success was achieved with stronger countries such as the US, or autocratic regimes such as China. At the same time, a surprising finding was that the EU is not always successful in its dealings with developing or weaker countries. This challenges common assumptions about the EU's power. We wish to know with more precision why this has been so. Can we generalize or predict which trading partners are more likely to take on the EU standards?

Under what conditions do trade negotiations lead to standardization? What limits EU influence?

In particular, our contributors point to the strength of relevant business interests, the items on the negotiating table, and low dependence on EU exports as major factors. But we note here the growing research on the changing importance of the EU market size in the global economy as it affects the material incentives of third-party governments when choosing to coordinate their regulatory measures (Meunier and Nicolaïdis 2006; Vogel 1995); the perceptions of third-party actors regarding potential outcomes (Drezner 2007); the EU's institutional features expressed through regulatory expertise and coherence (Bach and Newman 2007); and the importance of global value chains (Dür et al. 2020). Thus, more seems to be at work than what our volume could cover. Future research could generate a more comprehensive framework for understanding the dynamics around standardization between the EU and some of its weaker trading partners.

Second, and relatedly, we wish to reflect on the relationship between standardization (which obviously amounts to the harmonization of regulatory approaches between the partners) and mutual recognition. As we have discussed, standardization presents major benefits. Indeed, it is often justified on the basis of *forgone gains from trade* agreements (Kerr 2006). This underlies the WTO's own commitment to reducing regulatory barriers to trade (James and Anderson 2005) as well as commitments to regulatory cooperation in most major trade agreements, such as the Canada-US-Mexico Free Trade Agreement, Asia Pacific Economic Cooperation, and Association of Southeast Asian Nations (Yeung et al. 1999). It is also what has motivated the EU's internal effort toward standardization over the decades (Gaisford et al. 2003).

Yet, we have also seen that when dealing with strong economic partners such as the US and Canada, standardization has proven very difficult and at times insurmountable—with the result that mutual recognition was eventually considered (with the Transatlantic Trade and Investment Partnership and the Comprehensive Economic and Trade Agreement [CETA]) and selectively adopted (with CETA). The case of India also showed how pressures for standardization were resisted: major economic actors want their standards to prevail and are thus less likely to compromise. This invites reflections on whether mutual recognition will become a more viable option going forward. Some trends suggest that standardization remains an ambition even in the case of trade with major economic players. For instance, the

US and EU have set up a Trade and Technology Council in hopes of future agreements on standards in certain sectors. There is much to be gained by coming to agreements and possibly determining how everyone else in the world will have to adapt and regulate. Indeed, this is quite clear in the mind of EU, US, and other officials. Mutual recognition, moreover, presents its own challenges: lack of regulatory convergence raises suspicions of foreign products and services, while also raising fears of possible races to the bottom. Civil society in Europe opposed—with unprecedented intensity—mutual recognition around food and consumer regulation. Finally, the agreement with Japan suggests that standardization is possible.

At the same time, it is also quite clear that standardization comes with costs. It inevitably means that some economic actors have to adjust and conform to new requirements: not all preferences can be met. As standards expand to non-economic areas such as the environment and RoL, a host of other actors also experience adjustments. In turn, mutual recognition comes with certain advantages. Most obviously, agreement and adoption are in principle much easier than having to agree on, and then implement, shared standards. In addition, it may actually offer a more pragmatic path toward global standardization than is clear at first. If two major trading partners (such as the US and the EU) agree to recognize each other's standards, they, in effect, create a major incentive for firms and businesses elsewhere to comply with either set of standards—as this will give them access to that entire market. This is the principle of *erga omnes*, as De Ville (Chapter 6) writes. Thus, when it comes to major trading partners especially, we wish to know more about the trade-offs and difficulties associated with standardization. Can we predict what paths will be taken? What is the full array of factors at work?

Third, the findings encourage us to investigate further the relationship between the "Brussels Effect" and standardization in trade agreements. The former points to the influence of internal EU regulatory frameworks on external actors such as states, corporations, and international organizations. The idea is that, because of the size of the EU internal market, those external actors choose to adopt EU regulatory frameworks (and thus standards). The "effect" hence concerns the unilateral power of the EU to regulate global markets in indirect ways. By contrast, standardization in trade agreements, as our findings highlight, in many cases, can reflect the ability of the EU to directly project its own internal regulatory approaches onto third parties through international agreements. The Brussels Effect has been most visible in industries such as chemicals and automotive, where companies accept the costs of adopting EU rules to access the EU market. Those companies have imposed these rules not only on their operations in the EU, but also across their global businesses in order to avoid compliance costs with multiple regulatory systems. The "effect" is therefore across the world. Bradford (2020) writes that it has extended to other areas, including competition policy, food safety, environmental policy, and data protection. She further reasons that the emergence of the Brussels Effect has reflected five critical aspects of the EU: its substantial market power, regulatory capacity, preference for strict standards, inelastic targets (thus, relocation to regions with less stringent regulations is impossible), and non-divisibility of standards (i.e., not allowing the adjustment of standards to different markets).

The question becomes, given all this, what the relationship between the Brussels Effect and standardization will (or should) be. At stake is how the EU manages to project its worldviews across the globe. We have seen that EU efforts toward standardization have been successful but have also met roadblocks or outright failures. Perhaps, then, the two processes might complement each other as the EU tries to set standards across the world. For instance, in cases where the EU cannot achieve what it wants via trade negotiations, unilateral action might prove compensatory and effective. For example, when it comes to trade defense instruments, active measures of standardization have included provisions on anti-dumping, anti-subsidy, and safeguard rules to protect the EU businesses from unfair or overwhelming competition from third parties. But the EU has not always been successful in imposing its preferences on these fronts in trade agreements. As this has happened, the EU has moved unilaterally on a number of related fronts, as some of the writings in this volume indicated: foreign subsidy regulation, trade enforcement regulation, international procurement instrument, foreign investment screening mechanism, anti-coercion instrument, and carbon border adjustment mechanisms.

Several reasons, besides the difficulties with standardization, have encouraged the EU to adopt a unilateral approach. The most important of these reasons include China's growing assertiveness, increased American mercantilism, the paralysis of WTO negotiations, and changing preferences within the EU (e.g., German support for unilateral measures). Further attention should therefore be given to this complex relationship to determine if and how complementarity might be feasible, the conditions under which one approach seems preferable, and the implications of any given combination for the EU's position in the global economic and political order.

Our last point concerns China. Undoubtedly, the question of its rising influence will have to be addressed. Despite the significant trade with each other, the EU and China have yet to enter into any substantial trade agreement. In the meanwhile, China has emerged as an increasingly proactive player in the field of standardization from new technological fields, such as 5G and artificial intelligence, to traditional sectors such as health, agriculture, and energy. It has done so by pursuing a dual-track approach that involves integrating standards from entities such as the International Organization of Standardization and adopting a China-centered approach at the bilateral/regional levels, mainly through its Belt and Road Initiative. The first approach is based on international cooperation, but the second points to fragmentation (Seaman 2020). It remains to be seen which of these tendencies will prevail. In either case, the EU will face a major challenge. It surely will not want China to prevail in setting its standards. Quite likely, it will also resist a simple turn to international standards.

On this point, we can recall here how, in its February 2022 Communication to the European Parliament and Council, the Commission stressed the importance of implementing a strategic approach to shape international standards in line with the European values and interests by collaborating with like-minded partners (such as the US and Canada) and continuing the dialogue with China (European Commission 2022). What will the EU push for in this dialogue? What limits will it face? And what will the implications of unilateral initiatives by China be for standardization across the world?

Our hope is that this volume has offered valuable data and insights into the EU's standardizing efforts across the world. Any good investigation also leads to new questions. We have presented a few in this Conclusion. We close with an invitation for further work and discovery.

References

Bach, D., and L. Newman. 2007. "The European Regulatory State and Global Public Policy: Micro-institutions, Macro-influence." *Journal of European Public Policy* 14 (6): pp. 827–846.

Bradford, A. 2020. *The Brussels Effect: How the European Union Rules the World.* Oxford: Oxford University Press.

Drezner, D. 2007. *All Politics Is Global: Explaining International Regulatory Regimes.* Princeton, NJ: Princeton University Press.

Dür, A., J. Eckhardt, and A. Polett. 2020. "Global Value Chains, the Anti-Globalization Backlash and EU Trade Policy: A Research Agenda." *Journal of European Public Policy* 27 (6): pp. 944–956.

European Commission. 2022. "An EU Strategy on Standardisation: Setting global standards in support of a resilient, green and digital EU single market." COM (2022) 31. February 2. https://www.europeansources.info/record/an-eu-strategy-on-standardisation-setting-global-standards-in-support-of-a-resilient-green-and-digital-eu-single-market/.

Gaisford, J. D., W. A. Kerr, and N. Perdikis. 2003. *Economic Analysis for EU Accession Negotiations—Agri-Food Issues in the EU's Eastward Expansion.* Cheltenham, UK: Edward Elgar.

Hadjiyianni, I. 2021. "The European Union as a Global Regulatory Power." *Oxford Journal of Legal Studies* 41 (1): pp. 243–264.

James, S., and K. Anderson. 2005. "On the Need for More Economic Assessment of Quarantine Policies." In *The WTO and Agriculture*, Volume II, edited by K. Anderson and T. Josling, pp. 197–216. Cheltenham, UK: Edward Elgar.

Kerr, W. A. 2006. "International Harmonization and the Gains from Trade." *Estey Centre Journal of International Law and Trade Policy* 7 (2): pp. 1–10.

Meunier, S., and K. Nicolaïdes. 2006. "The European Union as a Conflicted Trade Power." *Journal of European Public Policy* 13 (6): pp. 906–925.

Seaman, J. 2020. "China and the New Geopolitics of Technical Standardization." *Notes de l'Ifri.* January. French Institute of International Relations. https://www.ifri.org/en/publications/notes-de-lifri/china-and-new-geopolitics-technical-standardization.

Vogel, D. 1995. *Trading Up: Consumer and Environmental Regulation in a Global Economy.* Cambridge, MA: Harvard University Press.

Yeung, M. T., N. Perdikis, and W. A. Kerr. 1999. *Regional Trading Blocs in the Global Economy: The EU and ASEAN.* Cheltenham, UK: Edward Elgar.

Young, A. R., and J. Peterson. 2006. "The EU and the New Trade Politics." *Journal of European Public Policy* 13 (6): pp. 795–814.

Index